THE NATURE AND TASKS OF A PERSONALIST PSYCHOLOGY

Edited by

James M. DuBois

University Press of America, Inc.
Lanham • New York • London

Institute for Personalist Psychology

University Press of America,® Inc.
4720 Boston Way
Lanham, Maryland 20706

3 Henrietta Street
London, WC2E 8LU England

Printed in the United States of America
British Cataloging in Publication Information Available

Library of Congress Cataloging-in-Publication Data

The nature and tasks of a personalist psychology / James M. Dubois.
(compiler).
p. cm.
Includes bibliographical references.
1. Christianity--Psychology. 2. Personalism. 3. Man (Christian theology) I. DuBois, James M.
PR110.N25 1995 233 --dc20 95-36961 CIP

ISBN 0-7618-0100-6 (cloth: alk: ppr.)
ISBN 0-7618-0101-4 (pbk: alk: ppr.)

The paper used in this publication meets the minimum requirements of American National Standard for Information Sciences—Permanence of Paper for Printed Library Materials, ANSI Z39.48—1984

Contents

Preface

Anyone who has attended an introductory level psychology course is familiar with humanistic psychology. Immediately the names Rogers, Maslow, and May, among others, come to mind. While humanistic psychology is no longer the dominant trend in psychology, it has unquestionably left a permanent mark on the fields of clinical and counseling psychology. Many of the changes which this movement initiated were very good and much-needed. The humanists rightly opposed earlier models of psychology which viewed the human person in a mechanistic fashion, or which insisted that all psychological claims be based on the findings of the natural sciences. Insofar as they recognized human freedom and dealt with a broad range of existential themes such as love, sense of self, anxiety, and religious experience, the humanists developed theories which more fully did justice to the personal dimension of human existence than had either psychoanalysis or behaviorism.

When one hears the phrase 'personalist psychology' perhaps no names come to mind. This is one reason why the members of the *Institute for Personalist Psychology* thought the name suited their mission particularly well. It allows them, so to speak, to make a new start. As when the humanistic psychologists first began working, so too now there are numerous representatives of psychology who defend reductionistic views of the human person, views which radically contradict the image of the human person which arises from everyday experience. Yet a simple renewal of the so-called humanistic movement in psychology is not what is needed today. In part, this is because the humanists also produced certain views of the person which can only be called reductionistic. For example, they frequently reduced human imperfections and evils to by-products of the individual's encounter with society, just as they reduced moral norms and moral right and wrong to the feelings of the individual subject or to social agreements. The result of this was that their view of human nature was, at least to some extent, naive, and their ethical theory was primarily subjectivistic or relativistic. These flaws in the theories of humanistic psychology led to flaws in its praxis, and its praxis contributed to the decline of many social structures in the United States, including education and marriage. These are some strong claims. However, some of the papers in this volume make significant steps towards substantiating them.

Nevertheless, it would be a mistake to conceive of the work of the *Institute for Personalist Psychology* as a reaction to other movements or as strictly critical in nature. The main inspiration of the *Institute* is to make positive contributions to psychology: to offer philosophies of the human person, of science, and of psychological practice, which will better serve people. This, however, requires us to pursue a dialogue between psychologists and philosophers. It further requires a willingness to confront a broad range of human issues, including religious issues, which are so often held to be taboo for psychologists. To this end, we organized our first conference, "The Nature and Tasks of a Personalist Psychology," held at Franciscan University of Steubenville in October of 1994. The papers collected in this volume have been adapted from those delivered at this inaugural conference.

The chapters of this book have been grouped into three broad categories: *Systematic Contributions, Critical Studies*, and *Introductions to Systems*. However, the reader must bear in mind that these headings are meant only to provide a general structure to the book. Many of the so-called critical and introductory studies make systematic contributions, and the papers called systematic often include numerous critical reflections. In what follows, I can only poorly summarize the general outlines of these papers.

Section I—*Systematic Contributions*—begins with the question, "Are Human Beings Innately Defective?" Although personalism is above all concerned to elucidate the personal perfections found in human nature, e.g. self-knowledge, freedom and love, DuBois argues that a sound psychology must also recognize that human beings are universally and by nature defective. The typical question asked by psychologists and philosophers, namely, whether human beings are intrinsically good or bad, misformulates the problem at hand. For we are not only concerned with moral shortcomings, we are concerned with the facts that human beings die, are subject to diseases, engage in self-deception, and experience significant restrictions on their freedom. Human contingency extends not only to our existence, but to our level of perfection. Although human beings possess many perfections by nature, the greatest of these perfections, the virtues, exist only as potentialities. Thus, the conclusion of the paper, which considers our response to human defectiveness, asks how and in what sense human beings should seek to develop potentials and become self-actualized.

In Chapter Two, Paul Vitz traces the development of the concept of person back to its Trinitarian roots in order to show how the notion of *being in relation* is essential to the Christian notion of person. He finds that one ought not to reject the Boethian concept of the person as *substance*, but one must supplement it with this notion of being in relation. This focus leads him to contrast a Christian and genuinely personalistic psychology with secular "self-psychologies." The former encourages one to trust and love God, as one loves and forgives one's neighbors; the latter encourage one to ignore God, and to trust in one's self and one's neighbors. The former encourages the development of the traditional virtues such as justice, courage, moderation, responsibility, perseverance and modesty; the latter has created its own list of virtues, which includes independence, self-actualization, and unconditional positive regard. As he develops his theory of relationships, Vitz offers much which both Christians and non-Christians will find insightful, including some reflections on forgiveness and interdependence.

Chapter Three is entitled, "Mediating Values: A Task for Personality Formation and the Preservation of Culture." In this paper Annemarie Buchholz-Kaiser argues that the theory of *Gemeinschaftsgefühl* as developed by Alfred Adler, as well as the findings of developmental and educational psychology, confirm the view of the human person that underlies the doctrine of natural law. This is a view of the person as self-determining and rational, acting both to fulfill his basic existential needs and to contribute to the well-being of others. Like Vitz, Buchholz-Kaiser argues that human beings mature as persons only in relation to parents and friends, and thus more emphasis needs to be placed on the social and relational dimensions of human life. This is also apparent in our relationship to perennial values, such as integrity, responsibility, concern for others, and willingness to help. While the values themselves are not derived from subjective awareness, they are also "not self-supporting, but can only be preserved by being consciously applied, cultivated and transmitted from generation to generation in a process of education and life in community."

Section Two—*Critical Studies*— opens with an essay by John Crosby, "Conscience and Superego: A Phenomenological Analysis of Their Difference and Relation." Crosby notes that a personalist psychology must be particularly interested in the phenomenon of conscience; for in conscience we encounter ourselves in a uniquely deep way. Thus, for example, we violate ourselves as persons when we compromise ourselves in a matter of conscience, and we show respect for others as persons when we allow them to act according to their own consciences, free from coercion. But what is conscience? In this paper Crosby wants to show that there is indeed a thing called a superego, or an authoritarian conscience. Children may well "introject" the parental voice of authority, and use this voice to guide their actions. However, Fromm rightly notes that there is a second, and in some ways healthier, form of conscience, one which he calls humanistic conscience. Crosby approves of the way in which Fromm resists the pathological identification with another which is implied in authoritarian conscience, but he finds that the humanistic conscience too is lacking something. Genuine conscience, as described by John Henry Newman and Dietrich von Hildebrand, involves two new moments: the experience of a categorical imperative or of a "magisterial dictate" and the moment of *understanding the content and source of the moral truth.* Given these two aspects, Crosby shows how we can understand both the authority of conscience and its compatibility with our nature as self-determining and rational persons.

Chapter Five, "Full Hearts and Empty Heads: The Price of Certain Recent Programs in Humanistic Psychology," is written by someone uniquely well-qualified to address his topic. William Coulson was a long-time colleague of Carl Rogers at the Western Behavioral Sciences Institute, and, together with Rogers, the co-editor of the seventeen volume series of books, *Studies of the Person.* In this piece, Coulson traces the influence of the ideas of Rogers, and to some extent of Maslow, on the behavior of Rogers himself, the behavior of the religious orders and schools which invited the implementation of human potentials psychology into their programs, and the behavior of Rogers' daughter, Natalie, who openly describes the role of 'Rogerian' theory in her leaving her husband and children to pursue a life independent of commitments to other persons and to objective moral norms. Coulson's report is frank, but not sensationalistic, and it is extremely well documented. It should be required reading for those who believe that human beings, once freed from inhibitions, prohibitions, and restrictions of all sorts, will blossom into beautiful, good and mature persons. It is an important study for the *Institute* insofar as it forcefully argues that psychological *theory* tends quickly to cease to be abstract; and once realized, it affects the lives of real human beings, either for better or for worse.

Josef Seifert's article, "Inferiority Complex and Response: Alfred Adler—Discoveries and Errors," comprises our sixth chapter. The title summarizes his paper very well. Seifert describes numerous sources of the human experience of inferiority (finitude, death, illness, ignorance, and the like), and credits Adler with rightly noticing a common response to this experience, namely, the will to power and the striving for prestige. Nevertheless, he does not think that Adler sufficiently well denounces this response; for this response, when carried out to its logical consequences, would lead to a hatred of God stemming from envy, and to a devaluing of all things superior stemming from resentment. A more proper response would be one of gratitude—for we need not exist but do in fact—and one of love towards the Creator. Similarly, Seifert finds that Adler's notion of overcompensation constitutes a poor response to personal guilt, and suggests instead the need for repentance accompanied by the hope for forgiveness. By analysing Adler's genuine insights into the human condition, and simultaneously suggesting new responses to the human condition, Seifert purifies individual psychology of certain overly-subjectivistic tendencies, and gives it a more personalist foundation.

Section Three has been entitled *Introductions to Systems.* The chapters in this section, each in some way, introduce the reader to a number of general characteristics of certain psychological or anthropological theories, thereby allowing the reader to see different ways in which a personalist psychology might become manifest. If a number of the systematic and critical contributions tend to focus on human finitude and imperfections (though not because these are the most significant human qualities), these contributions balance this volume by emphasizing a positive view of human persons and their perfections.

In Chapter Seven, Philip Sutton addresses "Personalist Themes in the Applied Thomistic Psychology of Anna Terruwe and Conrad Baars." At one point in his paper, Sutton tells us that Conrad Baars found that "the theoretical and practical goals of resolving repression by challenging or dismissing the conscience were so ethically and morally unacceptable that he considered leaving psychiatry." Baars remained in psychiatry largely because he succeeded in finding a partner in Anna Terruwe, with whom he worked to integrate the rational psychology of St. Thomas Aquinas into the theory and practice of psychology. Sutton compares the writings of Baars and Terruwe to the *Philosophical Principles* of the *Institute for Personalist Psychology* (found in an Appendix to this book), showing the fundamental compatibility and complementarity of their tenets. But undoubtedly Sutton achieves more than this as he presents the original work of Baars and Terruwe on the theory and treatment of repression, on the relationship of emotions to the will, on genuine affirmation versus pseudo-affirmation of oneself and others, and on the moral and religious spheres of life.

Chapter Eight is a paper by Fr. Adrian van Kaam, the founder of the science of formative spirituality, entitled "The Theology and Pre-theology of Empirical Christian Character and Personality Formation." I have included this in the *Introductions to Systems* section because in this paper Fr. van Kaam offers us a very helpful presentation of his system of formative theology, locating it within a range of psychological and theological theories of human nature, ranging from the non-transcendent, through the humanist and Christian transcendent theories. His own theory he describes as a *formative* theology for it aims not so much at providing *information* (this is the complementary aim of traditional theology), but above all at *forming* the individual's character and personality; or better at *transforming* human personalities into Christian personalities. However, Fr. van Kaam tells us that when the National Office of the USA Navy Chaplains took him and Dr. Muto around the world as team leaders, and they were confronted with persons representing 86 different faith groups, he found that much of his formative science could be applied at a pre-Christian level, relying primarily on lived-experience, while prescinding from specific religious doctrines. Naturally, to be able to do this is extremely valuable as one seeks a dialogue with all persons in a spirit of charity.

In the closing chapter of this book, Keith Houde presents us with, "Vision for a Personalist Psychology: Contributions of Paul Tournier and John Paul II." The paper begins with a brief introduction to the personalist movement in France, and with biographical sketches of Tournier and Pope John Paul II. Using as umbrella concepts five adjectives describing personalist psychology (wholistic, personal, dialogical, vital and integrative), Houde proceeds to consider a wide variety of topics relevant to personalist psychology, including the nature of causality, mystery, freedom, relations to God and others, power, love, vitality, stages in human development, depersonalization, spirit, religion, and the counseling encounter, among others. He closes his paper with a description of a "Personalist Agenda"—a fine agenda which could keep the *Institute for Personalist Psychology* and other like-minded organizations busy for a long while.

The "Philosophical Principles" of the *Institute for Personalist Psychology* have been published in an appendix to this book. Persons interested in learning more about the work of the *Institute for Personalist Psychology* are encouraged write to the address found below to receive free information on our newsletter and affiliate membership program.

Institute for Personalist Psychology
c/o Conference Office
Franciscan University of Steubenville
Steubenville, OH 43952-6701

James M. DuBois

Acknowledgements

This volume and the conference out of which it grew are the first fruits of the Institute for Personalist Psychology (IPP). I cannot possibly thank all of the persons who need to be thanked, so I ask for forgiveness from anyone who has been accidentally overlooked, with the assurance that your help has been appreciated. First of all, I thank all of the contributors to this volume for their fine contributions and to this book and to the discussions at the conference. I thank all those at Franciscan University of Steubenville who offered their support in connection with the conference and the founding of IPP: Nick Healy, the Vice-President of University Relations; Dr. Michael Healy, the Dean of Faculty; David Schmiesing, our Conference Coordinator; Justine Schmiesing, for help in typesetting; Dr. Andrew Hrezo, Associate Professor of Counseling and Secretary of IPP; and Fr. Michael Scanlan, T.O.R., President of Franciscan University. Thanks also to Michael Welker, John DuBois, and Jack Rook for their administrative help. Thanks to James Edwards for his time, advice, and support. Special thanks to all those who contributed financially to the Institute during its first year, thereby making our work possible. Here I would especially like to thank the International Academy of Philosophy which sponsored two of the speakers and provided support in editing this volume. I thank the members of the board of advisors and the board of trustees of the IPP for their participation in this project. Finally, I thank all of the participants in the opening conference of the IPP. Their presence made the conference a success, and gave these papers their first audience.

The Editor

I. Systematic Contributions

1

Are Human Beings Innately Defective?[1]

James M. DuBois

I. Introduction

In his book *Psychology as Religion*, Paul Vitz (1977) engages humanistic and self-help psychology with the following question: "Are we all that good?" As he concludes his reply he cites the former president of the APA, Donald Campbell, who claims that there is "social functionality and psychological validity to the concepts of sin and temptation and of original sin due to human carnal, animal nature" (p. 49).[2] I think that Campbell's statement is somewhat problematic insofar as it identifies being carnal as the source of "original sin," or of the aggressive tendencies connected with the concept of original sin. Nevertheless, it is interesting that Campbell finds the notion of original sin to have some validity. William Coulson (1972, 1990) also provides evidence that human defectiveness, as I shall call it, should be taken into account in the development of any educational or counseling program. A program which tries to unfold human potentials may succeed; only these potentials, he has found, are not quite as innocent and appealing as many would have us believe. Likewise, William Kilpatrick (1993), in his study *Why Johnny Can't Tell Right From Wrong*, finds that more attention needs to be paid to the defects in human nature. He argues that it is not enough to have persons clarify their values, nor even to find the right values. Persons additionally need examples and inspiration in order *to do* what is good. Although increasingly more people are recognizing this fact, he says that it is difficult for many to accept: "It violates the Romantic faith that children will do fine on their own, and—more to the point—it puts limits to adult self-expression" (p. 110).

The Institute for Personalist Psychology has proposed to develop a philosophy of science, a philosophy of human nature, and models of counseling which take into account the personal dimension of human existence. Philosophical personalism typically treats of a number of personal *perfections*: consciousness, self-determination, transcendence, world-openness, and many others. Yet, in the Institute's brochure entitled *Philosophical Principles*, it was necessary to include among the ten theses about the human person a statement on human limitations and imperfections.[3] Only in this fashion, it was thought, could our personalism avoid being naive, and succeed in portraying human nature accurately. In this brochure we do not claim that each of the ten theses is self-evident, rather we say that the Institute is dedicated to *demonstrating* these theses. The passages I quoted at the outset make it apparent that a number of the members of the Institute's board of advisors, Vitz, Coulson and Kilpatrick, have already addressed the topic of human defectiveness. Nevertheless, in the context of the inaugural conference of the Institute it seems appropriate to consider further the nature and the implications of this aspect of human nature. Many psychologists and educators influenced by New Age philosophies and enlightenment thought appear either to deny or to ignore the innate defects in human nature; and many who in principle admit that human beings are defective do not consider sufficiently well the implications of this fact for education and clinical practice.[4]

I will start my reflections by analyzing two concepts which appear in the ninth thesis of the Institute's brochure on philosophical principles: the concept of "imperfection" and the concept of "by nature." Gabriel Marcel (1973), Paul Ricoeur (1986), and numerous other philosophers have used philosophical methods to bring the phenomenon of defective nature to evidence. Undoubtedly they have shown that philosophical reflection has much to offer to an analysis of this problem. However, I will argue that the sense in which defectiveness characterizes human beings by nature excludes the possibility of a *direct philosophical insight* into human defectiveness; that is, there is no *self-evident* relation between being human and being defective.

If I am correct, then this raises certain questions of method. Many will recognize in the ninth thesis an affirmation of the doctrine of the Fall which is set forth in the book of Genesis. For those who accept the authority of the Hebrew Scriptures, there are no methodological difficulties connected with substantiating our thesis on human imperfection: the inerrant word of God teaches us this truth. However, there are several reasons why even Jewish, Islamic and Christian psychologists or psychiatrists might wish to substantiate the thesis independently of Judeo-Christian revelation. First of all, recognizing that human beings are fundamentally imperfect is relevant to all psychological praxis. Because many psychologists do not accept the authority of Scriptures, it is desirable to elucidate this phenomenon using noncontroversial empirical data, so as to make our conclusion accessible to as many as possible. Moreover, in the United States we live in a pluralistic society which forbids that teachers in public institutions of education draw upon revelation in presenting their class material. Thus, if we want our work to be valuable within the educational system of a pluralistic nation it must prescind from revelation and draw from data which can be examined by all persons, regardless of their faith perspective. Finally, for scientific reasons we might very well wish to distinguish between those propositions which we know through natural reason and those propositions which we believe on the basis of revelation or authority. For these reasons, I will try to offer evidence for innate defects in human nature based on what is given empirically. I will then answer a few basic objections to this project, and conclude by suggesting the relevance of our findings for a personalist psychology.

However, before attempting to demonstrate that human beings are innately defective, I would like to clarify what it is that I am trying to show. Those who defend a biblical account of the Fall are often (though I think wrongly) said to hold a view of human beings as basically evil, whereas many humanists hold that human beings are basically good. Regardless of how one interprets the biblical account, I think that this way of conceiving the debate is basically mistaken. The question goes far beyond good versus evil; it concerns additionally personal wholeness versus incompleteness, and personal health versus personal illness. Defectiveness is not only a characteristic of ourselves, it is something we *suffer from*, and *suffer with* throughout our lives. We will return to this point in the conclusion to this paper.

II. Finitude and Defectiveness

In the ninth paragraph of our *Philosophical Principles* reference is made both to the *limitation* of all human perfections and to *imperfections*. This is not a redundant form of expression; two distinct things are meant here, though they may easily be confused.

What is meant by "limitations" might best be understood with reference to the scholastic concept of *pure perfections*. This concept is said to have its roots in St. Anselm's ontological argument for the existence of God, but it is perhaps most fully developed in the writings of the Franciscan thinker, Bd. John Duns Scotus. These pure perfections are perfections which are absolutely good in themselves, and which do not exclude any other perfections which are absolutely speaking better to possess than not to possess. If we consider properties such as having real existence, being alive, being conscious, possessing knowledge, possessing moral goodness and so forth, we see that each of the perfections are absolutely speaking good in and of themselves, and none of them excludes any other perfection of this sort.[5] These pure perfections are opposed to *mixed perfections*, such as having strong muscles, i.e., to perfections which are not absolutely speaking better to possess than not to possess, partly because they necessarily exclude certain pure perfections. For example, having strong muscles excludes the perfections of being indivisible, indestructible, infinite, and so forth. According to the scholastic notion, there are some pure perfections which all real beings possess, such as having real existence; some which God and only some creatures possess, such as being alive and conscious; and some which only God possesses, such as having a necessary, real existence. Now of those pure perfections which God and creatures share in common, it was said that contingent and finite beings possess these perfections to a *limited degree*, and not, as God, to an infinite degree. When we refer to the human being as a *person*, we necessarily refer to a whole host of perfections. We do not refer to the human being simply as some kind of real being, but as a real being with the potential to be rational, to gain knowledge, to love, to determine one's own actions, indeed, to govern and determine one's very self. Yet it is clear that each of these pure perfections which come with being a person are possessed by human beings to a limited degree. I have knowledge, but not complete knowledge of all being. I can love, but my love is limited both in its quality and in the range of goods towards which it is directed. I am free to determine myself, but I am not determined only by my free actions, but also by my genetic make-up and my environment.

Some would say that already at the level of being finite or limited we are dealing with an imperfection in human nature. It is true that this kind of finitude implies a lack, and is a particular kind of imperfection. Nevertheless, when the ninth thesis of the Institute's *Philosophical Principles* refers not only to limitations, but also to imperfections, something more fundamentally imperfect about human nature is meant. What is meant here is that human beings are not only limited, but *defective*. I shall offer several examples in order to point to the difference between being imperfect in the sense of being finite and being imperfect in the sense of being defective. Consider the difference between possessing limited knowledge and *falling into error*, between bringing about a limited number of goods and *bringing about things which are evil*, between enjoying a limited number of pleasures in a limited degree and *suffering pain and anguish*, between being created in time and *being destined to die*, and so forth. In the cases of falling into error, bringing about things which are evil, suffering pain and anguish, and being destined to die, we encounter characteristics that are not perfections limited in accordance with our finite nature, rather they are characteristics of the human person which can only be denoted as defects.[6]

Were we to say simply that *most* human beings are *as a matter of fact* imperfect in this strong sense of being defective, then our claim would be quite easy to substantiate. One might simply listen to the evening news. However, this is not what has been claimed. Our claim was rather that human beings are *by nature* imperfect, and this is much more difficult to verify. In order to appreciate the difficulties to which I refer we must first clarify what is meant with the phrase "by nature".

III. Two Meanings Of The Phrase "By Nature"

Consider two instances in which we might correctly say something belongs to the nature of an object, in other words, that an object is by nature such and such. We might say:

1. that a human being by nature has two eyes, and
2. that responsibility by nature presupposes freedom.

In order to explain the significant difference between these two uses of the phrase "by nature," I would like to introduce a distinction made by von Hildebrand

(1991) between two different kinds of essential unities. In the first instance, von Hildebrand refers to *meaningful* or *morphic essences*. Examples of such essences would be the nature of the human body or the nature of water. Here we do not find a random unity of the various aspects of the essence, rather we find that the essence is meaningful. The essence comprises a kind, such that we may speak in general terms of things such as human bodies or pools of water. There are general truths which we may discover about these kinds, which for the most part comprise the "natural kinds" about which Aristotle spoke. That human beings have two eyes, that water freezes at 32 degrees Fahrenheit, appear to be generally true. But the nature of the human body is such that we can imagine exceptions, and we could never have intuited this truth simply by considering the nature of the other body parts. Yes, there are interconnections, but they appear contingent or nonnecessary, and they are knowable only through empirical investigation. According to von Hildebrand, these meaningful essences comprise the proper object of the *natural sciences*.

In contrast to these meaningful essences, von Hildebrand refers to *necessary essences*. Such essences are exemplified in the nature of a triangle, of propositions, of moral goodness, of promising, or of responsibility. These objects or essential unities comprise the proper object of the philosophical sciences. The truths about these objects have often been called *a priori*, and have been contrasted to the so-called *a posteriori* truths which characterize the meaningful essences proper to the empirical sciences. Von Hildebrand would claim that responsibility has a necessary essence, and that we may accordingly discover *a priori* truths about the nature of responsibility. The example I offered above was that responsibility by nature presupposes the freedom of the responsible subject. According to a Kantian interpretation, the necessity of our knowledge arises from a psychological source: we simply cannot think the state of affairs to be otherwise. But von Hildebrand, Reinach, Scheler and many of the early phenomenologists, believed that the necessity which characterizes our truth about responsibility finds its source not in our thought, but in the essence of responsibility, in the objective connection between freedom and responsibility which exists *prior to our thinking about it*.

Our concern in discussing the nature of philosophical essences is to see whether, in considering the essence of being human, we can arrive at a direct philosophical intuition of human defectiveness; or better put, whether we can apprehend a necessary connection between human nature and defectiveness which finds its source in human nature itself. It seems to me that we cannot. One might well describe human beings as *bodily persons*. There are many necessary truths which can be known about such beings. Such truths would concern the freedom and the rationality of these beings, the nature of consciousness, knowledge, moral goodness, volition, and so forth. Thus far we deal only with perfections. Insofar as they are bodily we encounter a whole new set of characteristics, finitude among them. However, while we may intuit the fact that such beings do not possess all pure perfections to an infinite degree, we cannot arrive intuitively at the fact that such beings are defective. This fact helps us, at least in part, to understand why many of the philosophers and psychologists who use intuitive methods of understanding human nature have often overlooked or ignored the defective side of human nature: this side appears to be contingent, and as such it cannot ground *a priori* truths; it cannot be the source of necessary states of affairs which are directly apprehended in a philosophical intuition.

Were necessary essences the only kinds of natures we recognized, then we could never speak of defectiveness as belonging to human beings "by nature." However, von Hildebrand's analysis allows us to recognize a second, legitimate kind of *nature*; namely meaningful, empirical natures which form general kinds, though the unity of their characteristics appears contingent and must be discovered using the methods proper to the natural sciences. In what follows I would like to argue that human beings are defective "by nature" in the same sense in which human beings have two eyes, and that the truth of the assertion about human defectiveness is known with at least as much certainty as is the truth of the judgment about human beings having two eyes. But just like the proposition that human beings by nature have two eyes, so too the truth of our proposition concerning human defectiveness is contingent and must be verified empirically.[7] One might also note here that it is not only the fact *that* we are defective which is contingent, but the particular way in which an individual person is characterized by imperfections is contingent and variable. Human beings necessarily possess, at least in potency, a number of perfections such as freedom, but the extent to which we actualize these perfections is non-necessary.[8] This fact must be borne in mind as one reads the following survey of human imperfections, and it becomes particularly relevant in section VI (c), which concerns self-actualization.

IV. Ten Items Of Empirical Evidence For Innate Defects In Human Nature

How do we discover that human beings are defective? I would suggest that it comes to the child as something of a surprise to find that human beings are defective. How easily the child is disillusioned! Children exclaim: "but that isn't fair!"—as though that fact alone ought to suffice for the nonexistence of the unfair state of affairs. Even when they come to see faults in others, they continue to be disillusioned when they find that even a priest, one supposedly devoted entirely to God, sins; or that the school teacher, one supposedly devoted to knowledge and education, has passed on an error; or that a doctor, one who supposedly has learned how to heal the human body, cannot save a loved one from death.

Yet who among us here today continues to be disillusioned by these same phenomena? Have we grown cynical, or have we simply come to recognize the unfortunate but universal condition of human persons? I believe the latter. But the process through which we come to recognize the innate and universal character of human defectiveness is slow and empirical.

I propose that each of the following ten facts about human nature, while they do not belong necessarily to the essence of being a person, and hence cannot be known through a pure philosophical intuition, are nevertheless evidently given in our experience of human nature. These facts are given in our experience of *human nature* (1) as it is directly experienced *in ourselves*, (2) as it is experienced in *other persons* around us, and (3) as it is found *described in pieces of literature, musical lyrics, and historical narratives* throughout *all* ages.

In no way are the following ten considerations meant to provide an exhaustive inventory of human defects. They are, however, meant to suggest the depth and the range of human defectiveness, and to show that these defects *go beyond anything which could be understood as strictly environmental or physical in nature.*

1. The first and most evident human defect is death. Human beings are *destined to die*. There is nothing about human nature as such which says that our bodies ought to deteriorate and one day cease to function, leaving others with no sensible evidence that we continue to live as conscious beings. Yet, with only a few claimed exceptions, denoted as supernatural, this is the case. Death has a tragic element which extends beyond the individual who is subject to death. Death separates parents from children, often during times of great need, and death almost always leaves behind itself a trail of tears. Even if there is an afterlife, death remains an evil; for at least temporarily it violently separates a person from his body, thereby destroying the unity which he deeply experiences. If there is no afterlife, then death is particularly evil, in that it thwarts a natural human longing and directedness towards the eternal, a directedness which animals do not reveal, even if they do exhibit a 'survival instinct.'[9]

2. Human beings are *ignorant* about issues *of the greatest importance* to their lives. I am not here talking merely of the finitude of human knowledge, but of *insufficient knowledge*, of dangerous or pathetic ignorance. We do not know whether the person we marry will be faithful and good to us; we do not know how to cure many things which ail us; we do not know, but rather must believe the content of our religious faith, content which concerns our future after death;[10] almost all of our greatest endeavors involve risk, and sometimes our ignorance proves particularly dangerous to our well being. Many great pieces of literature have been devoted to this theme, including Sophocles' *Oedipus Rex* and the Arabian tale of *Death in Tehran.*

3. Human beings *err and are subject to self-deception.* We not only err when dealing with abstract problems, we err in judging our own motives, our own moral status, our knowledge of different themes and persons. Psychoanalysis speaks here of rationalizing our behaviors, of projecting our feelings, of repressing certain facts, and in extreme case of suffering from delusions. Though it seems that few of us reveal all of the various forms of self-deception, it seems general to human nature that we deceive ourselves in at least some ways at some times.

4. Human behavior seems partially influenced by so-called *drives, innate urges, or tendencies*. Many of these would *encourage us to do things that we believe are immoral and, or, unhealthy*. It appears that most persons at some period in time

wrestle with at least some of the following urges: the urge to overeat, the urge to have sex irresponsibly, the urge to strike another person, the urge to abandon responsibilities to ourselves and to others in order to seek pleasure or to be lazy, the urge to make ourselves the center of attention in inappropriate ways at inappropriate times, and so forth. Even if we are free to fight against these urges, these urges are generally present as motivating factors which we must fight against if we are to preserve our freedom.[11]

5. Our *freedom of choice is limited* concerning many of the most *important factors which determine us*. We are not free to choose our genetic make-up, something which affects us so deeply in our physical appearance, our health, our intelligence, and our temperaments. We are not free to choose who raises us, who shall be our first teachers and what shall be the content of our education. We do not choose our religious upbringing or lack thereof. We do not choose the cultural milieu into which we are born, and so on. All of these restrictions of choice seem innate to the human condition, and yet they are severe defects insofar as these unchosen factors determine us, often in ways which are *not in our best interest*, and are *against our own subsequent desires*.

6. Human beings *abuse their free will*. Wojtyla has argued that our deepest sense of freedom lies not in a freedom *from*, but in a freedom *for*. When we speak of freedom we do not merely mean that we are free from being entirely determined by genetic and environmental factors. We mean additionally that we are free to will the good, to actualize new states of affairs beyond ourselves, and new values within ourselves. Yet this power to bring about new states of affairs and to determine our very being is sometimes used to bring about not good, but evil states of affairs, to actualize not values, but disvalues in ourselves. In this sense we abuse our freedom. And who can deny that he or she has ever done anything which was wrong, which one knew to be bad either in itself, or for oneself, or for another?

7. Human beings have *inappropriate emotional responses*. It is not only the case that we sometimes fail to grieve when we think we ought to, e.g. at a funeral, but we sometimes feel envy at another's good fortune, or joy at another's bad fortune. The point here is not that our emotional responses are not free, but rather than our spontaneous emotional responses often do not correspond to the value of the situations we find ourselves in.[12]

8. Whereas vices seem to develop without effort—we need only to go along with our urges—virtues are acquired and preserved only with tremendous effort. The greatest human potential is to become virtuous; yet all too often this potential to be virtuous is never actualized, and when it is, it is done only through a struggle against oneself. It may even be the case that by nature we possess certain virtues such as generosity or kindness, but if one grasps the unity of the virtues, the fact that all virtues are ordained for each other and can be destroyed through the lack of just one virtue, then we see that no one has an easy go of it in acquiring and preserving virtue.

9. Human beings are subject to physical illness, suffering, and pain. As we

suffer physically, we sometimes feel that it permeates our entire being. We may find that it colors our entire conscious life, and gives direction to our thoughts and actions. Yet, as Hume noted, the most intense sufferings are spiritual: fear, anxiety, guilt, grief, anger, loathing, and the like.

10. All human perfections are surprisingly *fragile*, i.e., easily lost or diminished. A bump on the head may cause us to lose consciousness; giving in to an addiction may cause a loss of freedom; giving in to immoral behavior may cause a blindness to certain moral values;[13] immoral behavior causes us to diminish in our moral goodness;[14] and our very life on earth is contingent upon so many trivial factors. Pascal noted this feature well, when side by side with his remark that man as a thinking being is more noble than the universe, he observes that man is "but a reed, the most fragile thing in nature."

I think that these ten defects characterize all human beings. We come to recognize these defects empirically, through our experience of ourselves, of others, and of human nature as it is recorded in literature and historical narratives. It is only at the level of religious faith that we might recognize exceptions, and even then these are not accepted as natural variations, but as supernatural variations.

V. Some Objections, Replies, and Unanswered Questions

Before considering the implications of human defectiveness for counseling and educational psychology, I would like to address two objections to my work thus far. The first concerns my method, whereas the second concerns the conclusion I have just drawn.

a. The Notion of Science Underlying this Project

It is clear that many psychologists will claim that this project was neither empirical nor scientific. If by 'scientific' one means based strictly upon what is observable to the senses, or what is strictly quantifiable, then obviously this project was not scientific, and nor, for that matter, is much of psychology, chemistry and physics. To some extent the question at hand concerns *what kind of a science* psychology should be. More specifically, one must ask whether psychology ought to take a "top-down" or a "bottom-up" approach to the human person. Many psychologists will argue that scientific assertions are to concern what is molecular rather than what is molar. They believe that science ought to begin with basic and noncontroversial observations, e.g. of behavior or of brain activities, and then attempt to construct a broader picture of human nature on the basis of this (i.e., work from the bottom up).[15] In the other camp stand those who believe that we can accept a wide number of *a priori* truths, truths which are self-evident, universal and necessarily true, e.g. the truth that one is responsible only insofar as one is free. Many within this same camp choose also to trust our commonsense beliefs, e.g. that I cry because I am sad, and not vice versa. These same persons will argue that a conclusion constructed out of molecular data which contradicts these sorts of self-evident claims has refuted itself through a *reductio ad absurdum*. What I have said so far ought to make it clear that the bottom-up versus top-down debate ultimately concerns what kinds of modes of gaining knowledge we ought to put our trust in. As far as I can tell, almost nobody in the contemporary debate questions whether we can trust the basic findings of the natural sciences, for example, that the brain operates largely through electrical and hormonal activities, and that these activities influence human behavior. Put in another way, almost nobody generally distrusts molecular observations. Rather, what is questioned is whether, *in addition to the findings of the natural sciences*, our commonsense beliefs about ourselves are warranted, and further, whether we can fully trust our philosophical intuitions regarding data such as human thought, free action, and so forth. Here I can only assert that I think we can and must trust commonsense beliefs and philosophical intuitions, and that if we choose to distrust these, we undermine the epistemological foundations of all science.[16]

Clearly, the approach taken in this paper has been a 'top down' or molar approach, one which chooses to trust our experiences of death, of self-deception, of illness, and the rest. However, the fact that one chooses to accept these data at face value does not mean that one is developing a naive or 'folk psychological' theory. The conclusions of this paper were not reached in a haphazard or noncritical manner, and they share several things in common with all scientific conclusions. Here I will consider only four marks of scientific knowledge.

1. Science seeks knowledge of propositions which concern patterns, percentages, or general laws.

Accordingly, we tried to find defects which characterize human nature in general, and tried to show that the phenomenon of being defective is innate and thus universal.

2. Science aims at providing a consistent and coherent body of knowledge.

Our reflections on imperfections found coherence insofar as they all stemmed from the same source: human nature. Our reflections are further consistent with the findings of Coulson's experiments with Carl Rogers, with Kilpatrick's investigation of the results of moral education programs, with several sources cited by Vitz which concern biological evidence, as well as the results gained from the study of Judeo-Christian theology.

3. Science draws from public evidence.

Our reflections are based on certain *data* which are not public, e.g. my inner experience of myself. However, the *method* used to gain this data may be used universally, namely, self-reflection. But furthermore, we drew from much data which are public: human nature as it is found in the multitudes capable of being observed at any moment, and as it is depicted in literature and historical narratives throughout the ages, i.e. accounts which are available for anyone to read and examine.

4. Many would add a fourth characteristic of scientific knowledge, namely, that the evidence it is based on must be empirical: it must deal with concrete,

observable data.

This is not a feature of all sciences, e.g. mathematics and philosophy, but as the data at hand are not of an *a priori* nature, it is perhaps a fair requirement. Thus, many will raise the following question: If we claim to be proceeding empirically, then why have we felt so free to draw conclusions independently of statistical analysis or experimentation?

The short answer to this question is that we do not need statistical analysis or experimentation in order to draw these conclusions. All people die and we know this. It is a *contingent and empirical* fact that human beings die, but it is a fact that can be apprehended independently of formal statistical analysis or experimentation. I would say the same of the remaining nine points. Even if data such as moral values and free choice are not bluntly apprehended via the senses, they are data which are apprehended empirically: they exist in time and in real particulars, and they are data which are present for all to apprehend, even if all do not apprehend them. Some of our considerations, then, require a broad notion of "observability," one which goes beyond visual apprehension, and the related senses. But it is precisely this notion of observability that rightly permits clinical psychologists to acknowledge the existence of *urges* such as the sexual urge, and *emotions* such fear or anxiety.

In short, our project here is based upon a *broad* notion of science, but one which does not violate any of the classical and non-arbitrary rules for science.

b. Social Arrangements and Human Defects

Of course, some will grant that our approach was legitimate, but nevertheless disagree with our conclusion. Among these there will be persons who will also grant that the above characteristics are defects, and further that these characteristics appear in all human beings. They will, however, claim that the term 'innate' should not be used because the source of the problem lies outside of the individual; it lies in our present social arrangements.

I would suggest that the initial appeal of this popular alternative theory arises from the common tendency to reduce the issue of defectiveness to the issue of moral evil, aggression, or something similar. However, we have resisted this from the start. Our innate defects go far beyond any tendency to do evil. Death is not the product of society. Pathetic ignorance concerning many issues of great importance does not arise from society. The structures of self-deception do not arise solely from society, they are only shaped by society. Our urges may be influenced by society, e.g. the prevalence of pornography may intensify, pervert, or more frequently give rise to the experience of a sexual urge, but there is no reason to believe that the urge itself derives from our society, that if society were arranged otherwise we might feel an urge to be chaste. The limitations on our freedom of choice are inherent to our biological nature and to our developmental status at birth, among other things. No alterations of society could change these facts about human nature.

The question as to whether the sources of moral evil stem from within human beings or from without cannot be fully treated here. However, the experiences of *being responsible* and of *being guilty* point to the fact that it is, not society, but I myself who brought about the disvalue or wrong state of affairs. Furthermore, a careful observation of children would seem to suggest that the influence of society has traditionally been to curb aggressive or evil tendencies, rather than to implant these tendencies. Finally, we may say the following. The fact that society has failed to rearrange itself so as to eliminate aggression and immorality would seem to derive either from a lack of knowledge as to how to accomplish this, a lack of ability to implement the new structure, or a lack of desire to bring about this good. In any case the failure to rearrange society into a genuine utopia proves that we are defective: we are either ignorant, impotent, or lacking good will, or a combination of these three. In any case we are defective.

Rather than to consider further objections, I would like to suggest two remaining questions which have gone unanswered, but which should be addressed within the context of a personalist psychology. First, could the innate character of these defects have a biological source? Would it be possible to find a "defect-gene," which could perhaps be eliminated through genetic engineering? A reply to this question would have to take into account the *nonphysical* characteristic of many of the defects, and further the *diversity* of the defects, such that they appear to permeate not only our intelligence, but all levels of our existence.

Second, what does the idea of innate defects do to our notion of responsibility? Ironically, our example of an *a priori* philosophical truth was that "responsibility presupposes the freedom of the subject." Is the universality of the abuse of freedom evidence that our will is not wholly free to choose good? And if so are we responsible for our immoral actions? It will not suffice to point out that an abused freedom is still a real freedom. The phenomenon of defectiveness leads us to ask whether the abuses of freedom stem from something determined, and whether this would alleviate us of responsibility. We see here a problem which involves levels of freedom, and levels of responsibility.

VI. Conclusion: The Implications Of Innate Defects For A Personalist Psychology

a. Inappropriate Responses to Human Defectiveness

Many different responses to human defectiveness are possible. One could, for example, try to go through life ignoring the various defects, while focussing exclusively on human perfections and possibilities. However, this approach is not only existentially superficial, it is also in very many ways deeply irresponsible. Each one of the ten defects discussed above requires a healthy response, and to ignore the defect is to exclude the possibility of an adequate response.

Other people naively choose to believe that human efforts will allow us to overcome these defects. Enlightenment, utopian, and New Age thinkers, each in their own way, defend this view. I think that I have already responded to this view in part by clarifying in what sense these defects are innate and universal, and to what extent they cannot be thought to be the result of social arrangements. These views have the problem that they encourage persons to engage in a form of self-deception, again, preventing the possibility of an adequate response.

At the other extreme there are those who "face the facts," but respond in despair. This sort of response can manifest itself in a variety of ways. One such manifestation is resentment. Scheler in particular has shown that when a certain good seems withheld from a person, the response of resentment may lead to the devaluation of the good at stake. For example, because death leaves no visible trace of the person, it appears to some that the good of eternal life is withheld from us. Accordingly, the response of despair, when coupled with resentment, involves a devaluation of human life. This response of resentment has been discussed not only by Scheler (1961), but also by Wojtyla (1981), and at a more popular level, by Aesop, who tells the tale of the fox and the "sour grapes." The response of despair may also manifest itself in various forms of *escape* from the problems of life, e.g., through drug use, excessive entertainment, sexual promiscuity, and suicide.

All this leads us to ask whether there are appropriate responses to human defects, and if so, what they would entail.

b. Appropriate Responses to our Metaphysical Situation

i. *Humble acceptance and the need for grace.* In his contribution to this conference, Josef Seifert discusses the fact that the appropriate responses to our metaphysical situation are gratitude and humility; gratitude for the gift of existence and a humble acceptance of the fact that we are not God. In considering the relationship of human defectiveness to the field of psychology, it seems appropriate to note that these responses of humble acceptance and gratitude are not only appropriate to our situation, they are also psychologically healthy. Frankl writes that the "acceptance of finiteness is the precondition to mental health and human progress, while the inability to accept it is characteristic of the neurotic personality" (p. 58, 1985). Recognizing our limitations and imperfections may help us to develop a healthy sense of patience with ourselves, because we may accept here and now that we shall suffer from, and suffer with, our own defective nature throughout our entire lives. Recognition of the fact that we are innately imperfect may also help certain persons to overcome scrupulosity. In the phenomenon of human defectiveness we recognize that we are not the free and responsible source of all of the bad which surrounds us, but only of a particular portion of it. Recognition of our defective nature may also help us not to act on certain urges and impulses. On the one hand, there is something quite natural about acting on the basis of an urge. But if we learn to distinguish in our own minds between those motivational inspirations which are in keeping with what is good and right, and those motivational inspirations which stem strictly from our defective nature, then we may be less tempted to act on the latter. If we can identify them as stemming from defects, then they will be stripped of a certain legitimacy that they claim as motivational forces.

I might note here that the approach to recovery of *Alcoholics Anonymous* entails not only a frank admission and acceptance of one's weakness, but its also requires the addict to turn to a "higher power." Hand in hand with the response of accepting one's own weakness, at least within the original *AA* model, goes an appeal for grace, an appeal for the gifts of strength and healing. Many Christian and non-Christian models are finding that the notion of grace needs to be more deeply explored in dealing with human problems, innate and non-innate, and this undoubtedly is an area which personalist psychologists cannot ignore.

ii. *Humor*. To summarize the results of section IV above, we could make the following diagnosis of human nature: Human beings are destined to die, are ignorant, self-deceiving, abusive of freedom, largely determined independently of their freewill, emotionally disordered, resistant to virtue, subject to illness, suffering and pain, and are fragile regarding all their perfections.

If some of us laugh upon hearing such a description, it is not without reason. C.S. Lewis (1960) points to the psychohygenic effects of laughter in his treatment of Venus, or the Spirit of Erotic Love. He writes that Venus

> ... makes a game of us. When every overt act is impossible and even glances cannot be exchanged—in trains, in shops, and at interminable parties—she will assail [two lovers] ... with all her force. An hour later, when time and place agree, she will have mysteriously withdrawn; perhaps from only one of them. What a pother this must raise—what resentments, self-pities, suspicions, wounded vanities and all the current chatter about "frustration"—in those who have deified her! *But sensible lovers laugh.* (p. 141)

Viktor Frankl, in his account of his experiences in the Nazi concentration camps, writes, "The attempt to develop a sense of humor and to see things in a humorous light is some kind of trick learned while mastering the art of living" (1962, p. 69). In these passages from Lewis and Frankl we see that laughter and a sense of humor may be more than the result of unconscious defense mechanisms, they may be consciously fostered, and—at least to some extent—they may be seen to be appropriate responses to certain discrepancies that we find in our own nature, e.g. the discrepancy between human dignity and the need to defecate. A proper sense of humor towards ourselves may be a healthy way of accepting without pride our defective state.

c. Defectiveness and Self-Actualization

At this point, however, some will rightly want to know whether I am here defending a view which says that we need simply to live with ourselves as defective, and that there is no place for a psychology of self-actualization. This I do not intend to say. We do need to accept our limitations and even some defects as innate. However, *the greatest human perfections, i.e., the virtues, exist in us only as potentialities*, and *it is our task to actualize them.* The real questions, then, which concern self-actualization are: *which* potentialities are we to actualize, and *how* this is to be achieved.

Concerning which potentialities are to be actualized we must recall Coulson's work with the human potentials movement, but also a classic line from Frankl (1985), where he writes:

> Socrates ... confessed to the potentiality within him to become a criminal and, therefore, if he had succeeded in fully developing his potentialities, the great defender of law and justice would have been a common law breaker. ... The potentialities of life are not indifferent possibilities; they must be seen in the light of meaning and values.

In this article, entitled "Beyond Self-Actualization and Self-Expression," Frankl actually gives us sound advice on *how* one becomes self-actualized. He claims, as Scheler and Kant did before him, that many human goods can come about only as by-products or side-effects. Among these goods he counts happiness, peace of mind, and a good conscience. Each of these arises only as we concern ourselves with something *transcendent*, with something beyond ourselves, e.g. as we love another person, or as we concern ourselves with certain tasks which appear to be uniquely ours. Again, this view is wholly consist with William Coulson's well-documented experience with the human potentials movement as reported in the present volume. The problems he cited did not arise from actualizing human potentialities *per se*; they arose from actualizing human potentialities without reference to the value-question concerning *which* potentialities should be developed, and from the tendency to go after self-actualization in a non-transcendent fashion, by turning inward on oneself, rather than outward towards other goods and other persons.[17] As I understand it, it is this latter tendency of many humanistic and psychoanalytic models which leads Coulson to speak of the TMP problem: the problem of Too Much Psychology.

To bring these reflections to a point: Psychologists and patients alike must frankly accept that human beings are defective. But they ought not to focus on this. To do so would be disheartening and would encourage an unhealthy occupation with oneself. To the extent that one ought to seek self-actualization, e.g. the actualization of virtues in oneself, this can only be done indirectly, by concerning oneself with objective goods which exist in the world, or with specific tasks which we are called to bring to fulfillment. In this sense, we can only agree with the logotherapists who focus on future positive tasks that the patient can actualize, rather than past traumas, or for that matter, one's own defects for their own sake.

d. Defectiveness and the Metaphysics of Meaning

Before concluding these reflections on innate defects, I would like to consider briefly one last claim made by Viktor Frankl, one which is directly relevant to our topic. Frankl too conceives of human defectiveness in a somewhat broad sense, referring to a tragic triad which is inherent to human life: pain, guilt, and death. But he does not conceive these phenomena as things which are merely to be accepted. He conceives them as things which must be *meaningful*. In *Man's Search for Meaning* he writes: "If there is a meaning in life at all, then *there must be a meaning in suffering*. Suffering is an ineradicable part of life, even as fate and death. Without suffering and death human life cannot be complete" (1962, p. 67, emphasis added). Is this true? In order for life to have meaning, must all aspects of human life have meaning, including those which are tied up with our defectiveness? Here we must distinguish two different senses of 'meaning'. In some cases, Frankl refers to meaning as something that we live for, or as that for which we are responsible. Meaning in this sense gives us purpose and direction in life. We do not, or should not live for pain, guilt or death; so they do not possess meaning in this sense.[18] However, we may also say something has meaning in the sense of existing for a reason, or being create for some end. In this sense pain, guilt and death may have some meaning. However, in my opinion, we are here confronted with mystery: if it is an obvious empirical fact that human beings are defective, it is not obvious *why* they are defective. In asking *why* human beings are defective we may inquire into both *efficient* and *final* causes: *what* made us this way, and to what *purpose* or end?

I would like to cite once again the Institute's *Philosophical Principles*. It says there that "it may well be that a nonreligious person cannot find adequate answers to the most fundamental questions concerning the nature and meaning of human life." Although human defectiveness may be discovered empirically, its ultimate origins, and the ultimate meaning connected with its persistence seem to escape natural explanation. Here we may find that the Judeo-Christian understanding of sin and atonement provides the key to understanding what could not be understood at a natural level. In Alan Wolter's introduction to Bd. Duns Scotus's treatise on "the necessity of revealed knowledge," he summarizes Scotus' position on the transition from natural reason to revelation:

> Since one part of every contradiction is true, it follows that either the face-to-face vision and enjoyment of God is our goal, or it is not. If reason cannot tell us which of the two alternatives is correct, at least we can see we are faced with a problem that cannot be reasonably ignored or concerning whose solution we dare remain in doubt. Reason, in a word, prods us to investigate whether or not God has revealed something supernaturally on this subject. (1951, p. 237)

By analogy, we might say that either pain, guilt and death are meaningful and serve a purpose, or they do not. We cannot recognize the ultimate origins and the purpose of these human defects; but, given the *tragic and innate* character of suffering and death, it appears that the meaningfulness and the sense of human life hinges upon finding an answer to this question. Hence reason prompts us to see whether or not their is a supernatural source through which we may come to understand what is presently our natural predicament. At the outset I offered reasons why personalist psychologists might prescind from Revelation; in conclusion I suggest there are reasons for the same to seek Revelation.

NOTES

[1] I am very grateful to the many participants who raised questions about, or made comments on, my paper, and to John White who did the same with a later draft. These questions and comments led to significant improvements in this text.

[2] Vitz is here citing Campbell (1974).

[3] See the Appendix to this volume for the *Philosophical Principles* of the Institute for Personalist Psychology.

[4] The former problem, of denying or ignoring human defects, is characteristic of most so-called humanistic psychologies. Perhaps Rogers (1961) defended a naive view of human nature most openly, but the same view is present to some extent in the writings of May, Maslow, and Fromm. Fromm's view is significantly more sophisticated, but Vitz (1977) nevertheless finds that it is not consistently realistic. The latter problem mentioned here, *viz.*, not considering sufficiently well the significance or practical implications of the intrinsic imperfections in human nature is perhaps more characteristic of so-called rationalistic approaches. Kilpatrick (1993) finds that Kohlberg's moral reasoning approach (especially during the early years of his research, e.g. Kohlberg, 1971), insofar as it is used not as a diagnostic tool, but as an educational tool, assumes too much. Kilpatrick argues that, at least implicitly, it assumes that human beings do not need to be taught right and wrong, but will simply arrive at the right answer, and it assumes that human beings will do what they know it right without the assistance of models, stories, and discipline.

[5] Wolter (1946) offers a fine introduction to the notion of pure perfections in Scotus.

[6] Some would prefer to call these defects 'evils.' However, due to the moral overtones which the word evil has taken on, I prefer the term 'defect.' This serves well to indicate that the human person is not as it should be, that it is lacking perfections that it ought to have. This is not a moral judgment, but it is normative. Insofar as I make this normative judgment, I do indeed presuppose that there is an ideal structure to the person. In this paper I am not able to defend the ontology which underlies this assertion, but I think that it has been adequately defended elsewhere. Cf. Seifert (1987), who explicitly identifies a structure of the person which is necessary and ideal, and Crosby (forthcoming) and Wojtyla (1977) who elucidate well many of the aspects of the structure to which I refer. When one thinks through it, the entire tradition of ethical realism presupposes that there is a structure of the human person which is at least (1) intelligible and (2) non-changing, if not necessary.

[7] By the way, although we have chosen not to rely upon the biblical account of the Fall, it is interesting to note in this connection that the book of Genesis confirms the fact that defects, as opposed to finitude, are not necessarily rooted in human nature, but are only as a matter of fact part of human nature. They resulted, according to this account, from a free and contingent human action. In contrast to this, *personal* characteristics, such as freedom, knowledge and moral agency—those through which we appear most "in the image and likeness of God"—*do* appear inherent to being human. It is especially these personal features, such as freedom and moral agency, which essentially set us apart from subhuman creatures such as apes or dolphins.

[8] Even though the essence of being a person entails that we possess perfections such as freedom, consciousness, self-possession, and rationality, it is clear that many human beings do not reveal all of these properties, e.g. the severely mentally retarded. Nevertheless, one can say at least that they possess these perfections potentially in that their nature as human beings is compatible with the actual possession of these perfections, whereas the nature of a rat or of a machine is not compatible with these perfections.

[9] D. von Hildebrand (1991a) develops many of these points very well.

[10] In citing this as a defect I in no way wish to deny that faith is a virtue. But this kind of faith is a virtue only in relation to our present defective state.

[11] It would be wrong to think that Freud's death instincts alone would belong to what I am calling human defectiveness. His so-called life instincts are characterized by a number of defects. For example, the sexual urge is clearly withdrawn from free control and is subject to perversions resulting from childhood traumas. Even healthy development allegedly involves passing through an oedipal stage, which can hardly be considered a perfection.

[12] It is often said that emotions, as states, cannot be right or wrong, they simply are or are not. However, Brentano (1969), Ingarden (1983), Scheler (1973), C.S. Lewis (1947), von Hildebrand (1953), and many other philosophers have seen that "intentional emotions", i.e. emotions that are "about" something (e.g. joy or sorrow about an event), can be appropriate or inappropriate. Emotions can correspond to the value of situation (both in quality and depth), or fail to correspond to the value of the situation.

[13] Von Hildebrand (1957) and more recently, Butchvarov (1990) have taken note of this phenomenon. It is my opinion that Meurseault, of Camus' *The Stranger*, exhibits precisely this sort of response to his own finitude.

[14] Cf. Aristotle, *Nicomachean Ethics* and Wojtyla (1993).

[15] Although I would not want to support the general theses of Sartre's existential psychology, his introduction to his book *The Emotions*, entitled "Psychology, Phenomenology, and Phenomenological Psychology" contains a fine evaluation and criticism of the idea that a molecular approach to the person could ever yield an adequate anthropology, or general view of the essence of the human person. Cf. Sartre, (1993).

[16] One of the clearest examples of the debate about what sorts of experiences and data ought to be admitted as trustworthy items of evidence has arisen within the further debate whether or not computers can think. Searle (1980), e.g. uses his famous "Chinese Room" thought experiment in order to support the intuition that thought presupposes more than syntax or formal operations. He argues (quite rightly) that it additionally requires semantic content and real intentionality. Ned Block (1980) and others have challenged this approach to the problem, and have thereby called into question the reliability of philosophical intuitions. However, I think that the foundations of human science collapse as soon as we begin to distrust such intuitions. In the *Prolegomena* to his *Logical Investigations* Husserl (1970) clearly shows how a radical empiricism which refuses to accept the intuition of self-evident *a priori* truths ultimately proves to be an absurd position, one which cannot be rationally justified.

[17] Perhaps the area of psychology in which these findings appear to be most significant is

the area of educational psychology. Because children also are marked by defects, and because human potentialities are both good and bad, children cannot be asked merely to clarify their values, nor to reason to the right conclusions. Even if they could innately arrive at the right conclusions (which is questionable), they need models and stories to strengthen their wills and move their hearts. Thus "character development" or "virtue-based" programs are much more in keeping with human defectiveness and the broad nature of human potentialities than are other contemporary models. For examples of character development approaches to moral education see Lickona and Ryan (1992), Lickona (1991) and Kilpatrick (1993).

[18] Frankl does argue that each of these tragic elements presents us with *opportunities* to actualize meanings, e.g. to face death in a dignified way, or to suffer nobly and provide a good example for others, or to respond to guilt by seeking forgiveness and reparation. But this in no way implies that the *defects themselves* are meanings in the logotherapeutic sense.

REFERENCES

Aristotle (1941). Nicomachean ethics. *The basic writings of Aristotle*. Ed. R. McKeon. New York: Random House.

Block, N. (1980). What intuitions about homunculi don't show. *Behavioral and Brain Sciences*, 3, 424-426.

Brentano, F. (1969). *The origins of our knowledge of right and wrong*. Trans. by R. Chisholm and E. Schneewind. London: Routledge and Kegan Paul.

Butchvarov, P. (1990). The demand for justification in ethics. *Journal of Philosophy, XV*, 1-14.

Campbell, D. (1974). On the conflicts between biological and social evolution and between psychology and moral tradition. *American Psychologist*, XXX, 1121.

Coulson, W. (1972). *Groups, gimmicks, and instant gurus*. New York: Harper & Row.

Coulson, W. (1990). Principled morality vs. consequentialism. *Questianity: Why the war on drugs drags*. San Diego: Research Council on Ethnopsychology.

Crosby, J. (forthcoming). *An essay on personal selfhood.*

Frankl, V. (1962). *Man's search for meaning. An introduction to logotherapy*. New York: Simon & Schuster.

Frankl, V. (1985). Beyond self-actualization and self-expression, in *Psychotherapy and existentialism*. New York: Simon & Schuster.

Hildebrand, D. von. (1953). *Ethics*. Chicago: Franciscan Herald Press.

Hildebrand, D. von. (1957). *Graven images. Substitutes for true morality*. Chicago: Franciscan Herald Press.

Hildebrand, D. von. (1991). *What is philosophy?* London: Routledge

Hildebrand, D. von. (1991a). *Jaws of death: Gate of heaven*. Manchester, NH: Sophia Institute Press.

Husserl, E. (1970). *Logical investigations*. Trans. by J. N. Findlay. New York: Humanities Press.

Ingarden, R. (1983). *Man and value*. Munich: Philosophia Verlag.

Kilpatrick, W. (1993). *Why johnny can't tell right from wrong*. New York: Simon & Schuster.

Kohlberg, L. (1971). Stages of moral development as a basis for moral education. In C. M. Beck, B. S. Crittenden & E. V. Sullivan (Eds.), *Moral education: Interdisciplinary approaches*. Toronto: University of Toronto Press, pp. 1-55.

Lewis, C.S. (1947). *The abolition of man. How education develops man's sense of morality*. New York: Macmillan.

Lewis, C.S. (1960). *The four loves*. London: Harcourt, Brace, Jovanovich.

Lickona, T. (1991). *Educating for character*. New York: Bantam.

Lickona, T. and K. Ryan. (1992). Character development: The challenge and the model. In T. Lickona and K. Ryan (Eds.), *Character development in schools and beyond*. Washington, D.C.: Council for Research in Values and Philosophy.

Marcel, G. (1973). *Tragic wisdom and beyond*. Evanston: Northwestern University Press.

Ricoeur, P. (1986). *Fallible man*. New York: Fordham University Press.

Rogers, C. (1961). *On becoming a person*. Boston: Houghton Mifflin.

Sartre, J-P. (1993). *The emotions. Outline of a theory*. New York: Citadel Press.

Scheler, M. (1973). *Formalism in ethics and non-formal ethics of value. A new attempt toward the foundation of an ethical personalism*. Evanston: Northwestern University Press.

Scheler, M. (1961). *Ressentiment*. New York: Free Press of Glencoe.

Searle, J. (1980). Minds, brains, and programs. *Brain and Behavioral Sciences*, 3, 417-424.

Seifert, J. (1989). *Essere e persona*. Milano: Universita Cattolica del Sacro Cuore.

Vitz, P. (1977). *Psychology as religion*. Grand Rapid, MI: Eerdmans.

Wojtyla, K. (1979). *The acting person*. Trans. A. Potocki, ed. A-T. Tymieniecka. Boston: Reidel.

Wojtyla, K. (1981). *Love and responsibility*. New York: Farrar, Straus and Giroux.

Wojtyla, K. (1993). In search of the basis of perfectionism in ethics. *Person and community*. Bern: Peter Lang.

Wolter, A. (1946). *The transcendentals and their roles in the metaphysics of Duns Scotus*. St. Bonaventure, NY: Franciscan Institute.

Wolter, A. (1951). Duns Scotus on the necessity of revealed knowledge. *Franciscan Studies*, XI.

2

A Christian Theory of Personality: Interpersonal and Transmodern

Paul C. Vitz

I. Historical and Theological Issues

To begin a rationale for a Christian concept of personality, let us consider some historical and theological issues. As many psychologists know, the word "person" comes from the Latin *persona* which meant "mask," as worn in the Roman theatre, and also the theatrical role that went with the mask. The Latin term translated the Greek word *prosopon* which had the same meaning and had first been used in this sense.

But this etymology of the word "person" is not, in fact, important or revealing. What *is* important is that the *concept* of a person, which is unique to Western culture, arose to prominence as a major philosophical and theological issue, in early Christian thought. The concept of a "person" was developed to express the doctrine of the Trinity: God as three "persons"—and of the Incarnation: Christ as both the second person of the Trinity and as its perfect embodiment in human form. This early theological use also placed a strong emphasis on dialogue; that is, it was largely through dialogue within the Trinity, often found in Scripture, that the plurality of persons in God was recognized. (This was much discussed before and at the Council of Nicaea, held in 325).

The historical antecedents of the concept of a person are under some debate: Aristotle apparently had some notion of the person, though the extent of its influence on Western (and in particular Christian) thought is unclear. Müller and Halder, (1969), have claimed, however, that the "concept" of a person was "unknown to ancient pagan philosophy, and first appears as a technical term in early Christian theology..." (p. 404).

Of course in certain respects the origin of the idea of a person is to be found in Judaism, where from the beginning God was understood as a person and not merely an abstraction. Yahweh was a personal God.

But in any event, after the early Trinitarian debates, the concept of a "person" then continued to develop within the framework of Christian thought for hundreds of years, and this concept still determines, to a great extent, the general understanding of the "person." In short, Christians have an historical and legitimate interest in the conceptualization of person—and hence of personality theory. Let me make it clear that I am not arguing that "persons" have existed only in Christian lands. What I am speaking of in this paper is the philosophical and psychological representation of person, in both a descriptive and an ideal understanding.

Nor do I assume that Müller and Halder are necessarily correct about the Christian theological origin of the concept "person." It may be that Aristotle and other Greeks had at least a basic notion of person in the relationship sense.

However, from a Christian perspective, it is essential to recognize that, because we are made in the image of a Trinitarian—and interpersonal—God, we are also made to be interpersonal. Human beings are called to a loving, committed relationship with God and with others. In a Christian theoretical framework, it is thus through free commitment to others that "persons" come into existence: that is, to a large degree, we *are* our interpersonal relationships.

The Protestant theologian T.F. Torrance (1983, 1985) has done much to illuminate the interpersonal implications of the Trinitarian concept of God in an historical framework. He identified two basic understandings of God as a person: the first view, the dominant one in Western philosophy, comes from Boethius. The other derives primarily from the patristic (primarily Greek) period of the church, and also from the 12th c. French philosopher and theologian Richard of St. Victor.

Boethius defined a person as "an individual substance of a rational nature." In this concept of "substance" there was a strong emphasis on separateness: on what divided one substance from another. The Fathers and Richard of St. Victor, in contrast, derived their concept of the person from the Holy Trinity. As Torrance noted, Richard defined a person "not in terms of its own independence as self-subsistence, but in terms of its ontic relations to other persons, i.e. by a transcendal relation to what is other than it, and in terms of its own unique incommunicable existence..." (1985, p. 176). In summarizing Richard's view, Torrance says: "A person is what he is only through relations with other persons" (1985, p. 176).

The essential feature of the Christian conception of the world, in contrast to the Hellenic, may be said to be that it regards the person and the relations of persons to one another, as the essence of reality, whereas ancient Greek thought conceived of personality, however spiritual, as a restrictive characteristic of the finite—a transitory product of a life which as a whole is impersonal." (Cited in Torrance, 1985, p. 172)

The Latin West's use of Boethius can thus be seen as a highly influential continuation of a pre-Christian Hellenic tradition, which apparently failed to accept personal relations as part of the structure of reality itself. The Trinitarian doctrine of the early Fathers of the Church, did take relationship to be part of the basic definition of the Trinity. But this Eastern Christian formulation, also found in Augustine, was largely displaced in the Latin West by the Boethian emphasis on substance, and did not receive further development at least until Richard of St. Victor—whose influence on subsequent Christian philosophy was far from dominant on this issue.

The contemporary Catholic theologian Joseph Ratzinger (1970, 1973) has taken a position strikingly similar to that of Torrance, though the two writers are apparently unaware of each other's thought. Ratzinger (1970, p. 132) wrote:

> ...Christian thought discovered the kernel of the concept of person, which describes something other and infinitely more than the mere idea of the "individual." Let us listen once again to St. Augustine: "In God there are no accidents, only substance and relation." Therein lies concealed a revolution in man's view of the world: the relation is discovered as an equally valid primordial mode of reality. It becomes possible to surmount what we call today "objectifying thought"; a new plane of being comes into view.

With a Trinitarian emphasis, Ratzinger (1973, 1990, p. 442) stated:

> ...person must be understood as *relation*...the three persons that exist in God, are in their nature relations. They are, therefore, not substances that stand next to each other, but they are real existing relationships... Relation[ship]...is not something added to the person, but it is the person itself. In its nature, the person exists only *as* relation.

The notion of person as relation has implications beyond the theological:

> ...the phenomenon of complete [relatedness], which is, of course, realized in its entirety only in the one who is God...indicates the direction of all personal being. The point is thus reached [where]...there is a transition from the doctrine of God into...anthropology (1973/1990, p. 445)

Ratzinger's use of the term "anthropology" is equivalent to the term "psychology."

Ratzinger (above) seems to imply that a person is *only* relation, and by implication that substance is not a necessary component. Elsewhere, Ratzinger (1990, p. 132) qualifies this by writing that relation and substance are equally valid primordial modes of reality. I also assume that person is both *substance* and *relation*. But the importance of relationship is central.

Much like Torrance, Ratzinger points out that the definition of "person" by Boethius, as an "individual substance of a rational nature," had unfortunate consequences for Western theology. He recognized that thinking of a person as substance emphasizes the isolated and autonomous notion of the concept, and that the lack of emphasis on person as relation was regrettable in Western thought. Ratzinger also commented that Richard of St. Victor was an important exception.

Some of the psychological evidence for the importance of relationship in the formation of the person should be noted however briefly. Relationships are necessary for normal human existence and development. It is literally true that without ordinary relationships, our very substance would cease to exist. A newborn child that has no mothering relationship with another human will die, even if physical needs are met. A person learns to speak through relationships with others, beginning in the first weeks of life, when the infant first listens to its mother's voice. Without relations, a human being does not know language and without language we are hardly human. Certainly there is no reason to think that either an "individual" or a "person" could come into existence who had no relationships with anyone else. This is not to deny the legitimacy of substance. In the present model, substance and relationship are each necessary, but not sufficient determinants of person.

Let's look at this issue from the different perspective proposed by Sampson (1981). He pointed out that "the Western epistemological tradition of Descartes and Kant that marks contemporary cognitive psychology involves an individualistic reduction centered around the 'I think.'" (p. 732) In this dominant psychological tradition, "objects are seen to be the products of individual mental operations; the world 'out there' is constituted by the individual's thinking and reasoning processes" (p. 732). Sampson interpreted this as an ideologically biased perspective and he argued that 'I think' should really be understood as 'we think' since our thinking is not just me thinking, it is initially a social construct before it is a private mental event. That is, for Sampson, 'we think' comes before 'I think.' (Here, Sampson is indebted to Vygotsky, 1978.) Specifically, Sampson wrote as follows:

> In describing the process of *internalization*, whereby external operations gain an internal representation, Vigotsky notes the key role of other people in a given social and historical context. In his terms, "an interpersonal process is transformed into an intrapersonal process" (Vigotsky, 1978, p. 57). In other words, the basis for the "I think" exists in the prior foundation of the social world; the interpsychological precedes and shapes the intrapsychological. (p. 732)

In a word, Sampson too (and Vygotsky as well) claim that that at least psychologically and epistemologically relationship precedes individuation.

II. Additional Psychological and Theological Characteristics

It is clear that, when Carl Rogers entitled his well-known book *On Becoming a Person* (1961), he was simply wrong. What he wrote was a book on becoming an *individual*, and in particular an autonomous, self-actualizing, independent individual. An individual is created by separating from others, by breaking away, by concentrating psychological thought, energy and emotion on the self instead of on God and other people. The founders of modern psychology clearly knew this. The first expression of the ideas that Rogers made more widely known can be found in the earlier writings of Alfred Adler and Carl Jung. Adler called his psychology

"Individual Psychology"; Jung called the central process of self-development "individuation." So Rogers should have called his book *On Becoming an Individual.*

Thus, in important respects a person is the opposite of an individual, for a person comes into existence by connecting with others, not by separating from them. That is, much of modern psychology, especially humanistic self-psychology is the anti-psychology or anti-structure of a Christian psychology.

Philosophy has long maintained the difference between the individual and the person. Jacques Maritain (1947), in particular, has articulated important distinctions between the individual and the person. Maritain did not focus on "relationships" for understanding the person. But he emphasized the spiritual dimension of the person which allows one to transcend individuality—the secular self. By contrast, modern personality theorists look inward to the self to decribe "individuality."

Furthermore, in our relationship to others, Christians are called to *love* and to *forgive*, while much secular psychology commonly calls on people to *trust* and to *forget*. Briefly, let us look at these two pairs of terms. First, one should ask whether it makes any sense to make trust in others (or in the self) the fundamental virtue. Clearly not. Jesus never asks us to do it. He was too much of a Jewish realist for that! He certainly never "trusted" others, and if he did not trust the apostles, it was for good reason: one would betray him, another deny him, and almost all the others abandon him. But he did love them! A mother may not always trust her child (she knows he can be naughty); a husband may not trust his (for example) alcoholic wife—but both can always love. After one has been betrayed once, much less "seventy times seven," one would be a fool to trust the other person—but it is still possible to forgive. In a word, secular psychology is being completely foolish to ask people first to trust, then to forget. It is impossible, and frequently unwise, truly to forget that another has hurt you. By contrast, to love and, when hurt, to forgive are, though difficult, realistic and possible.

But a Christian theory is not realistic just in some psychological sense, it is truly based on *reality*—that which exists outside the self. To become a person is to be respectful of external realities. By making the self the center of personality, all modern theories of personality remove people from reality, from the external world created by God and filled with real others. In short, these theories of the individual are intrinsically subjectivistic. A good example of this tendency is Carl Rogers (1980) whose theory is based in a thorough-going subjectivism: "there as many realities as there are persons"; we must prepare for a world of "no solid basis, a world of process and change ... in which the mind ... creates, the new reality" (p. 352). Other evidence of the subjectivism of much personality theory has been its reliable tendency to merge with Eastern religion, with subjective drug states and many kinds of occult world views that claim reality is the creation of each self.

Actually, the essential logic of becoming an individual—that is, of separating and distancing the self from others—eventually gets carried to its logical extreme. First, you break the "chains" that linked you to parents, then to others; then even to society and culture. Finally, you reject the self itself; that is, you separate consciousness from the illusion of the self. You end up by rejecting the self and all its desires—and thus the process of separation culminates in an experience or state of nothingness. Radical autonomy ultimately means separation from everything; it means total or ultra-autonomy, where even the self is gone.

The development of a person, being, in many respects, the "anti-process" of the development of the autonomous individual, often moves in a different direction. The person is created for union with God and others. It is love that brings this union, this enlargement. We see this in the words of Jesus, "I and the Father are One," and in his desire that his followers be one. The person knows not the "peace of nothingness," but instead the joy of union in love.

To summarize:

A *Person* is created by God in the Image of God.
An *Individual* is created by the self in the image of the self.

A *Person* loves and trusts God, and loves others as the self; persons forgive those who have hurt them.
An *Individual* loves and trusts the self, trusts others, and rejects or ignores God; individuals forget those who have hurt them.

A *Person* has the goal of committed relationships with others, and a state of union with God.
An *Individual* has the goal of separating from others, and eventually a state of separation from the self.

For a *Person* true freedom is choosing complete dependence on God who is completely free.
For an *Individual*, true autonomy is choosing complete dependence on the self.

A *Person* accepts the reality of God, other people, and the physical world.
An *Individual* rejects everything outside of the self as subjective, a non-reality.

III. In Defense of the Individual

The preceding set of comparisons is no doubt something of an exageration; it overstates things because no individual is apt to take these modern principles to such an extreme. Reality doesn't let us and most of us have a kind of psychological and moral commonsense that protects us from taking our theories too seriously. This is also a very idealized image of what a person is. We are all aware of how poorly even the best of Christians live up to such ideals. In the everyday world, it is often hard to distinguish between people who are presumably operating from these two—theoretically—very different models.

In addition, some positive things need to be said for the secular emphasis on independence and individuation. Freedom or independence from the unexamined views of others is an important virtue, not just for the secular world but in the Christian world as well. One of the major concerns of Christian theology is that of free will or free choice. God gives us the freedom to choose him or not. From Abraham to Moses to Jesus, this theme is central. In a certain sense, the emphasis on freedom found in the secular world of the last few centuries can be understood as the immanentizing of a basic Christian principle: that is, the theological concept of freedom is translated into the social and political world.

IV. A Trans-Modern Model of Person

In order to develop a new model of personality, it will be useful to describe three different models of the self, models developed by de Rivera (1989). His first model of the self he called "collectivist." In a collectivist society (he gave examples of Japan and China and pre-modern Europe) the self is derived from its place in the social order, especially the family. In this environment, the self complies with others to secure its support. Obligation to family or to one's social role is the basis of morality, and the purpose of the self is to maintain group harmony. This kind of self is part of a whole, and it values connections with other and the good of community. Its strategy is to use manners, social traditions and caring and feeling for others. The political system of such a society aims to secure the collective good. In the present context, this kind of society is close to the natural society found in mother and child relationships, and in the child's relationships to its family during its early years. It is in this kind of developmental stage and in this kind of society that the "we" precedes the "I." This is a *pre*-modern understanding of person.

De Rivera constrasted the collectivist self with the modern individualist self. This is the self that has been primarily criticized here (e.g., the modern secular self). In this kind of society, which de Rivera equated with the contemporary West, especially the U.S., the strategy is to look out for the individual self. Its society is ego-centric and contractual, not socio-centric and organic. Morality is based on abstract principles and the goal is self-integrity. This modern self values autonomy and individual rights which are secured by justice, reason, and law. And the goal of the modern political system is above all to protect individual rights. This is the *modern* self.

Both of these models are gravely flawed, according to de Rivera, and he has argued for what he calls a "mutualist" self, based on care for the other, love for the other, the transformation of fear into love, an emphasis on freedom in community, a deep concern for justice, and action that transforms real circumstances into more ideal conditions.

DeRivera's concerns are those of a social psychologist, who is, moreover, implicitly but not explicitly Christian. Here I speak from an explicitly Christian and more narrowly psychological or interpersonal point of view. In de Rivera's model, the first society presents a self which has relationships but no freedom; the second, a self with freedom but no true relationships. The Christian self, or person as it is called here, must combine both: relationship with freedom.

V. The Actual Process of Becoming a Person: "Personogenesis"

What *is* the process of becoming a person—or as Connor (1992, p. 47) calls it, "personagenesis"—within a Christian theory of personality? First, a Christian theory does not reject the person as substance, but gives equal or greater emphasis to the person as relation. In the language of Karol Wojtyla (now, of course, Pope John Paul II), a person is constructed on the "metaphysical site" of substance, but the process of construction involves the dynamics of relationships.

The first step in personagenesis "seems to be passivity, receptivity of love from another" (Connor, p. 45) In the natural world, this is normally the love a newborn receives from its mother. In the spiritual realm, which is at the core of person, it is listening to the call and love of God. Once initiated, the process of becoming a person continues. Wojtyla (see Wojtyla, 1969/1979) described the heart of this process as a "vertical transcendence" in which the person gives "the self to another" (Connor, p. 47). The process of lovingly giving the self to another both transcends the self and determines the self in the act of performing service. The giving of the self to another is how the self is transcended; it is also how one comes to know both the other and, from the perspective of the other, to know oneself much more "objectively" than one ever can from inside an autonomous self. This process is how one becomes a person. Wojtyla (1981) noted that free will is at the center of a person's self gift to another, for while man freely determines his action, he is "at the same time fully aware" that his actions "in turn determine him; moreover they continue to determine him even when they have passed." (Connor, p. 48)

When the other person receives one's gift of love and gives self in return, the highest form of intimacy results. In this context, intimacy has been lucidly described by the Christian philosopher Kenneth Schmitz (1986):

> Metaphysically speaking, intimacy is not grounded in the recognition of this or that characteristic a person *has*, but rather in the simple unqualified presence the person *is*... Indeed, it seems to me that the presence in which intimacy is rooted is nothing short of the unique act of existing of each person. Presence is but another name for the being of something insofar as it is actual, and in intimacy we come upon and are received into the very act of existing of another. We are, then, at the heart, not only of another person, but at the heart of the texture of being itself. No doubt it is true that the person is incommunicable in objective terms insofar as he or she is existentially unique. But in intimacy, as we approach the very act of self-disclosure, we approach the center of all communicability. It is this "secret" that we share with the other person. It is the sense of being with another at the foundation not only of our personal existence, but of being with each other in the most fundamental texture of being itself. Put in the most general

> terms—though we must not forget that each intimacy is through and through singular—the "secret" that we discover through intimacy is this: "*that reality is not indifferent to the presence of persons.*" (p. 45; emphasis in original)

Although Schmitz was describing the metaphysical nature of intimacy, the same understanding is at the core of psychological intimacy. Intimacy—with God and with others—thus becomes a major characteristic of a person. This intimacy is not cognitive knowledge based on abstraction, but knowledge based on experience, on union with the other. I call this model *trans*-modern because it goes beyond and transcends the modern autonomous self. It is a synthesis of the pre-modern and the modern understandings of the self

VI. Psychological Applications

One of the important tasks of any personality theory is to bring new or overlooked psychological aspects of personality into focus. Christian theorists have already been doing this. Some of the more important and distinctive contributions will be summarized here.

1. The Traditional Virtues

The traditional virtues—or positive character traits—have long been a concern of Christian thinkers. Of course there are other thinkers, primarily philosophers, who are concerned with the virtues; indeed, most religions have a deep involvement in these notions. But modern psychology has very reliably ignored the virtues—at least the traditional virtues.

There is a sense in which modern psychological theories each have their own set of what might be called "modern" virtues. After all, these theories have a strong moral or prescriptive character to them. Thus, a Rogerian set of virtues would include unconditional positive self-regard and the attainment of self-actualization; Jungian virtues would involve the quest for a balance between animus and anima, also a balanced expression of the four major mental activities (thought, sensation, intuition and emotion). There might even be said to be Freudian virtues, involving a general stoicism and self-knowledge that leads to the removal of repression and illusion.

Be that as it may, one can look through contemporary textbooks on personality theory and find no references to any of the following major traditional (or "cardinal") virtues: justice, courage (fortitude), moderation (temperance), wisdom (prudence). Such virtues as truthfulness, altruism, responsibility; perseverence, boldness, optimism; patience, modesty, flexibility; friendship and humility are mostly noticeable by their absence in contemporary personality theory. But Christian thought has reliably been concerned with traditional virtues because they are understood as psychological habits developed over time by the agency of the will. These habits then support attempts to live both a moral and a spiritual life.

In addition to the natural virtues, there are the theological virtues of faith, hope, and charity, which also have observable effects on people's lives, and to that extent are open to empirical investigation.

Examples of Christian psychological theorists who have contributed to this area of theory and research are Robert Roberts (1984, 1992, 1994), William Kilpatrick (1992), Thomas Lickona (1991).

2. Forgiveness

Probably the single most important clinical phenomenon that Christian therapists have introduced is that of forgiveness. Forgiveness is certainly a major therapeutic process, probably the most beneficial one that can take place between two people. In any case, secular therapy and theories of personality have largely ignored it. Forgiveness is, of course, central to Christianity, and in recent years many Christian psychologists have begun to conceptualize it and introduce it into psychotherapy. Some of the many who have made contributions to the understanding of forgiveness are: Augsburger (1970, 1981), Benson (1992), Brandsma (1982), Bonar (1989), Cunningham (1985), DiBlasio (1992), Enright and Zell (1989), Fitzgibbons (1986), Gartner (1988), Linn and Linn (1988), Pattison (1965, 1989), Pingleton (1989), Smedes (1984), Strong (1976, 1977), Veenstra (1992, 1993), Wapnick (1985), Worthington and DiBlasio (1990).

3. Relationships (Interdependence)

Let us look at a hypothetical family situation. Consider a widowed mother and son relationship. In our first scenario (A), the son is dependent on the mother, lives at home even as an adult, and it is obvious even to the casual observer, much less to a psychologist, that a neurotic dependency relationship has been established. The mother needs a "child," someone who needs her, while the son has become fearful of the outside world in which he never functioned, and he needs to maintain the warm support of his mother. The point here is that neither has freely chosen to love the other: they are controlled by psychological forces which they chose rather unknowingly years ago and without understanding the consequences or the strength of habit that would develop. One of this pair must choose to break this cycle of dependency, which contains only small amounts of genuine love. But it is not uncommon that people *do* make such a choice—witness the choice of many alcoholics to break their addiction.

In scenario A the mother and son have a relationship, but without freedom.

Another scenario (B) could involve a mother and son with a different outcome, in which the son, fearful of dependency and of being controlled by his mother, chooses to reject her, leave home and move far away, remaining at a considerable psychological and physical distance. Here the neurotic dependency has been broken. But the son remains afraid of being close to his mother for obvious reasons. He suffers from what might be called "neurotic independency." The mother, of course, is likely to feel hurt and rejected, but may continue to harbor the controlling needs that the son fears, which are based upon her own fears of being unneeded and unloved. In any case, the price of the son's independence has been the loss of any serious relationship with his mother, and of the mother with her son. In this scenario, the mother and son have freedom, but no relationship.

A third possibility (C), which is being held up here as the satisfactory solution, is for either the mother or the son—or preferably both—to have a strong relationship with God. This truly loving relationship with God frees a person from vulnerability to a neurotic need for love from another. That is, God's love frees us from an inordinate need for the love of any particular human being. This allows a person to freely choose to help and truly love the other, but to avoid pathological emotional involvements. There is in this situation no basis for dependency or fearful independency. In scenario C both mother and son have a relationship *and* freedom. They each freely chose to give themselves to the other.

Many psychologists might say: "Fine, you have avoided dependent relationships with other people, but at the price of a neurotic dependency on God—who may not even exist, and is just a fantasy composite of early parent introjects." As to God's existence: this is a matter of faith, just as the matter of God's non-existence is a matter of faith. The rejection of God is, in many psychologists, a neurotic fear itself (see Vitz, 1990). And the fear of faith is often the fear of being "duped," it is the fear of letting go of any autonomy, it is the fear of intimacy, it is the fear of giving the self in love to anyone or anything, it is the fear of losing one's pathological defenses. (Neurotic independency as in Scenario B.)

To return to the issue of "neurotic dependency on God": the very term of course implies something harmful to the person. But are the people whom we know to be close to God people who strike us as unhappy, maladjusted, and in general pathological? There may well be people who *claim* to be close to God who do communicate these traits, for example, religious fanatics. But real fanatics contradict their own religious ideals in that they do not love others and are filled with hatred. For the Christian, the love of God brings peace, tranquility, and the obvious love of others. True Christians, like Mother Teresa of Calcutta, attract all kinds of people because of this love and other positive qualities.

In conclusion, the core of a Christian theory of personality has a clear and distinctive rationale and a set of distinctive psychological emphases. This paper, of course, only touches on the task of developing such a theory, and important issues have not even been addressed here. For a stimulating discussion of many issues relevant to a Christian theory of personality, see Van Leeuwen (1987). In the future, all the various aspects of a Christian theory of personality will need to be addressed systematically by the Christian psychological community.

Some of the ideas in this paper first appeared in Vitz (1984, 1987a,b), and were presented at a Wheaton College Conference entitled "On Being and Becoming a Person," June 22-28, 1994.

REFERENCES

Augsburger, D. (1970). *Seventy times seven: the freedom of forgiveness.* Chicago: Moody.

Augsburger, D. (1981). *Caring enough to forgive.* Ventura, CA: Regal.

Benson, C.K. (1992). Forgiveness and the psychotherapeutic process. *Journal of Psychology and Christianity, 11* (1), 76-81.

Bonar, C.A. (1989). Personality theories and asking for forgiveness. *Journal of Psychology and Christianity, 8* (1), 45-51.

Brandsma, J.M. (1982). Forgiveness: A dynamic, theological and therapeutic analysis. *Pastoral Pstychology, 31,* 40-50.

Connor, R. (Fall, 1990). Relation, the Thomistic *esse*, and American culture: Toward a metaphysic of sanctity. *Communio, 17,* 455-464.

Connor, R. (1992). The person as resonating existential. *American Catholic Philosophical Quarterly, 66,* 39-56.

Cunningham, B.B. (1985). The will to forgive: A pastoral theological view of forgiving, *Journal of Pastoral Care, 39* (2), 141-149.

De Rivera, J. (1989). Love, fear and justice: Transforming selves for the new world. *Social Justice Research 3*, 387-426.

DiBlasio, F.A. (1992). Forgiveness in psychotherapy: Comparison of older and younger therapists. *Journal of Psychology and Christianity, 11* (2), 181-187.

Enright, R.D. and Zell, R.L. (1989). Problems encountered when we forgive one another. *Journal of Psychology and Christiantiy, 8* (1), 52-60.

Fitzgibbons, R.P. (1986). The cognitive and emotive uses of forgiveness in the treatment of anger. *Psychotherapy, 23* (4), 629-633.

Gartner, J. (1988). The capacity to forgive: An object relations perspective. *Journal of Religion and Health, 27* 313-320.

Kilpatrick, K.W. (1992). *Why Johnny can't tell right from wrong.* New York: Simon and Schuster.

Lickona, T. (1991). *Educating for character.* New York: Bantam.

Linn, D. and Linn, M. (1988). *Healing life's hurts: Healing memories through the five stages of forigiveness.* New York: Paulist.

Maritain, J. (1947). *The person and the common good.* New York: Scribners.

Müller, M. and Halder, A. (1969). Person: Concept. *Sacramentum mundi*, 4. New York: Herder & Herder.

Pattison, E.M. (1965). On the failure to forgive or to be forgiven. *American Journal of Psychotherapy, 31,* 106-115.

Pattison, E.M. (1989). Punitive and reconciliation models of forgiveness. In L. Aden & D.G. Benner (eds.), *Counseling and the human predicament: A study of sin, guilt and forgiveness*. Grand Rapids, MI: Baker, 162-176.

Pingleton, J.P. (1989). The role and function of forgiveness in the psychotherapeutic process. *Journal of Psychology and Theology, 17*, 27-35.

Ratzinger, J. (1970). *Introduction to Christianity*. New York: Herder & Herder.

Ratzinger, J. (1973/ Fall 1990). Concerning the notion of person in theology. *Communio, 17*, 439-454 (translation of the chapter "Zum personenverständnis in der theologie," in J. Ratzinger, *Dogma und verkundigung*, Munich: Erich Wewel Verlag, 1973, 205-223).

Roberts, R. (1992). Emotions among the virtues of the Christian life. *Journal of Religious Ethics, 20*, 37-68.

Roberts, R. (1993). *Taking the word to heart: Self and other in an age of therapies*, Grand Rapids, MI: Eerdmans.

Roberts, R. (1994). Forgiveness as a virtue. Unpublished ms.

Rogers, C. (1961). *On becoming a person*. Boston: Houghton Mifflin.

Rogers, C. (1980). *A way of being*. Boston: Houghton Mifflin.

Sampson, E. (1981). Cognitive psychology as ideology. *American Psychologist, 36*, 730-743.

Schmitz, K. (Spring, 1986). The geography of the human person. *Communio, 13*, 45.

Smedes, L.B. (1984). *Forgive and forget: Healing the hurts we don't deserve*. San Francisco: Harper & Row.

Strong, S. (1976). Christian counseling. *Counseling and values, 20*, 151-160.

Strong, S. (1977). Christian counseling in action. *Counseling and values, 21*, 89-128.

Torrance, T.F. (1983). *The mediation of Christ*. Grand Rapids, MI: Eerdmans.

Torrance, T.F. (1985). *Reality and scientific theology*. Edinburgh: Scottish Academic Press.

Van Leeuwen, M.S. (1987). Personality theorizing within a Christian worldview. In T.J. Burke (ed.), *Man and Mind: A Christian theory of personality*. Hillsdale, MI: Hillsdale College Press, 171-198.

Veenstra, G. (1992). Psychological concepts of forgiveness. *Journal of Psychology and Christianity, 11* (2), 160-169.

Veenstra, G. (1993). Forgiveness: A critique of adult child approaches. *Journal of Psychology and Christianity, 12* (1), 58-68.

Vitz, P.C. (1984) A covenant theory of personality: A theoretical introduction. In. L. Morris (ed.) *The Christian vision: Man in society*. Hillsdale, MI: Hillsdale College Press, 75-99.

Vitz, P.C. (1987a). Secular personality theory: A critical analysis. In T.J. Burke (ed.) *Man and Mind: A Christian theory of personality*. Hillsdale, MI: Hillsdale College Press, 65-99.

Vitz, P.C. (1987b). A Christian theory of personality: Covenant theory. In T.J. Burke (ed.), *Man and Mind: A Christian theory of personality*. Hillsdale, MI: Hillsdale College Press, 199-222.

Vitz, P.C. (1990). The psychology of atheism and Christian spirituality. *Anthropotes 6*, 89-106.

Vygotsky, L.S. (1978). *Mind in society*. Cambridge, MA: Harvard University Press.

Wallach, M. and Wallach, L. (1983). *Psychology's sanction for selfishness: The error of egoism in theory and therapy*. San Francisco: Freeman.

Wapnick, K. (1985). Forgiveness: A spiritual psychotherapy. In E.M. Stern (ed.) *Psychotherapy and the religiously committed patient*. New York: Haworth, 47-54.

Wojtyla, K. (1969/1979). *The acting person*. Dordrecht, Holland: D. Reidel. (Original in Polish, 1969, *Osoba i Czyn*, Cracow: Polskie Topwarzystwo Teologiizne.)

Worthington, E.L. and DiBlasio, F.A. (1990). Promoting mutual forgiveness within the fractured relationship. *Psychotherapy, 27* (2), 219-223.

3

Mediating Values: A Task for Personality Formation and the Preservation of Culture

Annemarie Buchholz-Kaiser

I. The Contributions of Psychology and Education to a Concept of the Human Person Consistent with the Natural Law

In times of arbitrariness and spiritual confusion the battle over the human person's essential nature becomes ever more intense and the present decline of values and increasing threat posed by totalitarian tendencies call upon us to take a fresh look at the need for a concept of natural law. In view of the attempts to determine social life by coercion it should be pointed out that no power has the right to constrain, curtail or disregard natural human rights. This is expressed in the United Nations Declaration of Human Rights. However, these rights are still far from being acknowledged throughout the world. The fact that they are in many places rejected or even attacked on ideological grounds bodes ill for the future. And this is unfortunately the case even though the recognition of Christian values, which are consistent with the natural law, has been instrumental in developing our liberal and democratic order. Moreover, it is the case even though the results of the human sciences, especially psychology and education, have time and again affirmed a concept of the human person which is consistent with the natural law.

At the very basis of the concept of natural law, especially as advocated by the well-known philosopher of natural law, Johannes Messner, is the idea that the values universally valid for mankind must be and will be found in the results of each of the human and social sciences.

It is the thoughts, feelings, and actions of individuals which shape and establish the civic order. Therefore, precise knowledge of the nature of the human being also enables more detailed and comprehensive insights into the conditions of human social life.

In other words: the human person as a natural being, not a slave of instincts, but gifted with reason, is endowed with a high level of self-determination and cognitive capacity. His personality can only develop fully in a social environment, just as the social environment can only find enrichment from the contributions of each unique individual. It is only in a long period of dependency that the child is introduced to social life. Within the family the child develops into a mature personality. His attitudes towards other persons, his value system, his conscience are moulded in the context of these first relationships. As Messner puts it: "Contrary to the common notion that man per se is a complete and rational being (an animal with a brain) whose social responsibilities are merely incidental, man only becomes a truly human being, mature personality and cultural being through communication and cooperation, first in the family, and then in the larger community."

The human person, being endowed with reason, is able to form judgments, to discern and adopt values and to come to decisions. According to Messner, the individual has the ability to adapt his life to, as he puts it, the "purposes of existence." Thus, the individual either chooses to govern his behaviour according to the law of nature or he does not. Johannes Messner points out that the human person is capable of consciously commenting on his own nature and his natural needs and of recognizing their purpose and content. The person only attains the full extent of his possibilities by adjusting his life to these purposes. Under "existential purposes" Messner includes the following:

> self-preservation including freedom from bodily harm, as well as social recognition (personal honor); man's striving for perfection in physical and mental respects (personality development), including the development of his abilities to improve his life and the provision of his economic welfare by securing the necessary property or income; the growth of experience, knowledge and the appreciation of beauty; reproduction by mating and the raising of the offspring; the benevolent concern for the mental and material welfare of one's fellow-men on an equal basis; association in society for promotion of the common good, which consists in securing peace and order as well as providing the opportunity for a fully human existence for all members of society, with an adequate share in the available goods . . ." (*Das Naturrecht*, p. 42)

Individual psychological theory and practice, as developed by Adler and his followers, and, above all, the findings of modern developmental psychology, turn out to be consistent with Christian and pre-Christian philosophies of natural law. The philosophy of natural law and Alfred Adler's individual psychology are both based on a personalist concept of human nature, and reject any mechanistic or materialistic concept of the human person. The human being is by nature a person and a sociable being, yet it is only by relating to his parents and, later on, to others that he is able to develop his individual personality, and thus becomes capable of participating in and shaping life in community.

As a personal being, the human being distinguishes himself from other living creatures by the possibility of living a life based on reason and knowledge. Neither drives nor instincts nor material social conditions determine him. He does not just have "needs" which must be satisfied but—as Messner puts it—he can learn to recognize the purposes inherent in his needs and adjust his style of life accordingly. Likewise, the person is not determined by his "subconscious," and this is probably one of the most important contributions of individual psychology. In sharp contrast to Freud, Adler does not understand the subconscious as a sinister drive repressed since childhood. He instead calls 'subconscious' those emotional reactions and behaviours which are simply not understood by the individual. Starting at birth, the child assimilates his impressions of life in a creative manner, thereby developing an image of himself and the world. In this process the person forms an idea of how to gain security and appreciation in the community. In the course of further development this condenses into an individual lifestyle, an individual way of solving the tasks of life, i.e., marriage and family, occupation and cooperation. This individual lifestyle also shapes a person's future behaviour and way of experiencing things.

In many studies modern developmental psychology reaffirms Adler's findings that the human child is born with a marked sociability, a disposition to associate with others. In the course of the earliest period of development the child spontaneously begins to establish a relationship to his parents, to seek their affection and approval, and to orientate himself to them. This disposition enables the human being to develop a way of life based on cooperation, empathy, and social responsibility. He tackles life's problems to his own and to other people's benefit. A developed sense of *social interest (Gemeinschaftsgefühl)* is the term under which Adler summarizes this idea. The term includes attitudes such as love of justice, peaceableness, confidence and courage, rectitude, respect for others, readiness to help, and altruism. Adler's term 'social interest' describes, as Messner would put it, the essential qualities of the individual who has become "a whole person," i.e., the mentally and emotionally healthy human being. What Adler called social interest, i.e., the fully developed ability to relate to others, provides the criteria by which the individual can examine and weigh the effects his activities have on himself and others.

In its broadest sense social interest can be seen as the result of a successful process of upbringing. Parents and others involved in upbringing and education can only convey the experience of cooperation to the child if they themselves possess a developed sense of social interest. Whether these people are well-balanced or nervous, the degree of their emotional maturity, as well the value system with which they judge the child's behaviour and influence him, accordingly determine the social environment which forms the child's emotional basis for life in community, his attitude towards others, and his ability to cooperate.

It is the task of parents to provide for a sound (in the sense described above) development of the child. Already in the infant period the child models himself on his parents in his mood and behaviour: in the emotional interaction with his parents he assimilates their norms and values. In the work of our Association, in educational counseling as well as in the care of children and adolescents we have found that parents and educators can be greatly helped when they understand the nature of a child's development. This understanding equips parents with numerous means of conveying, in daily life, a sense of the interrelatedness of human social life and a sense of right and wrong to the child in accordance with the needs and age of the child. This model of emotional experience within the family shapes the child's orientation in life. If this process of upbringing has been successful, it will lay the basis for a responsible style of life. Such a style of life is always oriented towards the common good and automatically includes the well-being of the individual.

The findings in various branches of psychology and education, which have only been briefly mentioned here, clearly confirm the concept of natural law. They demonstrate that a sound personality development is directly coupled with a commitment to the values which provide the basis of the natural law. Thus, these findings in psychology and education are of great relevance to the educator in his daily work. In view of the present decline of values and the resulting uncertainty, parents and adolescents would benefit greatly from taking into account and applying these findings.

II. Transmitting Perennial Values and Maintaining our Culture

Mediating perennial values, as well as sustaining these values, rank as today's most urgent tasks if we are to maintain a culture and society replete with human qualities in which life is worth living. The prevailing attitude of indifference and permissiveness towards value-relativism, value-decline, and value-destruction has not only already proved to be a grave error, but one which will continue to have disastrous consequences for the future.

Contrary to the growing tendency to consider all values as purely subjective, we maintain that the findings of the human sciences have proven that there are values whose foundations lie in human nature itself and which therefore transcend all forms of modernism, trends, political conditions, and arbitrariness.

The wealth of material gained from observations made in developmental psychology, and the research work of individual psychology, which corresponds with fundamental anthropological work like that of Adolf Portmann *et al.*, have one thing in common: a high level of individual personality formation, the development and survival of a humane culture and a society committed to man's well-being—all these achievements of mankind depend upon the existence of certain fundamental values and their transmission from generation to generation. Values such as responsibility, social interest, concern for others, willingness to help, the ability to cooperate and contribute through one's own efforts to the general welfare, as well as independence of mind, courage, integrity, tolerance, the ability to solve conflicts without resort to violence and respect for the dignity of the human being, result from the fact that all of human life is embedded in a social structure. In this sense these values are neither fortuitous nor are they the result of certain historical or economic conditions. Everything in the history of Western civilization that has proven its worth for human society finds its confirmation—as I have already mentioned—in Messner's theory of natural law.

The psychological and educational training and counseling within our Association are entirely rooted in the tradition of a personalist theory of human beings. This theory stands in clear contrast to that of Freud, as well as to the various theories which reduce the human personality to a product of historical-materialist conditions, or which consider it as a function of biological-organic drives. Using Alfred Adler's work as a starting point we included the entire findings of developmental psychology and in this manner attained a differentiated theoretical basis for practical work. The human being's main characteristics are his relatedness to fellow human beings and his ability to be creative in developing his own life and the culture in which he lives. His capacity for reason and empathy, for concern for others and responsibility also allow him to live by a moral code. Human conscience and a sense of morality are therefore abilities originating in human social nature.

The need for a social framework is clearly evident in the newborn child's helplessness, but it is also apparent when the weak young child is confronted with the problems arising from the child's immediate environment. In a long period of childhood the human being is dependent upon the caring and protecting support of a fellow human being, as well as on the secure and lasting foundation offered by a protective community, its language, its values and culture. Adolf Portmann termed this support by the community during the child's early years the "Social Uterus." The human being only matures to a being capable of existence, thereby shaping his individuality and sense of identity, in emotional interaction with significant others. The language, norms and values of the social environment are gradually acquired by the human being in his life in the community. In this way the individual becomes a member of civilization who in turn later transmits those same values to other human beings.

The development of a human personality is from early childhood on a complex emotional process which takes place in personal interaction between the child and his family's social and cultural environment. In this process the developing human being acquires an ingrained attitude towards life, towards fellow human beings, towards the world and life's tasks. This ingrained attitude influences a person's actions, thoughts and feelings. In psychological terms, therefore, values are emotionally ingrained aptitudes which have become an integral part of personality. As fundamental attitudes they serve as guiding principles in specific situations. They are part and parcel of what gives meaning to a person's life.

Care is taken to point out in both our theoretical and practical work that a constructive attitude towards life and towards other people cannot be divorced from a well-developed ability to relate emotionally to one's fellow human beings. This ability corresponds, as has already been mentioned, with responsibility, concern, courage and independence of mind—to remind of just some of the main principles. Again, these qualities we subsume under the general term of *social interest*. From this concept a theory for moral education and personality formation, as well as a sound emotional development, may be derived. The feeling of solidarity with one's fellow human beings, one of the most important abilities in our time—here we are reminded of the necessity of avoiding such developments in society as the war in the former Yugoslavia—is part of the concept of social interest.

The basis for such concern and social feeling must be developed from early childhood on, within the family as well as among friends and classmates. Social interest, the fully developed ability to relate to one's fellow human beings, manifests itself in an individual's actions and finds its expression in empathy and concern for others, a willingness to help others and to cooperate with others, as well as in a sense of responsibility. A person's ability to realize his own wishes and aims in a sound and meaningful way, while taking into consideration the well-being of others, is the sign of a genuine ability to relate. At the same time, a further consequence of well-developed social interest is reflected in the individual's refusal to accept threats to, and violations of, not only his own integrity and dignity, but that of fellow beings. Instead, such threats and violations are met with indignation and resistance. Values cannot be conveyed in a merely rational way. They can only become an integral part of a young person's emotional life if that person actively strengthens social feelings and concern for others and increases his social interest. Moral education is therefore a task of personality development and includes the fostering of a person's social feeling and social interest, which is called *Gemeinschaftsgefühl* in German. It is this and nothing else that lies behind the endeavors of the psychologists and psychotherapists in our Association and their wish to assist others in personality development in accordance with the principles of psychology and the science of education.

Fostering social feeling, however, involves a conscious expression of these aspects and the development of a distinct position on ethical questions: Emotional development and the awareness of the interrelatedness of the above factors go hand in hand. Although values do not derive their validity from subjective awareness, but are rather discovered as objectively valid, they are at the same time not self-supporting but can only be preserved by being consciously applied, cultivated and transmitted from generation to generation in a process of education and life in community. This forms the basis for stability in social life and is a prerequisite of cultural progress. Thus, moral education is also a factor in cultural preservation.

Human coexistence can only be guaranteed if man's hard-won ethical and moral achievements in the course of centuries are not sacrificed. Their abandonment, if only for the period of a generation, will have decisive and dire consequences. The example of Russia has shown us how disastrous the consequences can be when cultural developments are arbitrarily broken off at some point and cultural traditions are cast aside. If, in a certain culture, a generation is permitted to grow up devoid of the values necessary for social life—necessary because they are rooted in human nature itself—the continued existence of that culture will be gravely endangered. This "logic of human coexistence," as Adler put it, which is the solidarity between the individual and society, the ties which bind us to past, present and future, gives human life its crucial meaning in the flow of time, resulting in the fulfillment of one's humanity and enabling a culture to survive.

Personality formation and the preservation of culture thus come together to form a single unit. They do not come into being of their own accord, but only if we develop them and put them to practice. This is the basic insight which underlies the ethics and morality of individual psychology.

LITERATURE

Adler, Alfred. *Social Interest—A Challenge to Mankind.* London 1938. New York 1964.

Adler, Alfred. *What Life Should Mean to You.* First published 1931. Reprinted London 1971.

Buchholz-Kaiser, Annemarie. *Individualpsychologische Bildungsarbeit. Aspekte der analytischen Bearbeitung von Persönlichkeitsproblemen in Gruppen. Das Gemeinschaftsgefühl bei Alfred Adler im Vergleich zur Therapie der Psychosen bei Frieda Fromm-Reichmann.* Zürich 1991.

Buchholz-Kaiser, Annemarie. Standortbestimmung, in: *Jahresbericht 1988*, Hrg.: VPM. Zürich 1989.

Buchholz-Kaiser, Annemarie. Eigenständigkeit und Beziehungsfähigkeit I-V, in: *Zeitschrift Menschenkenntnis* —Psychologische Zeitschrift für Ehe-, Erziehungs-, Berufs- und andere Lebensfragen. Nr. 9/89; 10/89; 11/89; 12/89; 1/90. Hrg.:VPM. Zürich.

Kaiser, Annemarie. *Das Gemeinschaftsgefühl—Entstehung und Bedeutung für die menschliche Entwicklung.* Eine Darstellung wichtiger Befunde aus der modernen Psychologie. Zürich 1981. Engl. trans., *Social Interest—Its Formation and Significance for Human Development.* A Presentation of Important Findings of Modern Psychology (forthcoming.)

Kriele, Martin. Das Naturrecht in der Neuzeit, in: *Naturrecht und Politik.* Philosophische Schriften Band 8. Hrg: Karl Graf Ballestrem. Berlin 1993.

Messner, Johannes. *Das Naturrecht—Handbuch der Gesellschaftsethik, Staatsethik und Wirtschaftsethik.* Innsbruck, Wien, München 1984.

Messner, Johannes. *Social Ethics—Natural Law in the Modern World.* London 1965 (First published 1949. Reprinted.)

Messner, Johannes. *Ethik und Gesellschaft.* Aufsätze 1965-1974. Köln 1975.

Nussbaumer, Elisabeth. Wertevermittlung im VPM, in: *Zeitschrift Menschenkenntnis* - Psychologische Zeitschrift für Ehe-, Erziehungs-, Berufs- und andere Lebensfragen. Nr. 7-8/93. Hrg.: VPM. Zürich.

Portmann, Adolf. *Biologische Fragmente zu einer Lehre vom Menschen.* Basel 1944.

Theoretische Grundlagen zur psychologischen Tätigkeit im VPM. Hrg.: VPM. Zürich 1991.

II. Critical Studies

4

Conscience and Superego: A Phenomenological Analysis of Their Difference and Relation

John F. Crosby

A personalist psychology is bound to be particularly concerned with doing justice to conscience. It is widely understood that when some question affects us strongly in our conscience, we quicken as persons. We enter into the inner sanctuary of our personhood when we work through some question of conscience. We violate ourselves as persons when we compromise ourselves in some matter of conscience. We show respect for others as persons by abstaining from any coercion in all that concerns their own judgments of conscience. We need not waste many words on the relevance of the topic of conscience to our newly formed Institute for Personalist Psychology.

It is widely thought by psychologists and philosophers that conscience is nothing more than what Sigmund Freud called the superego. Indeed, Freud himself thought this, or more exactly he thought that conscience is one of several functions of the superego. I want to argue that one can never hope to understand the deep personalist meaning of conscience if one reduces it to the superego, and that a truly personalist philosophy as well as a personalist psychology have to distinguish between superego and conscience as fundamentally different things. I call my paper a phenomenological study, because it belongs to the genius of phenomenology to resist all forms of reductionism, and to let each thing be itself. I want to show why we have to let the superego be the superego and let conscience be conscience and must never reduce the one to the other.

But though I want to defend conscience against being absorbed into the superego, I think at the same time that there is such a thing as the superego, so I begin the work of my paper with an attempt to characterize the superego. Only in the second main part of my paper will I come to conscience and its relation to the superego.

I

Since one would need to know Freud better than I do in order to speak with confidence about what exactly he does mean and does not mean by superego, I propose to follow the presentation of the superego in the writings of the Freudian analyst and psychologist, Erich Fromm, especially as found in his book, *Man for Himself: an Inquiry into the Psychology of Ethics.*[1] Though he himself transcends Freud in his own theory of conscience, Fromm is familiar with the Freudian concept of the superego, which he deals with under the heading of authoritarian conscience.

Let us begin with the small child whose parents prohibit various things which the child would like to do. The parents uphold their prohibitions by threatening different punishments in the event that the child does not comply. At the earliest stage of moral development the child will of course do the prohibited things if it can escape undetected and go unpunished; but the prospect of being caught and punished usually suffices to deter the child from the prohibited behavior. One can find a very similar stance towards authority in the way many people relate to the law of the state; one complies in order to avoid state punishment, but otherwise one does what one wants, even if that means violating the law.

Such a child can proceed in its moral development to the point of understanding the reasons for the parental prohibitions and in this way it can make these prohibitions its own. Then the child avoids the prohibited behavior, but not because it is prohibited and is threatened with punishment, but because the child, understanding what it now understands, does not for its part want such behavior. It now sees the behavior in question as the parents see it, and no more wants it than they do; and just as they do not need to be threatened in order to not want it, so neither does the child now need to be threatened in order to not want it. It is in his own name that the child wants to avoid such behavior, and no longer just in response to parental pressure. This is one way of developing beyond the stage of fear of parental threats.

But if it does develop in this way, it would not develop a Freudian superego; it is a very different moral development which leads in the direction of the superego. For this the child has to internalize the parental prohibitions in a way that is different from understanding them and learning to will them for himself. It has to perform what psychologists call an "introjection" of the parental authority. You know what it is to project your inner feelings on to another, as when you are irritated at someone and proceed to project something blameworthy onto him or her. Well, there is also the reverse movement—not projection but introjection—whereby you take some other into yourself, identifying yourself with that other.

For understanding introjection I find it helpful to think about a certain way in which a person can live in the expectations of others. Max Scheler has described this under the title of "heteropathic identification" with others.[2] Such a person experiences so strongly the expectations of others that he loses any expectations of his own for himself and comes to be dominated by, and to live only for and live only in, the expectations of these others. Their expectations replace the expectations which he would normally have for himself; he yields in a sense to the others the place which should be occupied by his own self, and in this sense he identifies himself with them. Such a process of identification is obviously different from the case where a person comes to understand for himself the justice of the others' expectations and on this basis expects of himself what they expect of him. This way of agreeing with others involves a clear recognition of his difference from them and involves therefore no heteropathic identification with them. But such identification involves a certain loss of oneself in the dominant others, or an introjection of them into oneself.

Scheler gives an intriguing instance of how heteropathic identification can occur even among animals.[3] He relates the case, which he read about, of a large snake opening its mouth and moving towards a squirrel to eat it. At first the squirrel wants to run away, but it hesitates, and then does the last thing you expect it to do, it jumps into the mouth of the snake. Scheler interprets this as follows: the squirrel felt in an abnormally strong way what the snake wanted of it, and it began to want the same thing. But wanting to yield to the snake conflicted with the squirrel's instinct for self-preservation. It was this inner conflict which made the squirrel hesitate. As the empathizing of the squirrel with the desire of the snake continued, it began to suppress the squirrel's instinct for self-preservation; eventually it took over completely, and led the squirrel to act spontaneously in complete agreement with what the snake wanted. Scheler sees here in the animal world a case of something very like the human phenomenon that he calls heteropathic identification with others.

Scheler's concept of heteropathic identification provides us with a helpful approach to the superego. As I understand it, the superego arises from a certain identification of the child with the parental authority, perhaps especially with the paternal authority. Freud describes the identification like this in *The Ego and the Id*: "When we were little children we knew these higher natures [that is, our parents], we admired them and feared them; and later we took them into ourselves."[4] Instead of remaining outside of the child and in need of being supported by threats, the paternal authority is now taken into the child in such a way that threats become superfluous. The child who introjects the paternal authority will comply with the paternal prohibitions all on his own, even at those moments when he knows that the father is not looking. The father now has his own representative in the mind of his son or daughter; this representative observes the child even in the absence of the father.

One begins to see how someone might confuse conscience with the superego, for the latter begins to look like conscience in some respects. The superego as it emerges in our discussion seems to have the inwardness as well as the authoritativeness of conscience; it also has the element of someone watching me from above within myself. But let us not get ahead of ourselves; only later will we come to the question of discriminating conscience from the superego. We are not yet finished with our characterization of superego.

In his discussion of the superego, Fromm rightly stresses that the superego represents something depersonalizing for the child, or for the adult with a superego for that matter. This is in part because the commands and the prohibitions of your superego are not understandable to you. Recall that the introjecting of parental authority is something very different from understanding for yourself the justice of your parents' commands and prohibitions. Now if you are bound to act according to norms and principles which you in no way understand and cannot make your own by means of understanding, then you suffer thereby a certain depersonalization. Thus in one place Fromm compares being oppressed by a superego with the situation of the man in Kafka's novel, *The Trial*.[5] This man, called K, is charged with a crime of which he knows nothing, and he is brought into a mysterious court whose laws and procedures are impenetrable to him. So it is, according to Fromm, in the inner life of someone who has taken into himself norms which he does not really understand.

But there is more in Fromm on the depersonalizing tendency of the superego; he suggests that the superego can develop only on the basis of a certain unwillingness of a person to be a distinct personal self.

> He has found inner security by becoming, symbiotically, part of an authority felt to be greater and more powerful than himself. As long as he is part of that authority—at the expense of his own integrity—he feels that he is participating in the authority's strength. His feeling of certainty and identity depends on this symbiosis...[6]

We can verify a certain truth of this if only we look in the right place in our own experience. I venture to say that we have all had the experience of a conflict between the pressure of the superego and what we ourselves understand to be good and choose on the basis of our understanding. We have felt parents' and other people's expectations pulling us in one direction, and we have felt something in ourselves resonating with their claims; but at the same time we felt our own insight drawing us in another direction, and we felt something else and something deeper in ourselves resonating with this insight. In this inner struggle, which may repeat itself in the course of a person's moral development, we are aware of being challenged to dare to be ourselves by following our own insight, and are aware at the same time of being exposed to the temptation to play it safe and to remain sheltered in the symbiotic relation to the introjected authority. Perhaps the conflict in us is heightened by the illusion that we commit a morally reprehensible rebellion against the superego by following our own insight against its demands. But at the same time we know that if we remain captive to the superego, we do so at the expense of living fully our distinct personal selfhood, or in other words at the expense of a certain personal integrity, as Fromm says.

This depersonalizing tendency of the superego derives not only from the person who seeks shelteredness just at the point where he should be living as a distinct personal self; it can also derive from the authoritative persons who are introjected by that person. Fromm reminds us of the famous passage in the *Antigone* of Sophocles where King Creon speaks about the kind of children which every father wants:

> So it is right, my son, to be disposed—in everything to back your father's quarrel. It is for this men pray to breed and rear in their home *dutiful offspring*—to requite the foe with evil and their father's friend with honour, as did their father. Whoso gets children *unserviceable*—what else could he be said to breed, but troubles for himself...[7]

This expresses a parental attitude which does not regard children as distinct persons, but as extensions of the parents. Such parents are only too glad to keep their children tethered to themselves by means of a superego in their children; in this way the children are made to exist as moral extensions of the parents. These parents will be quick to interpret as ungrateful and immoral rebellion any attempt of their children to develop their own moral understanding and to act in their own name.

We can say, then, that a person can fear being a distinct personal self, and that others, too, can fear him being a distinct personal self, and that these two fears can support each other in the formation of the thing that we are here calling the superego of such a person.

It follows from our discussion that an authority can be depersonalizing not only in the obvious case where it remains outside of me and has to resort to threats against me to secure my compliance; it can be no less depersonalizing when it is inside of me and has been so internalized by me as to have no need of threats.

Let me bring out just one further feature of the superego. Fromm observes that the superego is a repressive force in the life of a person. The creative energies and the spontaneity of a person are crippled by the dependency on the introjected other. They might be released if the person were to learn to form and to act on his own judgment, but they remain painfully pent up in the person as long as his superego blocks such growth in moral independence. These frustrated energies of personal existence, denied their natural outlet, become inner demons; they give rise to a certain cruelty against oneself which is so often found in the working of the superego. Fromm writes that the person who is dominated by a strong superego,

> being more or less crippled in his productiveness, develops a certain amount of sadism and destructiveness. These destructive energies are discharged by taking over the role of the authority and by dominating oneself as the servant. In the analysis of the Super-Ego, Freud has given a description of its destructive components which has been amply confirmed by clinical data collected by other observers.[8]

Here, too, we seem to touch upon a mark of conscience, especially of "bad" conscience, which, as we all know, can accuse a person in the most merciless and relentless way.

We can no longer defer the question whether conscience is nothing more than the superego, whether it is adequately and exhaustively explained in terms of the psycho-dynamics of introjection and heteropathic identification, as Freud and many others think. I am quite convinced that there is such a thing as the superego in many persons, I think in fact that most of us know it from past and perhaps even from present experience. I further think that for the cultivation of our conscience it is very important to know what a superego is. But I think that this is important for the very reason that conscience is not the same as superego. We turn now to conscience and the kind of contrast it forms with the superego.

II

Fromm has the merit of marking a certain distinction between superego and conscience. On this point he is better than his master, Freud. More exactly, Fromm calls the superego "authoritarian conscience," which he contrasts with "humanistic conscience," which is for him conscience in its healthy form. Let us see what he means by humanistic conscience.

> Actions, thoughts, and feelings which are conducive to the proper functioning and unfolding of our total personality produce a feeling of inner approval, of "rightness," characteristic of the humanistic "good conscience." On the other hand, acts, thoughts, and feelings injurious to our total personality produce a feeling of uneasiness and discomfort, characteristic of the "guilty conscience." *Conscience is thus a reaction of ourselves to ourselves.* It is the voice of our true selves which summons us back to ourselves, to live productively, to develop fully and harmoniously—that is, *to become what we potentially are.* It is the guardian of our integrity; it is the "ability to guarantee one's self with all due pride, and also at the same time *to say yes* to one's self" [Nietzsche]. If love can be defined as the affirmation of the potentialities and the care for, and the respect of, the uniqueness of the loved person, humanistic conscience can be justly called *the voice of our loving care for ourselves.*[9]

It certainly seems to be true that in conscience we have to do with ourselves, with our integrity. You typically say in a crisis of conscience that you will not be able to live with yourself if you act against your conscience. In Robert Bolt's play about the life and death of St. Thomas More, *A Man for All Seasons*, there is a scene in which Thomas More says to his friend, Norfolk: "I will not give in because I oppose it—I do—not my pride, not my spleen, nor any other of my appetites but *I* do—*I*!"[10] Just as Fromm suggests, Thomas More seems to be concerned with the integrity of his very self, his I. In authoritarian conscience, or superego, one loses oneself in a certain sense in the introjected authority, suffering thereby a serious de-personalization; here in conscience rightly understood one preserves and protects one's self, and one thrives in one's personal selfhood.

But does this suffice on the distinction between superego and conscience? Has Fromm told us all we need to know about conscience in its contrast to the superego? I think not. On the basis of what Fromm has given us, one can hardly understand why conscience and superego have so often, and so plausibly, been identified; in his presentation they are obviously different and no one can miss the difference. Fromm has given us only one aspect of authentic conscience, and has left out another, all-important aspect of it, and has quite wrongly assigned this other aspect to authoritarian conscience, or superego. What am I referring to?

Do we not encounter in conscience something demanding, something unconditionally binding, something authoritative, something calling for a kind of obedience? In his famous phenomenology of conscience John Henry Newman speaks of conscience as a "magisterial dictate"[11]; in another place he speaks of it as "a voice, or the echo of a voice, imperative and constraining, like no other dictate in the whole of our experience."[12] It is well known how Kant explained the imperativity of that which binds us in conscience. He distinguishes between categorical and hypothetical imperatives. The latter say to us in effect, "if you want to attain a certain result, then do this or that." Which means that if you do not care about the result, you need not bother about doing this or that. But categorical imperatives say simply, "do this" or "You shall not do that." No if-clauses, no conditions, no way to get out of the imperative by declining the pursuit of some goal. The categorical imperatives do not even say, "if you want to be happy, fulfilled, integrated, then do this or that"; even such significant conditions play no role with categorical imperatives. Thomas More did not hear in his conscience, "if you want to be ultimately happy, then do not give in to the king." He heard instead the sterner imperative, the unconditioned imperative, what Newman calls the magisterial dictate: "thou shalt not give in, it is absolutely wrong to yield to the king." Or recall the great drama of conscience portrayed in the play of the Russian writer, Puschkin, entitled *Boris Godounov*, which was put to music in the great opera of the same name by Moussorgsky. Boris killed the child Dmitri, the true heir to the throne, and, as the opera opens, has been reigning as Tsar of Russia for some years, but always tormented by his conscience, and most of all when he is surrounded by his own children. He shudders at the vision of the dead child which keeps rising up to accuse him. You could never explain this shuddering of Boris on the assumption that he had only violated some hypothetical imperative; no, it all makes sense only on the assumption that he is aware of violating some higher law which bound him not hypothetically but categorically.

You will not find in Fromm anything about this imperativity and this authoritativeness of the moral call addressed to us in conscience, or about the moral accusation heard in a guilty conscience. He has something much tamer in mind when he speaks of conscience as "the voice of our loving care for ourselves," which would be an absurdly harmless way of describing the conscience of Boris Godounov.

Fromm expresses his own atheistic humanism by saying, "No power transcending man can make a moral claim upon him. Man is responsible to himself for gaining or losing his life".[13] Recall the title of his book, *Man for Himself.* Conscience should be a matter only of a person in relation to himself; it becomes deformed as soon as it involves obedience to an imperative, in fact it then falls back into authoritarian conscience, or superego.

It must be admitted that conscience as portrayed by Newman, as experienced by Tsar Boris Godounov, has certain points of resemblance with a superego which Fromm's humanistic conscience lacks; looked at from the outside Newman can be suspected more plausibly than Fromm of having described nothing more than a superego. How is it that the imperativity of a moral call differs from the pressure of introjected authoritative persons making their demands of me in the form of a superego?

Out of all that might be said by way of distinguishing these two things, I call your attention to one supremely important point of distinction: *we are capable of understanding moral imperatives, of understanding where they come from and why they can bind us; we are capable of approving them with our own insight. This means that in obeying them we need not be yielding to the pressure of another person, whether of another outside of us or of another introjected person speaking in our own mind, or rather speaking in place of our own mind; we are quite capable of obeying in such a way as to think with our own mind and act in our own name.* One might have gathered this liberating power of our own insight, from Fromm's own characterization of authoritarian conscience. As we saw, he repeatedly points out that the person afflicted with this pathology of conscience lacks understanding for the inner justice of the commands and prohibitions which he accepts. We said that his introjection of parental authority is something utterly different from coming to understand the point of the parental directives and so to will them in his own name. The introjection leads to a certain blurring of the difference between his will and his parents' will; he wills what they will only because of the way in which their will replaces his own. But his act of understanding enables him to will what his parents will and to remain completely intact as a distinct person; his understanding lets him act with his own will. This remains true even when that which he understands is a moral imperative calling for a kind of moral obedience.

Notice that it is not exactly the moral truth which liberates our personhood in relation to moral imperatives; it is *our understanding of moral truth* which alone liberates. The norms that are internalized in the depersonalizing manner of a superego may well be perfectly true and valid moral norms; the truth liberates only through our understanding of it.

But you will ask, what exactly is it that we understand when we grasp a moral imperative in our conscience, or when, having violated an imperative, we are burdened with a guilty conscience? Kant gives a profound answer to this question when, after searching for the ground of a categorical imperative, he says that this ground will have to be something having absolute value; that which has value only in relation to our needs can bind us only hypothetically but never categorically. He asks where absolute value is to be found, and he answers that it is first and foremost found in persons; each human person has absolute value, which we commonly call dignity. We are, therefore, categorically bound to show respect for persons, and never merely to use them for our own purposes. If we understand the worth and dignity of persons, then we understand the categorical imperative to respect them which makes itself felt in conscience. Boris Godounov understood the value which the child Dmitri had as person and so he understood perfectly—in contrast to the hero of Kakfa's novel, *The Trial*—why his conscience was accusing him so relentlessly. Thus it is that imperativity and obedience and accusation enter into our life of conscience without any least tendency to degrade our conscience to a mere superego.

But we have to go farther in showing how unlike conscience in the sense of Newman is from a superego, and how wrong Fromm is to identify them. Notice that Thomas More says "I" so emphatically just at the moment when he responds with unconditional obedience to a moral imperative. It is too little to say that the imperative does not harm his I; we have also to say that it gives Thomas More a supreme experience of his I. This experience of the quickening of one's deepest self in relation to a moral imperative has been well described by Dietrich von Hildebrand:

> A moral call is addressed to someone to intervene in a certain situation; perhaps another is in danger, or perhaps he has to refuse to do some evil which is asked of him. He grasps the morally relevant value, he understands its call, he is aware of the moral obligation, which appeals to his conscience. On the one hand, we have here a high-point of transcendence in the pure commitment to the morally relevant good. But on the other hand, this call, insofar as it is morally obligatory, pre-eminently contains the element of "tua res agitur" ("the thing concerns *you* personally"). In a certain sense this call is my most intimate and personal concern, in which I experience the uniqueness of my self. Supreme objectivity and supreme subjectivity interpenetrate here. One can even say that we have here the dramatic high-point of the "tua res agitur" in our earthly existence. On the one hand, I commit myself to something which in no way stands before me as merely "an objective good for me," but rather as something which appeals to me as valuable in itself; but on the other hand, since a moral obligation in its unique impact is here at stake...my decision to follow the call or not, eminently reaches into the innermost center of my own existence (*Eigenleben*). When the moral call is addressed to me and appeals to my conscience, then at the same time the question of my own salvation comes up. It is not just the [objective] "issue" which is at stake; I and my salvation are just as much at stake.[14]

You see that Fromm's talk of conscience as the "voice of our loving care for ourselves" is in a way present here in von Hildebrand's account of conscience; it is present in his talk of the supreme subjectivity which is stirred up in conscience, as well as in his talk of the "tua res agitur" of conscience. But at the same time this concern of me with myself in conscience is placed in a new context and is in a way transformed in von Hildebrand *because of the presence in his account of that which Fromm excludes, namely the imperativity of moral obligation and the call for a kind of moral obedience.* Von Hildebrand wants to show that it is just this imperativity which potentiates the subjectivity of conscience, transforming Fromm's harmless "loving care for myself" into a concern with something much more ultimate for myself, a concern with a kind of salvation for myself. Far from drawing me off of myself, or absorbing me heteropathically into another, or in some other way doing violence to my distinct selfhood, the moral imperative reveals depths of my interiority and of my deepest well-being of which Fromm knows nothing. The subjectivity which resonates with the moral imperative is immeasurably deeper than the subjectivity which, as in Fromm, has only to do with itself. Conscience as portrayed by von Hildebrand does not, because of the strong theme of obedience, tend to become a superego, as Fromm thinks it must; just the contrary, it becomes more and more opposed to a superego as the theme of obedience grows, it becomes an ever deeper experience of personhood through the imperativity of the moral call. Fromm's "man for himself" is a flat and one-dimensional creature compared to man as he really exists, namely as called to the service of that which is good in itself. Thus Fromm's "humanistic conscience" is a pale and anemic thing compared with the throbbing, living conscience which resonates with the moral law and its categorical obligations.

If we are asked how it is possible for obligation to weigh so heavily on us without harming us as persons, we have only to think through again the answer which has already been given. It is because we understand the goods and values out of which obligation grows. At the beginning of the passage just quoted from von Hildebrand we read: "He grasps the morally relevant value, he understands its call." This understanding lets us internalize the moral call, not in the sense of introjection, but in the sense of being able to will *all in our own name* the right response to the call. Everything turns on the capacity of persons to understand goods and values and to understand what kind of commitment we owe to them. This is why relativism and subjectivism regarding value and the good are so devastating for our image of the human person; if these philosophies are true, then there is nothing to be understood about good and value, and we have no way of going beyond a superego, or going beyond Fromm's humanistic conscience.

Perhaps one will object that I have left no room for any moral authority to which one might submit in leading one's moral life; the insight which liberates us for conscience seems to render moral authority superfluous. But it is not difficult to allow for moral authority on my principles. It is only necessary that one at least understand the trustworthiness of the authority that one follows; then one has enough of one's own understanding to avoid acquiring anything like a superego as a result of accepting norms that one does not yet entirely understand. Of course, moral authority will have the tendency to phase itself out by fostering in the person his own moral understanding about the norms themselves.

One more step, and our analysis is complete. It is almost impossible to experience conscience as I have presented it in all its imperativity and yet not to experience a religious depth in it; it is almost impossible not to be aware of encountering God in conscience. I know of no major thinker who recognizes the imperativity of moral obligation and who at the same time holds fast to a merely humanistic account of conscience. Once you find in conscience Newman's "magisterial dictate," you cannot help also finding something like his God. It would belong to another study to unfold that which lies behind this religious intuition. What concerns us at present is that with this breakthrough into the religious sphere there need be no least movement towards a superego. Of course it will seem to some as if the resemblance with a superego has only increased; the God appearing in conscience may look suspiciously like an introjected human father. *But as long as the moral requirements felt in conscience are understood, then the God who emerges as the ground of them is also understood, and the human person who understands does not get absorbed into God, but rather encounters God person to Person, never so alive as distinct person as in his relation to the divine Person.*

Let us conclude. We have developed a personalist criterion for distinguishing between superego and conscience. The superego commonly represents a pathology of individual personal existence and always represents at least a deficiency of personal existence. Conscience, by contrast, which is fundamentally more than Fromm's humanistic conscience, represents the most authentic, awakened personal existence; it is, as we said at the outset, the inner sanctuary of each person. Precisely a personalist psychology should never conflate these two things, should never reduce conscience in the sense of Newman to superego in the sense of Freud. A personalist psychology will know how to distinguish these things in theory and in practice; it will know how to help patients beyond the moral immaturity of the superego, towards the fullness of personal life in conscience.

NOTES

[1] Erich Fromm, *Man for Himself: an Inquiry into the Psychology of Ethics* (New York, 1947), 145-175.

[2] Max Scheler, *The Nature of Sympathy* (Hammed, Conn., 1973), 18-23, and especially 42-45.

[3] *Ibid.*, 21-22.

[4] Freud, *The Ego and the Id* (New York, 1962), 26.

[5] Fromm, *op. cit.,* 171-175.

[6] *Ibid.*, 151.

[7] Quoted by Fromm, *op. cit.*, 157.

[8] *Ibid.*, 155.

[9] *Ibid.*, 163.

[10] Robert Bolt, *A Man for All Seasons* (New York, 1990), 38-39.

[11] Newman, *An Essay in Aid of a Grammar of Assent* (London, 1898), Chap. 5, sec. 1, p. 105-106.

[12] *Ibid.*, p. 107.

[13] *Ibid.*, 174.

[14] My translation from von Hildebrand, *Das Wesen der Liebe* (Regensburg, 1971), 274-5. Here is the German text: "Es ergeht an jemanden der Ruf, in einer bestimmten Situation einzugreifen, sei es, dass sich ein anderer in Gefahr befindet, sei es, dass...jemand etwas Boeses, das von ihm verlangt wird, zu verweigern hat. Er erfasst den sittlich bedeutsamen Wert, er versteht seinen Ruf, er wird sich der sittlichen Verpflichtung bewusst, sie appelliert an sein Gewissen. Einerseits liegt hier, in der reinen Hingabe an den sittlich bedeutsamen Wert in sich, ein Hoehepunkt der Transzendenz vor. Andererseits aber enthaelt dieser Ruf in eminenter Weise das Element des "Tua res agitur", insofern dieser Ruf sittlich verpflichtend ist. Dieser Ruf ist in gewissem Sinne sogar meine allerintimstse und persoenlichste Angelegenheit, in der ich die Einzigartigkeit meines Selbst erlebe. Hoechste Objektivitaet und hoechste Subjektivitaet greifen hier ineinander. Man kann sagen, dass hier der dramatische Hoehepunkt des "Tua res agitur" auf Erden vorliegt. Einerseits gebe ich mich an etwas hin, das in keiner Weise als "objektives Gut fuer mich" vor mir steht, sondern als etwas, das nur als in sich wertvoll mich anspricht; aber weil dabei meine sittliche Verpflichtung in ihrer einzigartigen Tragweite im Spiel ist, also im letzten der Ruf Gottes an mich, ragt anderseits die Entscheidung, ob ich dem Ruf folge oder nicht, in eminenter Weise in mein Eigenleben hinein. Wenn der sittliche Ruf an mich ertoent, an mein Gewissen appelliert, dann wird damit auch gleichzeitig die Frage meines eigenen Heils aktualisiert. Nicht nur die "Sache" steht auf dem Spiel, ich und mein eigenes Heil stehen gleichfalls auf dem Spiel."

5

Full Hearts and Empty Heads: The Price of Certain Recent Programs in Humanistic Psychology

W. R. Coulson

Consider the misbehavior Jason Berry reported in his articles three and four years ago and in his book *Lead Us Not into Temptation.*[1] He reported it had cost the Catholic Church in America 400 million dollars in financial settlements—likely more by now. Talkshow hosts Phil Donohue and Geraldo Rivera exposed the problem on television and called it priestly pedophilia. But I think "pedophilia" is a mistaken identification. There is reason to say that most such cases betray not a mental illness called pedophilia but the influence of bad philosophy: an application of humanistic psychology if you will. In the 1960s and '70s, there developed atop this psychology a philosophy of personal development and interpersonal relationships called the human potentials movement. A recent study initiated by the Franciscans of the St. Barbara province in California[2] suggests that four-fifths might be the proper proportion of non-pedophiles—*non*-pedophiles—among priests who have misbehaved sexually with altarboys, choirboys and other children; for it has been reported by the provincial office that psychological testing labels only two of the eleven offending friars in the sex abuse scandal at St. Anthony's seminary as certifiable pedophiles.

St. Anthony's was the scandal that deserved the front-page treatment it got in *The New York Times* December 1, 1993. The runover headline on page A-12 sums up the story: "Friars Sexually Molested Boys at California Seminary, Church Inquiry Says." To the credit of the Franciscans, they requested and paid for the inquiry; and their provincial superior called the findings "horrific."[3] Thirty-four boys were said to have been molested over a 23-year period; fully one-fourth of the faculty participated in molesting boys.

We have to go back a bit to understand how Catholics were vulnerable to the lessons of human potentials philosophy. If we had been less gullible after Vatican II, we might have seen what was coming down the pike. I was at WBSI, the Western Behavioral Sciences Institute, when the California Franciscans invited us to deliver to them a series of programs capturing our own version of human potentialism. It was the Rogerian-Maslovian version, named for Carl Rogers and Abraham Maslow,[4] the men who with James Bugental and Rollo May (and others lesser known) had recently launched the American Association for Humanistic Psychology.

When I now suggest we should have seen what was coming, I am thinking of a letter received at WBSI from a West Coast Franciscan seminary professor in 1968. We had recently done a human potentials workshop at his school, the sort of event that Rogers later characterized by the term "the person-centered approach." The idea was to try to help friars get beyond their friarhood and students their studenthood—to turn them all into persons and all therefore equally available one to the other. This person-centered approach of Carl Rogers was a latter-day synonym for his well known client-centered psychotherapy.

Shortly after the workshop at his seminary, the friar-professor wrote that his vocation had changed direction: "I am behaving like mad, with true self blossoming all over the place. Killing me."

We took it that his tongue was in his cheek; later we realized that he spoke more truth than the WBSI staff was capable of facing. Maslow was the exception, though the severity of his judgment against the whole approach didn't emerge until his *Journals* were published much later.[5]

Was the behaving-like-mad friar one of the notorious eleven child-abusers reported in *The New York Times*? We'll probably never know: except for two who have gone to jail, the names of the men are being kept secret, and it isn't really important to know: something was wrong with the very idea of huggy-kissy priests in the first place, something wrong with applying heavy-duty human potentials lessons to religion.

Later Carl Rogers was to describe the movement as having been "thoroughly insidious in religion."[6] The audience to whom he said this consisted of facilitator trainees taking part in a tape-recorded discussion with him in 1976. They laughed heartily to hear the remark, but really, it wasn't funny. In an article published October 8, 1967, *New York Times'* reporter Richard Reeves (since the author of a well regarded book on the escapades of John F. Kennedy) described some of the unfunny developments he saw humanistic psychology stimulate in a religious setting. It was among Anglo-Catholics in a human potentials workshop at Grace Episcopal Cathedral in San Francisco that fall.

> In one "happening" ... a nun told of her struggles with sexual desires and an overly-considerate woman, taunted in an encounter group as "super mama," erupted for the first time in a rage against her husband. The principles are similar in most of the movement's activities ... In body awareness, people may get down on the floor and roll over each other, pretending they are animals at play. In role-playing, a man may act out before a group some unpleasant behavior of his wife.

In describing to the group the unpleasantness of his wife (and earning their gratitude for being open about a private concern), the man gains one attachment and loses another. Loyalty to the standards of the group—primarily its advocacy of openness—becomes more important than loyalty to the person of the wife.

In addition to talking about religion, Carl Rogers referred to his marriage in the 1976 meeting with the facilitator trainees. To hear what he said about his wife is to hear of the destructive power of the human potentials movement. He was later to write that as she lay dying (three years after he opened up in front of the trainees), his feeling was: "I wanted to care for her, but I was not at all sure that I loved her."[7] Confessions of this kind were offered throughout the period in which he made a real effort to put himself in a bad light with the public. The problem for the reporter who likes and respects Carl Rogers is that there is no way to reproduce his words without putting the man in the same bad light today. But it seems to be what he wanted: one of his motives, he said, was to find release from the habit of being good—also from *seeming* to be good. His parents had set him up to be and seem good in public. When it became clear it was at odds with the person-centered system of psychology, being good became a burden. This was his sense of things: Being good keeps me apart from people; some of the most interesting people aren't very good.

In a filmed interview he put it as follows: he wanted to be like his clients—particularly (if you look at the record) the naughty clients, naughty, that is, as his parents and other elders of the devout, family oriented Protestant tribe would have judged. In the film (called "Reflections" and previewed at the 1976 facilitator training meeting) he told interviewer Warren Bennis,

> If I've had a mentor, it's been thousands of mentors, the people I've tried to help. I think I have learned from them the tremendous sense of satisfaction they feel when they move from being phony or defensive or working behind a façade into a more real type of behavior ... It is so much more satisfying to be real ... Put it this way: I provided the conditions which oftentimes helped them to grow in ways that I hadn't yet grown. And that's a very challenging kind of thing. It makes you think, "Why can't I do that? Why am I not that way?"[8]

Interviewer Bennis drew out of him a main reason he wasn't "that way." It was because of his parents. They got him to do "the right things," a focus that got in the way of being real.

> *Rogers:* I was a very good boy. I always got good grades in school. I did the right things.
> *Bennis:* You were a good boy?
> *Rogers:* I was a *very* good boy. I wasn't rebellious at all. It appalls me sometimes to think what a good boy I was.
> *Bennis:* You were a good boy for 20 years?
> *Rogers:* Yes.
> *Bennis:* Did you know you were a good boy? Were you doing it begrudgingly, doing the good-boy work?

> *Rogers:* One of the fascinating things about my parents' control was that it was so subtle that it did not seem oppressive. I was a good boy, but that seemed to be the way I should be. It didn't seem as though I had to be this way against my will.
> *Bennis:* Yeh, that's neat. Marx said the sign of a truly oppressed person is when they don't know they're oppressed.
> *Rogers:* There's a lot of truth to that.
> *Bennis:* But how did they do it?
> *Rogers:* We never had playing cards in our home. We rarely went to movies. Even soda pop was looked on as a little bit sinful, and drink, of course, was unspeakable. And yet I don't remember great diatribes against all that. It was just, "That's not the way we do things. Those are things that we don't go in for."
> *Bennis:* Your family seems so unlike the kind of world you've invented.
> *Rogers:* Yes,...the kind of way I have of working with people, the non judgmental quality that I encourage, the attitude of intellectual and personal exploration, all of that would really be anathema to my parents and my family.

Now, it will help to keep in mind Rogers' expression, "It appalls me sometimes to think what a good boy I was"—also Bennis' report on Marx, "The sign of a truly oppressed person is when they don't know they're oppressed." They help clarify the dynamic of abuse among the Franciscans and, in an equally telling example, the Sisters of the Immaculate Heart of Mary. Consider the published report of Sister Mary Benjamin, IHM.[9] Her religious vocation had been a family affair. One of 11 children of a Polish-Irish-American family, she had been gathered up in 1962 by her parents, brothers and sisters *en masse* and delivered to the Immaculate Heart novitiate at Monticito, California, where WBSI would later deliver the first in its of its large-scale experiments in humanistic psychology for Catholics. Upon arrival at La Casa de Maria, the life of a religious novice became "like a honeymoon" to Sr. Mary Benjamin. "I loved the early morning hours, the walk to chapel through the citrus grove in the fading starlight. We gathered in silence and gently began chanting the psalms" (p. 183). She didn't know how oppressed she was in this activity. Oppressed? Yes, for it was not by choice that she arose in the dark, marched in line to the chapel and prayed in chorus—it was what all nuns did and had done for hundreds of years. So it wasn't authentic. She wrote that following "sensitivity training, my order's first venture into the human potential movement" (p. 186), she came to believe religious life was *per se* oppressive. She also came to see her parents as initiators of the oppression. It was they who had habituated her to Catholic practice and belief. Nothing that followed her earliest childhood had therefore been free; it had been, rather, the expression of habit. Looking back at her upbringing, she said she had discovered "a secret desire" all along: "to rid myself of my baptism and my parentage" (p. 182). She believed her real wish all along had been to be "born a pagan with the freedom to live by my own instincts" rather than the Catholic code. Concerning this discovery, she might have borrowed from Rogers and said, "It appalls me to think what a good girl I was"—appalling her the more, actually, for not having been experienced at the time.

Good was no longer what you were given to be but what you *chose* to be. The choice was to be made on your own terms alone, or those of your favorite therapist-author.

Here is how it worked out at St. Anthony's seminary. For years there had been catalogues of rules in friaries. Some of the rules were designed to make the exchange of intimacies unlikely. That the rules were of long standing made them, *eo ipso,* invalid from a human potentials perspective. "Childish" and "rule-bound" is what Rogers, expressing this judgment, had called Catholic institutional life. He said this in a 1967 review of Father James J. Kavanaugh's *A Modern Priest Looks at His Outdated Church.*[10]

The protective Catholic framework got set aside at St. Anthony's. It seems to have been seen as a form of oppression. Among the unspoken corollaries of the discarding of old-time rules were that everybody could now have sex. Or if they didn't feel like having sex, at least they could practice acceptance, understanding, and permissiveness about other people having sex. According to the investigative report of the situation at St. Anthony's,

> The board of inquiry was assured that no student was ever allowed into the private rooms of the friars. But time and again in the course of the investigation, we learned that the opposite of this was actually true. Doors and rules were intended as physical and psychological barriers. But they were ignored. The perpetrators often brought students into their private rooms to molest them there. One offender had taken a private room in a house next to the seminary. There he had children in his room overnight. The board of inquiry learned that on several occasions, two young boys who were not seminarians, were brought by him to the table occupied by the friars in the refrectory. They were there for dinner and they were there for breakfast the next morning.[11]

That is what the independent board of inquiry learned. Rules were for breaking. Catholic rules were for Catholics to break. To break them established that one had grasped the revised, more psychological concept of goodness; it was measured by how real, non-childish, and independent of external authority one was. Those who didn't break the rules personally practiced nonjudgmentalism while others broke them, romancing town boys in the refrectory.

Nonjudgmentalism was the recommendation of *Client-Centered Therapy,* 1951. Rogers authored the book. Thomas Gordon contributed a chapter which offered a formula to supervisors who would withhold supervision for the sake of organizational therapy. Gordon, who had been Rogers' student at Ohio State in the '40s and his faculty associate at Chicago in the '50s, put the formula as a question about "acceptance, understanding, and permissiveness."[12] He wrote,

> Staff members carrying on therapy at the Counseling Center at the University of Chicago have persistently raised the question whether such factors as acceptance, understanding, and permissiveness would have effects equally therapeutic for

> groups as for individuals. Would it be feasible to try a therapeutic approach in situations outside of the clinic office? What would be the effect upon a group if its supervisor tried consciously to create an accepting atmosphere in which its members could work? (p. 320).

Gordon's questions became a proposal; eventually the proposal became a method, marketed as Leader Effectiveness Training.[13] Rogers got behind it under the rubric of "therapy-for-normals," a theme that occupied the rest of his life.[14] When the Rogerian research team moved from Chicago to the Wisconsin Psychiatric Institute in 1958, Rogers was successful in soliciting a grant from the National Institute on Mental Health (though the subsequent test of therapy for normals was unsuccessful at Wisconsin[15]). In 1964, he and a smaller research team left the Midwest for San Diego. The focus of research on therapy-for-normals became group work, with funding now provided *ad hoc* by agencies and institutions whose staff members were willing to volunteer for treatment. The first such institutional arrangement was made in 1965 following the Watts riots. It entailed group work for staff of the Catholic Welfare Bureau of Los Angeles. A series of workshops for other Catholic institutions followed, all of them in their own way originating in Thomas Gordon's questions of 1951, "Would it be feasible to try a therapeutic approach in situations outside of the clinic office? What would be the effect upon a group if its supervisor tried consciously to create an accepting atmosphere in which its members could work?"

The answer at St. Anthony's is evident now: the group wouldn't get supervised. Eventually there could be the scandal of sex abuse.

Eventually there could also be scandal close to home. Recall that Rogers talked about his wife in front of the facilitator trainees in 1976. She had become ill four years earlier.[16] Recall that he wrote later that he wasn't sure he loved her any more. Why didn't he know if he loved her any more? I think he'd been in too many groups like the session with the trainees, where the demand had been to "get real" and thus, among other things, to account for his life, including his marriage.

Finally he couldn't give account. Married since 1924, Carl and Helen Rogers had become part of one another. There was no way to explain. To remain married a half century was an anomaly among modern American mental health specialists. Perhaps, it was thought, his enduring marriage meant he hadn't really gotten aboard "the group process," with its emphasis on "change." Pressed too often to account for fidelity to a woman whose invalidism would be judged as holding him back, he became "not at all sure that I loved her."

He'd joined the human potentials movement. To put it another way, he'd paid the Polanyian Penalty. Scientist-philosopher Michael Polanyi and his wife Magda had been acquaintances of Carl and Helen Rogers. In *Personal Knowledge* in 1958 Polanyi had written of the great cost of detachment from commitments:

> ...man stands rooted in his calling under a firmament of truth and greatness. Its teachings are the idiom of his thought: the voice by which he commands himself

> to satisfy his intellectual standards. Its commands harness his powers to the exercise of his responsibilities. It binds him to abiding purposes, and grants him power and freedom to defend them.
> And we can establish it now as a matter of logic that man has no other power than this.
> He is strong, noble and wonderful so long as he fears the voices of this firmament; but he dissolves their power over himself and his own powers gained through obeying them, if he turns back and examines what he respects in a detached manner. Then law is no more than what the courts will decide, art but an emollient of nerves, morality but a convention, tradition but an inertia, God but a psychological necessity. Then man dominates a world in which he himself does not exist. For with his obligations he has lost his voice and his hope, and been left behind meaningless to himself.[17]

Detach himself Rogers did. He volunteered the following to the 1976 audience of trainees:

> A situation that I'm in is very difficult for me. It is that [because of] my wife's illness ... she's dropped ... her own interests and isn't physically able to carry out many of the things that we used to do together; and so her love becomes a much more clinging love. And I've had to really work through for myself: where does this stop? I feel I have got to live my life; I've got to be my own person if I'm to be of any help to her—that if I simply said, "All right, you need me so much, I'll stay with you all the time; I'll sacrifice my life to take care of you," that would probably destroy both of us—because if I give up my life or my personhood to take care of her, then I'm going to become bitter, I'm going to become angry inside at what I've given up, I'm not going to want to be be with her—it would be out of a sense of duty—and that isn't the kind of relationship I want, it isn't the kind of relationship she would appreciate either, though she might think now that she would. And so I feel I've got to be my own person and live my own life, and in that way I'll be much more free to be a person *with her* and be caring for her—and really care for her—when I am with her.[18]

His wife had never been unwilling to sacrifice her "personhood" when necessary for his sake. I would hesitate to mention this comparison (and other problems I am on a path to reveal) but for the fact that, as I said before, Rogers knew he was in a bad light and didn't care. To get comfortable in a bad light was one of the developments of the human potentials movement that Rogers learned about first hand and wanted revealed. Thus, the tape recordings of 1976 have him saying that, any more, "I really don't give a damn what anybody thinks about what I do, and that's a very releasing feeling."[19]

It is hard to fathom how it was releasing. The record as a whole reveals that he was in a bad place throughout much of his California period; the bad light it puts him in to describe that era now is a reflection of the place. By bad place I mean *wrong place,* a place where no one should go, a place for doing one's own thing when what one should be doing is what one has promised to do. To compare how Helen Rogers behaved when her husband needed her support in 1949, and how he behaved 25 years later when she needed his, is to compare, as it were, the old church in America with the new. Members of the old church were less focused on fulfilling their needs as individuals than attuned to accepting their commitments. They were like Helen Rogers. Her husband's autobiography of 1967 describes the 1949 espisode that later came to be known as "our runaway trip":

> There was a deeply disturbed client ... with whom I had worked at Ohio State, who later moved to the Chicago area and renewed her therapeutic contacts with me. I see now that I handled her badly, vacillating between being warm and real with her, and then being more "professional" and aloof when the depth of her psychotic disturbance threatened me. This brought about the most intense hostility on her part (along with a dependence and love) which completely pierced my defenses ...

Rogers told friends that the woman "began to take up a bigger and bigger part of my therapy time ... She would sometimes appear on our doorstep." He added, "I somehow gave up *my* self in the relationship."

The efforts of colleagues at the University of Chicago Counseling Center to help him were of little avail. He said, "Gradually I realized I was on the edge of a complete breakdown myself and then suddenly this feeling became very urgent. I *had* to escape." So, he said, "I went home and told Helen that I must get away, at *once.* We were on the road within an hour and stayed away two or three months on what we can now calmly refer to as our 'runaway trip'."[20]

Most important, it seems to me, was the selflessness of his wife and his consequent assurance that, when he needed it, she existed only for him. It was "I," "I," "I," "I," "I," then "we": "*I* realized," "*I* was on the edge," "*I* had to escape," "*I* went home," "*I* must get away." This famous *I*—recently the president of the American Psychological Association and winner of all kinds of awards—was quite helpless. Whom did he tell? No longer his therapists: for all their training, none of the psychologists and consulting psychiatrists at the famous university clinic had been able to help. It was to his wife that he said, "I must get away, at *once.*" "Then we shall," said Helen. "I," "we"—it was all the same to her.

Helen Rogers described the trip: "We finally came to roost at our hideaway at Seneca Lake and spent a month roughing it in our cabin in the cold temperatures of May in New York State. There were periods of real despair which we weathered together....We roamed the hills and I taught him all I could about painting. We spent many hours enjoying and exploring and painting the countryside."

Her husband added a postscript: "... throughout this whole period Helen was certain this state of mind would pass away, that I was not insane, and showed in every way how much she cared. Wow! That's the only way I can express my gratitude. That's what I mean when I say she has stood by me in critical periods."[21]

When it was his turn to stand by, he said, "I feel have got to live my life; I've got to be my own person."

But let's go back to Richard Reeves' *New York Times'* report of a man speaking ill of his wife at a church workshop in San Francisco. The exercise Reeves saw—people rolling over each other in the cathedral hall, "pretending they are animals at play"—is part and parcel of the wife's dismissal. With the censor out of the way, the man is free to play animal games with strangers (and God knows what next). A related image is found in news reports coming out of Santa Barbara, where seminary faculty had freed themselves of supervision. A *Santa Barbara News-Press* article of December 5, 1993, for example, describes a faculty-student camping trip. An amorous teacher, responding appropriately to non supervision, one supposes, climbed out of his sleeping bag to lie atop a boy in the middle of the night: "The frightened boy," the paper reported, "pretended to sleep. He rolled over and dislodged the aroused friar. The boy stayed awake all night out of fear. Thinking no one would believe him, he remained silent about the incident."

Pope St. Leo the Great said this in the fifth century: "What makes it impossible to stay silent is precisely what makes it almost impossible to speak."

Speak we must. The truth is that there has been a lot of misbehavior by ministers of many different denominations in America (not just Catholics), misbehavior which cannot be traced, by any means, solely to a dictionary of abnormal psychology. Certain lines of abnormal theorizing in the 1950s, '60s and '70s—Maslovian-Rogerian theorizing, I am saying—are implicated in the misconduct. As the woman at Grace Episcopal Cathedral was goaded into erupting at her husband for the first time, so too were some of the Franciscans—and the Jesuits and the Immaculate Hearts and the Sisters of Mercy, the Maryknollers and more—goaded into erupting at Holy Mother Church. "There, there, doesn't that feel better?" the facilitators were known to say. And maybe it did feel better. But self-expression became the norm, and self-containment got put on the back burner.

Martin Buber said this: "Religions are mansions into which the spirit of man is fit, that it might not break forth and burst open its world."

Worlds burst open in the wake of human potentialism. Earlier generations of Franciscans might have been "repressed." But at least they didn't roll over high school boys in the middle of the night.

Howard Kirschenbaum and Valerie Land Henderson, who edited *The Carl Rogers Reader* in 1989, have pointed out that Rogers wanted to make of his personal life in California a case study. They write that "As Rogers began to emphasize the importance of the congruent therapist, teacher, or professional in all helping relationships, this led naturally to his wanting to be as personal and authentic as possible in his own professional communication."[22] He developed a popular talk featuring the following ideas: "I want to be real" and "I want to encounter realness in others." He gave the talk widely, including to Congressional staff in Washington.[23]

Being real, for Carl Rogers personally, developed along the lines of the present report: with some backing and filling, an ambitious, responsible, straight-shooting

Midwestern social scientist became "a person" and no longer "gave a damn" what anyone thought. He sketched this on tape in the same session in which he talked with trainees about his disappointment with his wife, and he allowed the report to be widely circulated. To a young German, who spoke about wanting to be less attentive to her mother, he was heard to say on the tape,

> I responded particularly to the part where you said that you'd have to take care of yourself because that's been a lesson that's been very hard for me to learn ... [In a recent] workshop, I was not in very good shape, either psychologically or physically when I went there, and I realized, "I must take care of myself." And for the first time in my life, I did. Ever since I was thirty, I suppose, I've always been in charge of things, and I'm a conscientious person and I feel responsible for them, so I feel responsible for what's going on. Even though I trust the group and all that, yet there's some inner feeling of "Yeah, but I'm responsible." And this time, for the first time, I could say, "I'm going to take care of myself first. I've got to be a person or I can't really be any good to the workshop. And so I really did take good care of myself. I skipped meetings when ordinarily I would have felt, "Oh, I should be there." I skipped staff meetings, which were sacrosanct. Then I found that, as a result, I was much more free in being myself with the workshop group.[24]

It was hard for him not to make a case for irresponsibility—irresponsibility, that is, as a responsible act. He wanted to convince people (not least himself) that a Carl Rogers workshop goes better with an irresponsible Carl Rogers. In other words, he wanted irresponsible behavior to be seen as moral.

His ultimate goal, though, was not to explain himself but to stand at last naked and unjustified. When pieced together, the report becomes not altogether wholesome, but Rogers thought it needed telling, which is one reason, as his biographers say, that "In his last twenty years, he almost always began his books, essays, or speeches in a personal vein."[25]

Here was his motive.[26] Rightly honored by the American Psychological Association as a preeminent experimentalist,[27] he wanted the long-term pattern of experimental results made clear. If he wanted to say how he fit into the pattern personally, it's because he had been such an effective, and eventually troubled, advocate of a dubious proposition. The proposition of course was therapy-for-normals. The tragedy includes that it was a program into which his children were drawn as well, most publicly daughter Natalie, who applied it to her marriage and wrote her sad-angry book about the outcomes. Son David, a prominent medical educator, also got involved and wrote articles applying his father's theories to medical practice; like his sister, his own "full share of marital difficulties" eventuated, as noted in *Becoming Partners,* Carl Rogers' book on "marriage and its alternatives."[28]

In *Carl Rogers on Personal Power,* the author described an encounter that came up in the course of his personal program of therapy-for-normals. It involved him with a client whom he described as "Michele, an attractive woman in her late thirties ... She is lonely ... and both wants and fears closeness with a man. She finds this conflict unbearably present here at the workshop."

The workshop took place in the summer of 1975 and was entitled "A Person-Centered Approach: The Process of Individual Growth and Its Social Implications." Rogers was the leading light, as at all the person-centered workshops, and he also facilitated the encounter group of fifteen participants to which Michele was randomly assigned. In the second session,

> I found myself thinking about Michele and the painful tug of war within her. I felt a very strong impulse to hug her. This set off a dialogue within me, my mind being full of reasons why I should do no such thing. "Isn't sexual attraction one reason you want to embrace her? What makes you think she would accept it when her greatest fear is of closeness? This is only the second meeting of the group and it would seem by some (and perhaps correctly) as a ridiculous 'Touchie-feelie' thing. She hasn't indicated any desire for anything of that sort, so forget the whole stupid impulse!" And then I found myself saying to her (in a somewhat cowardly and indirect expression of what I was feeling): "Michele, if I should tell you I'd like to give you a good *hug,* what would you say?" To my astonishment, she quickly replied, I'd love it." So we stood up and gave each other a strong, close embrace in the middle of the circle. We returned to our places, I feeling definitely embarrassed, but somehow pleased that I had been able to follow an inner feeling, whether right or wrong.

(Maslow, when he was revising his work before his death, referred to the idea of following an inner feeling whether right or wrong as "the mystique of the sacred impulse," in which "controls, editing, critique of all kinds are evil, bourgeois, capitalistic, etc." Some of his early ideas (as in the first edition of *Motivation and Personality*) might support the idea of following an inner feeling whether right or wrong. But he'd learned something; he put it this way: "it occurred to me that my unconscious was *not* the boss. My impulse is *not* sacred and irrefutable."[29])

Rogers' description of the encounter with Michele continued. Having acted on his impulse to deliver a hug, he said,

> I was bowled over by her quiet statement, almost an aside: "Maybe I won't fly home tomorrow after all." I could scarcely believe that my intuitive impulse, so scorned by my intellect, had been so much on target. I certainly could not have dreamed that I was acting out, in myself, what was to be a major learning for the whole community...that intimacy is safe.[30]

But it wasn't. Carl and Helen Rogers had been married 50 years at the time of this encounter. In the 53rd year of their marriage he put the report on Michele before the public. It was the second such episode that had been published.[31] In 1967 he'd made a film of a sixteen-hour encounter workshop. Called "Journey into Self," the edited version was submitted to the Academy of Motion Picture

Arts and Sciences and won an Academy Award for best short documentary of 1968. Toward the end of the film, a certain exchange, problematic from an ethical perspective, was recorded. It took place between Rogers and a young woman, Roz, a glamorous Eurasian bride, the wife of a Naval officer stationed in San Diego, who had volunteered for the filming. In the final session of the group she said to the 65-year-old facilitator,

> Carl, I don't mean to make your position right now more difficult for you. The way I love you is not as Carl Rogers and all your prestige, because I don't know that much about it ... but you have responded so warmly to me and you have given me love. I think when I walk away from here I know that you will be a part of me and I'll always remember you and the experience.
> *Rogers:* There is something very warm and very human on the part of both of us ... I felt needed and I felt useful and real and a lot more expressive. I was brought up in the kind of background a lot of you have been brought up in: you don't touch anybody and so forth. And I just hugged you.

Richard Farson, who was Rogers' co-facilitator for the film, said, "And you loved her."

> *Rogers:* You bet I did.
> *Roz:* And I loved you. And I *love* you, not just for the day.
> *Rogers:* So do I. I love you. A few years ago I couldn't have said that in a group or certainly not to a good looking young gal like you. I could not have.

And the camera shows him brushing away a tear.

Helen Rogers saw the preview showing of "Journey into Self." I cannot but think she asked herself, "What's going on?"

She became an invalid in 1972 and died two years after the publication of the Michele episode. My wife and I had known her since 1963 and recognized her for a strong woman. (Privately, Carl Rogers' graduate students at the Wisconsin Psychiatric Institute referred to her with affection as Big Mama; we imagined her lifting up her husband when he came home from a hard day at the clinic and placing him gently in his rocking chair with a drink and the evening paper.)

As it turned out, Carl would live eight years beyond Helen. Perhaps she didn't care to hold on. Daughter Natalie sees her as having felt not only an invalid but invalidated.

For her part, Natalie may well have wanted to even the score. She herself adopted the doctrine that intimacy outside marriage is safe—leaving her family in the name of growth or empowerment. That is to say, she left them in the name of the same process her father's famous 1961 book had called *becoming a person.*

One wasn't supposed to be a wife and mother, a husband and father, a priest or nun or brother. One was supposed to become a person. The movement called for those who would "grow" to follow the path of becoming open and real.

In the name of openness and realness, a year after her mother's death, Natalie published excerpts from the private notes and journals in which she'd been challenging the world view of her parents' generation since attending Brandeis.[32] Before Helen died, Natalie wrote a letter of rebuke to her. But she never sent it. She excerpted it in *Emerging Woman:*

> I see you as having given up your interests and needs to create an environment of support for your husband's career and his fame. That has angered and frightened me ...
> I believe you are worth putting yourself first ...
> I am disappointed that you did not make a claim for yourself and your interests when your children left home! You continually put your husband's profession first. Between age forty and sixty you missed an opportunity to become more fully you—more independent ...
> Mother, I see you as having held in your resentments and angers for years! ... I see those resentments oozing into your sore joints, your aching body. The scars on your milky white torso, the swelling of your joints, the bone marrow that won't manufacture red cells ... I am sensing your pain as repressed rage ...[33]

Unfortunately, if the expression of rage becomes one's thing, there may be no end to it, just as there may be no end to the faux intimacy of weekend workshops, whether rolling over people to simulate animals at play or delivering a strong, close embrace to a lonely young woman in the middle of the group. To have taught that feelings will substitute for principles in the New Age is to have created endless problems for our society, our children, and ourselves.

Carl Rogers knew this might happen.[34] Here is how he illustrated the contrast between the Protestant, fundamental upbringing his parents provided him and his five siblings, and his own later, full-hearted system of human development: "I think of my mother ... If she had problems, well, she didn't know of anything that scrubbing a few floors wouldn't help. That was her answer to psychological difficulties. So that all of the things that I have developed are really the antithesis of the kind of climate in which I grew up."[35] And here is how Garry Shirts, a colleague at WBSI, remembered what it was like among the staff when Rogers and Maslow were in residence at WBSI, consulting with one another on the philosophy of science: "[P]eople cried and you shared your feelings with them and tried to be closer."[36] Neither Rogers nor Maslow was intellectually impaired; neither man found much value, personally, in spending time in tears. But each developed theories of optimum human functioning that led to the imposition of this emotionality on others—and therefore led their impairment: "full hearts and empty heads."

Maslow and Rogers, we can say, did more to introduce the human potentials movement to decent people than anyone else. They were decent men themselves, who drew off one another's work.[37] As carriers of themes from humanistic psychology into everyday life, they were without peer. They came to popular attention in the 1960s, Maslow with a book titled *Toward a Psychology of Being* (1962) and Rogers with *On Becoming a Person* (1961). In education, their work led to a distinctively American turning point, which today affects not only America but the world. It has to do with the ideal of universal self-actualization. It is evident how much integrity has been lost to education in the Western world because of the overly psychological influence of this ideal. In some countries—England and America quickly come to mind—education, even in graduate-school departments of social science—has become like a virtually endless series of discussion circles or amateur group psychotherapy sessions.

In 1961, Maslow spent seven months in the San Diego area of Southern California, on a visiting fellowship at WBSI. Rogers was not yet on the staff but was on the board of trustees; meeting some of Rogers' students and followers, Maslow wrote in his journals that he was less than impressed. Sigmund Koch, editor of a scholarly textbook series, *Psychology: A Study of a Science,* was in residence at WBSI at the time; Maslow wrote of a "pleasant rapprochement with Sigmund Koch ... Brilliant man. Others here are not brilliant." [38]

What Maslow observed at WBSI was not unlike what he'd begun to see among his psychology students at Brandeis, a progressive university in Massachusetts, operated primarily by and for Jews.

Developments at Brandeis troubled him. He'd grown up with what he called "my Jewish heritage of libraries and books." But he found that many of his students, Jews like him, were being denied the same heritage. The problem was not independent of the theory of universal self-actualization. His students didn't think they needed to bother with the hard work of learning. In a conference on counseling held at the University of Florida in 1961, he said, "Some of my students read a paper or two on self-actualization, and then have a kind of sudden conversion experience, and on Thursday at two o'clock, they decide they're going to be self-actualized *as of that moment.* Then, I find I've let loose in the world people who have jumped to the goal too quickly."[39] So Maslow realized there were major problems with the ideal he called self-actualization. Visiting WBSI again in the summer of 1962, he wrote as follows: "My motivation theory was published 20 years ago, and in all that time nobody repeated it, or tested it, or really analyzed it or criticized it. They just used it, swallowed it whole...."[40] This left Maslow impaired along with his followers; for in dealing with his students, he wrote,

> I feel ineffective, not well used, not using my full power. It's as if I took a job in a chewing-gum factory ... What am I being paid for? Listening to *them?* I might as well be a chemist then. My knowledge and experience are wasted ... I'm doing therapeutic work, not teaching psychology.[41]

Maslow's journals didn't see print until 1979, nine years after his death. By then, much energy, secular and religious (not excluding among the Catholics), and no small amount of money, had been invested in failed attempts to make of self-actualization a universal reality as well as a universal ideal.

Maslow penned his comments about working in a chewing-gum factory in

October 1968, about 20 months before his death. In 1969 he wrote an exasperated review of *Turning On* by journalist Rasa Gustaitis. The book reported on her experiences at WBSI, Esalen Institute, and other centers of the burgeoning human potentials movement. She'd had a contract to do a book for Macmillan called *Turning On Without Drugs,* but one of the first things she did after getting involved with the movement was to try drugs. So the book had to come out with a different title. In reading the book, Maslow said it struck him that

> everything and everybody she admired added up the way of life of psychopaths—living only in the here-now, not thinking also of past and future and of the world in which the here-now is placed, of being impulsive and admiring any impulse or whim or words and the *acting* on it, of a kind of contempt of the straight and square, putting them on and panhandling from them, of having shifting, fluctuating, transient, inconsistent interpersonal relationships, sexual or non sexual, of being unpredictable, unreliable, without loyalties (stealing from each other), "expression-is-all" and totally without controls, even of human [excrement], of dirt, of sores, garbage, etc., of implied irresponsibility to their children (all of these attitudes = lousy child care = lousy wife care)....
>
> My vague impression is that this is much more a male wish-fulfillment than female. The male fantasy is of unlimited [sex] without responsibility of any kind to woman or child, a modern version of the older "stag" fantasy—fool 'em, f— 'em, and forget 'em. Women and children get the short end of things here, as I remember discussing with X, who yearned for continuity, a home, and a child instead of [having sex with] some transient male every once in a while, which she didn't even enjoy ...[42]

Much of what he complains of later came to pass within a wide circle of American youth, not just along the growth center circuit. By then, Abe Maslow was dead and without voice; his criticisms of transient sex and lousy child care wouldn't see print until the publication of his *Journals* in 1979. By that time Carl Rogers, relatively unchallenged, had written a string of articles, chapters and books which amounted to a defense of the transient sex and lousy child care going on (among other places) at his daughter's apartment (as she later wrote). One example from this string of defensive writings is the book *Becoming Partners,* privately described by the author as a salvage job.[43] What had to be salvaged included daughter Natalie's reputation. Transient sex and lousy child care were recast as being on the leading edge of social change, a manifestation of what he called "the person of tomorrow."[44] Rogers wrapped up the book with the following appeal for what he called the freedom to be experimental:

> It fascinates me that as I look over the list of names of the people who have so honestly filled this book with themselves, the great majority of them have, in their struggles for a better partnership, engaged—either in the past or present—in practices which federal, state, or local laws would class as illegal. To give them their old-fashioned names, "living in sin," "committing adultery," "lewd and las-

> civious conduct," "fornication," "homosexuality," "ingesting illegal drugs," even "soliciting"—these have all been present in these pages, though when they are actions engaged in by individuals struggling to find a better pattern of partnerships, the old-fashioned names are, frankly, ridiculous.
> So perhaps one thing we as a culture might do which would preserve this enormously valuable laboratory, these pioneering ventures into new relationship space, would be to relieve them of the ever-present shadow of moral reproach and criminal action.
> If only we dared to say, "We will not interfere," this would be an enormous step forward in facing reality.[45]

Related developments were seen in the incursion into the work of the Sisters of the Immaculate Heart of Mary. It was called the Educational Innovation Project. It began at the Western Behavioral Sciences Institute and transferred with Rogers and his research team to the new Center for Studies of the Person in 1969.[46] The sisters, 560 in number at the peak of project activity, ran a system of 60 schools, including a college. It did not survive the project. Also, many of the nuns left the Church. Withal, the impairment that emerged among the nuns, their lay faculty associates and their students was similar to what Maslow had already observed at Brandeis University and what Rasa Gustaitis had experienced at Esalen, WBSI and elsewhere.

Immaculate Heart College was the nuns' flagship school. It ceased to exist. Said a mother, pulling her daughter out, "She can lose her faith for free at the state college." What went wrong—call it the emptying of heads—is illustrated in the case of a professor of literature at the college who attended one of the encounter weekends as part of the Educational Innovation Project and afterward redesigned all her courses. She wrote to the WBSI team to say,

> My classroom behavior is radically different now. I have been able to confess anxiety to my classes and consequently feel more comfortable in the classroom than ever before. I invited the girls to call me by my first name, and after a couple of weeks they are doing so. This allows for a lot of free exchange. I am not giving grades and I am not even giving exams. They are writing their own questions—the ones that are meaningful to them. Then they are discussing them.[47]

It's what I mean by the emptying of heads. A student of Immaculate Heart College wrote that

> The whole idea of sensitivity groups sounded beautiful to me, both when reading Dr. Rogers' paper on self-directed change and at the talk today. However, in actual practice, something doesn't seem to be quite right about it. A lot of times I've heard that faculty felt they were being forced in these groups to say things they didn't want to say; I myself feel very uncomfortable about being shut in with people who break down and say things I feel I shouldn't have heard. I think it

> creates a kind of embarrassment, which would seem to be a hindrance in relationships rather than a help. Still, I do feel that I gained a lot of insight into other people's behavior (pp. 55-56).

Another student wrote that "I felt at a loss today in that encounter group: very naked, as though everyone knows too much about me" (p. 59).

A third student wrote, "I think you've got a goodly dangerous thing going and it is very necessary. It's like taking the risk of being ripped up in order to grow. I cannot foresee the end results. I think it is more important that there is life in the 'Now.' I want to thank you" (p. 57).

Were the faculty literally forced—by Carl Rogers!—"to say things they didn't want to say?" It would be surprising. Descriptions of his clinical approach always picked up on the permissiveness. But if we put ourselves in Michele's shoes when she was offered a celebrity hug, we can see how the faculty might have felt pressured. How do you turn down a famously good man? Maybe in the moment, they wanted to do what they guessed he wanted them to do; maybe they were too polite not to; or maybe they thought he was needy—who knows? In any case, they provided what was wanted. Rogers wrote a field report that reveals a process that was probably experienced by the faculty as force, even though, by and large, they went along with it. The report concerned a session for faculty members and parish priests of one of the Immaculate Heart elementary schools:

> In the final meeting, Sunday night, Joann was the first major focus. One of the priests in the group confronted her with some of her lack of feeling. The group all chimed in on this. It was fantastic to watch the slippery and elusive way she could avoid ever expressing herself or any of her feelings, always focusing either on intellectual things or on some other members of the group. As the confrontation became more and more direct, she said she just didn't know what was being asked of her. Finally, however, she admitted to being griped at many of the things which the principal does and particularly at her emotionality. She expressed her positive feeling for the priest, though she felt she had to remain aloof, "because of my position." She resented some of the things that Millie said to her. She interacted in a real and emotional way with my cofacilitator, and finally she wept a bit, became more feelingful, not too quickly defensive in her reactions. Several members of the group, but particularly the principal, practically cheered when she expressed some of her feelings. They had felt that she was so cool and aloof.
>
> One of the members had brought a bottle of bourbon. It was broken out at this time and there were very affectionate—and some critical—reactions to each other, very spontaneously shared, meaningful and warm.[48]

To use the college student's expression, such is the life of "being ripped up in order to grow"; such is *the process* as it is often called, the process of first resisting the expression of feelings, then yielding, and finally of being applauded for having "grown."

I wish to build the balance of my remarks around what the Immaculate Heart

College student called "end results" and said she couldn't foresee. My focus will be the autobiographical case study of life in the Now provided by Natalie, Carl and Helen's daughter. It is found in *Emerging Woman.*[49] In that book, written between 1975 and 1980, she reported on tragic developments which followed graduate studies in humanistic psychology—interestingly enough, with Abraham Maslow (1958-60), whom she describes as her mentor at Brandeis.[50] She enrolled toward the end of Maslow's expansive phase, 1958-60. In his expansiveness he wasn't yet fully prepared to appreciate, for example, why X, who had sex with transient males, wouldn't even enjoy it. Leaders of the college student generation of that era had begun to favor liberation (some of them citing Maslow's writings for support), but within a decade, Maslow was ready to ask this question in his journals: "Who should teach whom? Youngsters teach the elders, or vice versa? It got me in a conflict about my education theory. I've been in *continuous* conflict for a long time over this, over Esalentype, orgiastic, Dionysian-type education."[51] That was late in his career, 1968, just two years before his death. But earlier, during Natalie's term as a student, he was more or less still in his Esalen-orgiastic-Dionysian period. Gradually, the results began to come in, results that included what was happening to the daughter of his colleague. That development helped turn him around.

Here is what happened to Natalie. When she enrolled at Brandeis, she was Natalie Fuchs, the wife of a faculty colleague of Maslow, Professor Lawrence H. Fuchs. He held a Harvard Ph.D. in American Government and taught courses in political science. In *Emerging Woman,* the wife described how things were in the early years of the marriage:

> When I look at our photo album I see pictures of a loving honeymoon in Europe with our tiny English car, hikes and picnics with the kids, birthday celebrations and travels. There is warmth in our faces, radiance and laughter in the children. Together. As many hours of as many days as possible, together. We shared our lives focusing on the world and the children. Bedtime stories, Saturday walks, family art projects on Sundays. Together we build a nest, a house out of which each of us could fly, only to return to its safety and warmth.[52]

That is how it was before she got involved in humanistic psychology.

Natalie's father and three colleagues were team-teaching a graduate course in the summer of 1968 when he broke down and cried in front of the class. One of the students later wrote a note to the course coordinator,

> My immediate response was a feeling of awkwardness in not knowing what to do to help him regain his composure. I expected one of Carl's colleagues to distract the group from what I was sure was the "old man's" momentary loss of control. Nothing of the sort happened. That incident got my rapt attention. I was to return to it many times in the next few weeks.

Why didn't the team come to the senior colleague's rescue? Because they were therapists. Therapists value tears. They had gotten what the course may well have been about.

Only later were this student and others able to learn what had made the professor cry: the story became public in 1980 when *Emerging Woman* appeared. And although Carl Rogers' closest associates knew at the time, more or less, the personal trauma that had reduced him to tears, they were no less shocked than anyone else when Natalie's book told openly what she believed she had achieved. In careful detail did the book describe a woman abandoning her children, abandoning her marriage, pursuing other women's husbands, and rebuking a protesting wife in humanistic language. Here is an example of what the breakup with her husband and children permitted her to seek:

> I spent two very important weeks with a man I was growing to love. He was a competent, independent, adventurous person who knew something about sharing his feelings.... Together we were exploring the out-of-this-world consciousness and transcendence through sensuality and sexuality ...
> Complicating matters... was the fact that this man was married ...
> My old fears of being abandoned if the wife found out returned. He promised that our togetherness would not stop if she discovered the truth ...
> We both wanted a non-monogamous relationship and wondered how jealous we would feel if another sexual partner came into the picture. Our relationship was exciting and meaningful ...
> So how is it that as I was feeling very high on this love, I let another love into my life? It seemed very natural to me. There is something about living and loving intensely that attracts other people.
> Into my life comes a wild, free-spirited, rebellious, tender, sinuous creature. I had simple, pure love to give and an openness to receive ...
> This second lover was also partnered ...
> I respected his wife when she walked into my house with flashing angry eyes. She accused me of being needy and without compassion ... She said, "You invaded our relationship." I said, "I responded to his overtures. I was open to loving and so was he."
> Afterwards I thought ..., "He loves you and is loving me. Why should I not act on my own feelings? I am open to hearing yours, and relating to you, also."
> I also pointed out to her that I was putting myself in a very vulnerable position ...[53]

And what did the man's wife say? She said she hadn't considered the possibility her husband's mistress might be vulnerable, too—"I hadn't thought of that."

If I may interject a judgment, the world was less rich once she did think of it.

Gregory Bateson commented on similar patterns of communication observed when teaching at a humanistic college in California in that era. His students had learned to express themselves in what he called "a horrible touchy-feely jargon." The college was an experimental program of the University of California system. In *Gregory Bateson: The Legacy of a Scientist*,[54] David Lipset reports that in 1973 the famed anthropologist Bateson

> affiliated himself with Kresge College, the most radical of the Santa Cruz experiments in undergraduate education. Founded in 1970, with an ecological focus to "explore educational innovation through a human relations approach," the college program was inspired by the humanistic psychology of Abraham H. Maslow and Carl Rogers ... In content, education tended toward crafts, meditation, utopias, gardening ... women's studies, politics, and the California sun (p. 280).

In June 1974, sociologists Gerald Grant and David Reisman sat in on Kresge's first graduation ceremony. They reported on the experience in their book *The Perpetual Dream: Reform and Experiment in the American College:*

> Members of the class that had created Kresge sat in a wide circle on the wooden floors, some wearing sandals and others in blue jeans, formal gowns, or jackets and ties. Their parents and friends sat ringed about them in chairs ...
> [Professor] Michael Kahn stepped forth in a crimson Harvard gown bearing a large seashell in his hands as though it were a holy vessel ...
> Coming into the circle, Kahn explained that the nautilus was a creature that lived in the depths. Now holding the shell at eye level, he passed slowly before them. Anyone wishing to speak about something "deep down" would hold the shell while they spoke ... [An] Asian student reached for it and went to the center of the circle with four other students. They hugged and kissed each other and then sat down again. A girl in tangerine slacks held the shell, tried to speak, could not, cried, said thank you, cried again, and sat down. One or two others held the shell silently. A boy cried and said he was sad that he would not see his friends for a long time ...
> A heavy girl wearing a patchwork denim skirt spoke somewhat giddily, saying she was "not much into academics" ([followed by] long laughter from students) ... Then she leaned her head back, let loose with an ear splitting scream, shaking her arms and body as though possessed and then sat down. After a pause, students applauded her, followed more hesitantly by parents, unsure as we were whether she was parodying the college or was an expression of it ...
> No honors were distributed; there was no valedictory; no students were singled out for achievements. Pondering this on the way out, we recalled our interview with Gregory Bateson ... In his view, at Santa Cruz in general and Kresge particularly, students tended to be uninterested in striving for honors or in getting ahead. Not many in his large course on the ecology of mind were engaged with ideas ... Papers done in the course were generally deplorable. It was hard to get students to take seriously what was being said or for them to take themselves seriously when writing something. It was an amiable life at Kresge. It was pleasant. It was kindly. Students spoke a "horrible touchy-feely jargon," Bateson said, but in actual behavior they were unusually kind, but that didn't help you learn very much in Latin grammar or any other serious subject.[55]

If, on the subject of psycho-social experimentation in the '60s and '70s, one were to read only Carl Rogers' daughter—if, that is, one didn't know about the denim-skirted girl with the ear-splitting scream, or about other participants in other experiments later described by a dismayed Carl Rogers as a pattern of failure—

one might be inclined to credit the daughter with authenticity.[56] However, much of what she reports was not so much authentic but sought uniformly by youth in that era—sought as well by the would-be youth of the human potentials movement then and since. *Emerging Woman* reports on a mother's repeated acts of personal irresponsibility. Child abandonment, drug use, and husband stealing are the most obvious examples. But she makes clear her belief that misconduct of this kind can signify what she calls "transformation" and what she calls "personal empowerment." Human potentialists believe they are responsible only to the self.

They are probably mistaken. Human potentialism was (and remains) a social trend, a fashion. The self-directed sessions of primal screaming Natalie inflicted on herself in the name of growth are remindful of Kresge and of the standards implicit in many other reports on the human potentials movement filed in the 1960s, when the fashion was new. I mentioned that Richard Reeves covered it for *The New York Times* in 1967. Jane Howard wrote about it for *Life* magazine the next year and followed up with a book, *Please Touch.* The *Life* article was titled "Inhibitions Thrown to the Gentle Winds: A New Movement to Unlock the Potential of What People Could Be—But Aren't." It recorded events at Esalen. Esalen-style education, she wrote, called for groups of participants "to recite dreams, confess secrets, don masks, go naked or gaze with unswerving honesty into each other's eyes for a full 10 minutes." Then,

> before we knew it, we were making up individual, impromptu dances. "Let what wants to happen, happen!" cried [group leader] Josie, the only real dancer among us. "Stay with the feeling! Make whatever noises you want to make, in time with your heartbeat! Flow!" Flow we did, or tried to. We swung, swooped, flailed and soared, shouting our rhythmic nonsense words. Mine sounded like a balloon caption from some Paleolithic comic strip: "Froonga! FROONG-*GA!*" [57]

In its unremitting explicitness about sex, *Emerging Woman,* Natalie's book, goes beyond the Grace Cathedral happening that Reeves wrote about and goes beyond the froonga session at Esalen. But the same territory is covered and the same theory expressed in all three—and I'll bet you know of elementary schools where they're running variations on the same approach today. What makes *Emerging Woman* valuable is its proud confessional nature. Laid out in intimate detail are the author's sexual conquests, her personal approach to masturbation and her personal method of ingesting LSD; from not knowing "where I was" to losing all sense of "where I was going," she tells everything. *Theory* was the cause; not weakness but theory.

Originally, as I have said, the theory was that of her teacher, Maslow. Here is a brief example from the *Journal of Psychology.* Published in 1949, the article manages to predict Natalie's idea that a justification for multiple sexual partners is that "it seems very natural." Maslow's article was titled "Our Maligned Animal Nature." Central was the following claim: "I can report empirically the healthiest persons in our culture...*are most (not least) pagan, most (not least) 'instinctive,' most (not least) accepting of their animal nature.*"[58]

Following this implicit advice, Natalie Rogers dropped her family in order to allow her animal nature free rein. That she felt "irrational terror" in the process (as she writes) helped persuade her and her friends in the movement that she was on the right track. That's how crazy the whole thing was. She put it as follows in *Emerging Woman:* "It is not just being *dependent* that deprives us of our sense of self-direction. It is also being *depended upon* that gives us the excuse not to search and *be* for ourselves."[59]

What had stunned her father, causing him to cry in public, was the implicit claim that authenticity demands unreliability. Carl Rogers may have wanted to be authentic himself, but seldom at the price of unreliability. In a 1966 interview published in *New Directions in Client-Centered Therapy,* he commented on Maslow's place in humanistic psychology. It lay near the origin of his beloved daughter's problems:

> I think Maslow is probably the most visible and the most verbal and most out-in-front of the humanistic psychology trend. He embodies within himself some of the things that both stimulate me and concern me. A lot of his ideas are very exciting, and he's continually formulating new ideas. But I think he has very little concern with tying humanistic psychology to science.[60]

In other words, Maslow had little concern at the time with tying humanistic psychology to truth telling. Actually Maslow was to agree. In a journal entry of September 29, 1969, he referenced the "anti-intellectual, anti-scientific dangers" inherent in his earlier theories of self-actualization:

> Slowly crystallizing into consciousness: to cosmocize and universalize my critique of Esalen into an examination of benefits and booby-trap not only of Esalen and its whole chain, but also of the hippie culture, psychology 3 [his own "Third Force Psychology"], Synanon, NTL [National Training Labs, the sensitivity training network]—in fact the whole Eupsychian network.[61] Much of it is a *misuse* of my thinking. But the misuses are all old philosophies and issues: romanticism, pro and con; anti-intellectual, anti-scientific dangers.[62]

Maslow's thinking—as also Carl Rogers' thinking—turned out to have *invited* misuse. It was not only anti-intellectual and anti-scientific but anti-family. Maslow's published journals reveal how deeply he regretted this. That he was correct to have regretted it is demonstrated by Natalie Rogers' own journals of the 1960s and '70s, which she samples in *Emerging Woman.* We can make a sad excerpt of 1968 our conclusion. She wrote:

> I can't believe this is me ... that I did it! I have actually pulled out of our house and away from my children ... Will I ever have breakfast with them again? As I write this I sob. I feel totally cut off from who and what I am—the mother, wife, housekeeper, party-planner, birthday-party giver, counselor to children and husband ...[63]

What she *really was,* she said, was mother, wife, and so forth. The odd thing is that she gave up what she really was in favor of so-called self-empowerment, in favor of (as her father's book title had it) becoming a person. It makes no sense to trade the living reality of the family for a psychological variable as clinical and abstract as this *personhood.*

She said that in searching for an apartment she had noticed prospective landlords "look critical, like, 'Can you pay your bills?' or 'Are you abandoning your children?'"[64]

Are you abandoning your children? Well, yes. By now there are large numbers of abandoned children, even if many appear still to live at home. Some live in material poverty, of course, but others are found in homes sufficiently affluent to have afforded trips to Esalen, WBSI, and other centers where self-fascination was taught in the '60s. And now it is also being taught in seminaries and neighborhood schools.

NOTES

[1] NY: Doubleday, 1992.

[2] "Report to Father Joseph P. Chinnici, OFM, Provincial Minister, Province of St. Barbara" (P. O. Box 1065, Santa Barbara, Calif. 93102: Independent Board of Inquiry, November 22, 1993), 72 pp. plus appendices.

[3] Joseph P. Chinnici, OFM, "Pastoral Response to Report on Sexual Abuse at St. Anthony's Seminary" (Oakland, Cal.: St. Barbara Province, November 29, 1993), p. 1. The tenor of the statement can be drawn from the conclusion: "We as Christians, as followers of St. Francis, and members of the Roman Catholic Church, are not afraid of the truth; nor are we afraid to repent and reform ..." (p. 2).

[4] Rogers and Coulson were members of the permanent WBSI staff; Maslow was present on occasion as a visiting fellow and consultant on the philosophy of science.

[5] In public, Maslow tended to mute his criticisms of the excesses of humanistic psychology. Toward the end of his life, he began to write copy that he felt was "blunter, more honest, more naked, more true and correct," but it was largely confined to his journals, which were unpublished until 1979. Even at the time of writing them, he suspected his notes on humanistic excesses were "hedged, fudged, appeasing, diplomatic, polite." See Richard J. Lowry, ed., *The Journals of A. H. Maslow.* (Monterey, Calif.: Brooks/Cole, 1979), Maslow's entry of July 19, 1967, p. 776 (hereafter identified as *Journals*).

[6] From an audiotape series, *Carl Rogers at the La Jolla Program* (La Jolla, Calif.: La Jolla Program, 1977).

[7] Carl Rogers, *A Way of Being* (Boston: Houghton Mifflin, 1980), p. 91.

[8] See the autobiographical film "Reflections" (La Jolla, Cal.: Western Behavioral Sciences Institute, 1976).

[9] See her chapter, "Revolving Doors," in Rosemary Curb and Nancy Manahan, eds., *Lesbian Nuns: Breaking Silence* (Tallahassee, Fla.: Naiad Press, 1985), pp. 181-93.

[10] In *Psychology Today,* July 1967, p. 13.

[11] "Report to Father Joseph P. Chinnici ...," p. 46.

[12] See Gordon's chapter in Rogers' *Client-Centered Therapy* (Boston: Houghton Mifflin, 1951), pp. 320-83.

[13] In the 1970s, Gordon developed parallel programs called Parent Effectiveness Training, Teacher Effectiveness Training, Leader Effectiveness Training, and Youth Effectiveness Training. All of them supplied positive answers to his questions about therapy conducted outside the clinic.

[14] "Whether psychotherapy can be made available to the person who has no conception of it, and no conscious desire for it" was the key Rogerian research question of the late 1950s and following. This question is found (p. 57) in Rogers' article "A Study of Psychotherapeutic Change in Schizophrenics and Normals: The Design and Instrumentation," in Richard M. Steinhilber and George T. Ulett, eds., *Psychiatric Research Reports,* Vol. *15* (Washington, DC: American Psychiatric Association, 1962), pp. 51-60.

[15] In the the Wisconsin study, Rogers said it was soon confirmed that "very few individuals [whether schizophrenic or normal] feel any conscious need for help." This proved to be an insurmountable barrier. See Rogers, "Significant Trends in the Client-Centered Orientation," in Lawrence E. Abt and Bernard F. Riess, eds., *Progress in Clinical Psychology,* Vol. *IV* (NY: Grune & Stratton, 1960), pp. 85-100 (the quoted passage is at p. 93). Rogers' book about the project, *The Therapeutic Relationship and Its Impact* (Madison: University of Wisconsin Press, 1967) indicates that, by and large, the normal volunteers who stuck with the scheduled sessions—unlike those who dropped out because they were "rather fearful of interviews" (p. 66)—regressed on the therapeutic variable of "openness to experience." Contrary to expectation, that is, they became *less open* as each interview proceeded. Rogers wrote of this as an evident tendency of the normal subjects "to execute a defensive retreat from therapeutic engagements" (p. 83). Whether retreat was defensive or prudent was unsettled at the time, however, and in moving west, where his focus became groupwork with normals, Rogers sought more data. In 1981, i.e., with 17 years of further experience, he said of therapeutic groupwork that as "the working process goes more deeply, it can bring great personal pain and distress. Nearly always the pain has to do with insights into self or with the fright caused by a change in the self-concept, or distress over changing relationships. So there are experiences of frustration, distrust, anger, envy, and despair in the group. In the individual there are the personal experiences of suffering through change, of being unable to cope with ambiguity, of fear and loneliness and self-depreciation. But both group and individual experience these sufferings as a part of a process in which they are involved and which they somehow trust, even if they could, at the moment, give no rational reason for doing so." In other words, what research subjects feared in the early '60s, they tended later to trust. Perhaps it was the difference between Wisconsin and California; or maybe (as there is reason to believe) America had become more accepting of therapy. In either case, on Rogers' 1981 analysis, we can speculate that normals who embrace the offer of therapy *will be dealt a lot of pain but, against reason, will continue to seek it.* In this light, the retreat from therapy-for-normals seen in Wisconsin in the early '60s was less fearful than prudent. (For the quote about pain, see "Communities," a chapter by Rogers in Alberto Villoldo and Ken Dychtwald, eds., *Millennium: Glimpses into the 21st Century*

(Los Angeles: Tarcher, 1981), pp. 135-146; the quoted passage is at p. 140.)

[16] She lingered for seven years and died in March 1979, in the 55th year of their marriage.

[17] Michael Polanyi, *Personal Knowledge* (Chicago: University of Chicago Press, 1958), p. 380.

[18] *Carl Rogers at the La Jolla Program.*

[19] *Ibid.*

[20] From Rogers' autobiography, in Edwin G. Boring & Gardner Lindzey, eds., *A History of Psychology in Autobiography,* Vol. V (NY: Appleton-Century-Crofts, 1967), p. 367.

[21] Quoted in Howard Kirschenbaum, *On Becoming Carl Rogers* (NY: Delacorte, 1979), p. 234.

[22] Howard Kirschenbaum and Valerie Land Henderson, eds., *The Carl Rogers Reader* (Boston: Houghton Mifflin, 1989), p. 4.

[23] Rogers' associate Harold C. Lyon Jr. was a high official of the U. S. Department of Education in the Carter administration and later co-edited a textbook manuscript with Rogers, *On Becoming a Teacher* (a project subsequently aborted). Having earlier done a best-selling volume in *Studies of the Person,* the education textbook series Rogers helped edit, Lyon became in turn Rogers' sponsor in Washington, where he was in a position to help him with what Lyon saw as his senior colleague's great interest "in getting into the straight world with his ideas. I brought him to D.C. to lead a seminar-encounter group for Congressional staff—about 30 people. He talked about his work and then opened people up. It was funded by the Ford Foundation as part of a series. I was also on the board of Quest, a D.C.-area growth center, and we arranged a lecture at George Washington University at $5.00 a person. The audience numbered more than 5,000. Rogers gave a very vulnerable talk about his life" (Lyon, personal communication, Oct. 8, 1987). One of several published examples of the vulnerable talk is the chapter on "Being in Relationship" in Rogers' *Freedom to Learn: A View of What Education Might Become* (Columbus, Ohio: Charles E. Merrill Pub. Co., 1969), pp. 221-237. It was given first as a lecture on interpersonal relations at a convention of the American Personnel and Guidance Association, the nation's largest school counseling body. Rogers commented that "I was dumbfounded that the auditorium, holding several thousand persons, was crammed full at 8:30 in the morning (!) to hear a talk on interpersonal relationships" (in *Freedom to Learn,* p. 221). There has long been hunger for Rogers' ideas on personal liberation among educators, the same hunger exprienced in Washington during the Carter years. And today there are the so-called Renassiance Weekends attended by the Clinton family.

[24] From *Carl Rogers at the La Jolla Program.*

[25] Kirschenbaum and Henderson, *op cit.,* p. 5: "Eventually he also began to use his own life as a case study....In his last twenty years, he almost always [etc.] ..."

[26] It is necessary to add "I think." No one can be sure of Carl Rogers' motives. He wanted it that way. He was proud of the fact that, as he put it, "Nobody knows where I'm going until I've gone so far they can't stop me, that's one thing." He said, "I'm in a way sort of stealthy." Warren Bennis, who interviewed him for the "Reflections" film, said,

"That is really interesting. I'm serious, this is very important. Stealthy—who would have ever thought Carl Rogers would—" and interrupted himself with a laugh. Believing that psychologists such as himself, who specialize in OD (Organizational Development), are "change agents," Bennis was fascinated by the admission. Bennis said he thought Rogerian stealth offered a "theory of change" (*op. cit.*). A side effect of Carl Rogers' stealth, however, is that no one can know with assurance what he had in mind to achieve, for "no one knows where I'm going until I get there." When Rogers and a colleague described to a magazine writer their consulting aims in starting a new organization (Center for Studies of the Person)—"Helping organizations achieve more of *their own purposes* rather than ours"—the description may not have been entirely accurate. (See Harold Keen, "Encounter Groups on the Move," *San Diego Magazine,* June 1969, pp. 36-41, 108-115.)

[27] In 1957, he was one of three recipients of the first Distinguished Scientific Contribution awards of the American Psychological Association.

[28] Carl Rogers, *Becoming Partners: Marriage and Its Alternatives* (NY: Delacorte, 1972), p. 29.

[29] *Journals,* entry of June 11, 1969, p. 1158.

[30] *Carl Rogers on Personal Power* (NY: Delacorte, 1977), pp. 163-64.

[31] The third if one counts *Becoming Partners.* It spoke of his marriage at a time when "I formed a real attachment to another woman ... I am grateful that our grown-up daughter [Natalie] helped Helen to recognize her true feelings [of anger at her husband more than jealousy, he thought] and to reestablish communication between us ... Helen and I both remain good friends of the woman who was such a threat to her" (p. 25).

[32] Privately published, the book is Natalie Rogers, *Emerging Woman: A Decade of Midlife Transitions* (Santa Rosa, Calif.: Personal Press, 1980; 2nd edition 1989). It is available through the Person-Centered Expressive Therapy Institute (P. O. Box 6518, Santa Rosa 95406), which the author describes as "a living extension of the work of my father, Carl Rogers" (p. 10). The work there extended, however, is less the work for which her father was honored as a scientist (and trusted by Catholics) than work following upon acceptance of the principles of individualism practiced in the circle of the daughter, friends, and lovers. As an honored scientist, Carl Rogers knew only psychotherapy. As a participant in the person-centered circle, he (like the others) was supposed to know everything, i.e., everything of importance. Thomas Gordon exemplifies knowing everything when he writes of the "principle of separateness" that it "rules all human relationships"—*all human relationships.* But the principle was derived not from the study of relationships in all their variety but one very peculiar kind of relationship, namely, the permissive relationship between therapist and client. See Gordon's *Teacher Effectiveness Training* (NY: Wyden, 1974), p. 336.

[33] *Ibid.,* pp. 176-77.

[34] In his autobiography he wrote of a certain "smugness or assurance which has crept in." It appeared in writing the autobiography. It was a good feeling—still, a *feeling.* "Intellectually," he wrote, "I know with equal assurance that I and my thinking may be shown to be completely erroneous; that the directions in which I am moving may prove to be blind alleys ..." (*op. cit.,* pp. 382-83). He knew not only that long-term experience

might reject his theories but that people might be hurt. To an audience of facilitators involved in the project with the Immaculate Heart Sisters, he acknowleged that "we really are engaged in a new cultural enterprise which places value in behaving differently in social groups than individuals have customarily behaved. And do we know for certain that that's a better way to behave? Well, we think so. But I don't believe we can say that we *know* so. So we are involved in a risk. And so are the other people, I think" (from a tape recording, December 17, 1967, in the author's possession).

[35] From the film "Reflections," *op. cit.* His "all of the things that I have developed," included "the nonjudgmental quality that I encourage, the attitude of intellectual and personal exploration." Experience suggests that this combination, when carried directly from the clinic into life, is "TMP," Too Much Psychology. (The term is found in an interview conducted by Linda Nicolosi, "Reflections on the Human Potential Movement," *NARTH Bulletin* [National Association for Research and Therapy of Homosexuality], in press.) Ordinarily Rogers didn't practice TMP. He knew better than to treat people who were not his clients as if they were. A story told by Logan Fox exemplifies. Fox, who helped edit the Japanese edition of Rogers' works, taught at Ibaraki Christian College in Japan and, like many other Christians, wanted to be more like Carl Rogers, at least the Carl Rogers he'd read. A good Rogerian is thought to be thoroughly nonjudgmental and empathetic. But it was hard: "I so often failed to be accepting of people." He felt guilty about this—until Rogers arrived in Japan to conduct workshops at his invitation in 1961. One evening, after a day-long session, Fox and Rogers got together to compare notes, and the conversation turned to the annoying behavior of a certain participant. When judgments were unleashed, Fox teased Rogers about failing to practice acceptance. Rogers replied, "What the hell, he's no client of mine." (Quoted in Kirschenbaum's biography of Rogers, *op. cit.*, pp. 296-97.)

[36] Quoted in Jeannette DeWyze, "School without Rooms," *San Diego's Reader,* June 30, 1983, p. 1.

[37] Rogers, for example, cited a paper by Maslow ("Our Maligned Animal Nature," referenced below) to support his shift from skepticism about people having "a real affection for themselves" to confidence a decade later. See Rogers, *On Becoming a Person* (Boston: Houghton Mifflin, 1961), pp. vii, 73, and 91.

[38] *Journals,* entry of June 21, 1961, p. 107.

[39] From "Some Frontier Problems in Mental Health," unpublished paper in the Maslow collection, History of American Psychology Archives, University of Akron, Maslow's emphasis. Quoted in Edward Hoffman, *The Right to Be Human: A Biography of Abraham Maslow* (Los Angeles: Tarcher, 1988), pp. 261-62.

[40] *Journals,* entry of August 30, 1962, p. 190.

[41] *Ibid.,* entry of October 22, 1968, p. 935.

[42] *Journals,* entry of November 6, 1969, pp. 1193 and 1195.

[43] Rogers, letter of April 16, 1972, to W. R. Coulson.

[44] There were a dozen writings by him on this theme throughout the 1970s. The first was a graduation address, "The Person of Tomorrow" (1969), at Sonoma State College, and the last was a chapter cited above in a collection called *Millennium: Glimpses into the 21st Century.*

[45] Rogers, *Becoming Partners,* pp. 213-14.

[46] These developments are reported in an interview with the author in *The Latin Mass,* January-February 1994; reprinted in *Theologisches* (Germany), June 1994, pp. 275-287.

[47] Quoted in Carl R. Rogers and W. R. Coulson, *Interim Report of the Educational Innovation Project* (La Jolla, Calif.: WBSI, 1968), p. 66.

[48] Quoted in W. R. Coulson, *Groups, Gimmicks, and Instant Gurus* (NY: Harper & Row, 1972), p.115.

[49] Let me add to the earlier reference to *Emerging Woman* that the book remains in print, has been translated into five languages, and can be ordered at $9.95 plus postage by calling the Person-Centered Expressive Therapy Institute, at 800/477-2384.

[50] Natalie Rogers, *The Creative Connection: Expressive Arts as Healing* [Palo Alto, CA: Science and Behavior Books, 1993], p. xv.

[51] *Journals,* entry of May 5, 1968, p. 919, emphasis in original.

[52] *Emerging Woman,* p. 22.

[53] *Ibid.,* pp. 129-131.

[54] Prentice-Hall, 1980, p. 280.

[55] Chicago: University of Chicago Press, 1978, pp. 119-121.

[56] May I speak again of gratitude for Natalie Rogers' openness (even though I question her authenticity)? She reports that publishers turned down *Emerging Woman* in manuscript, telling her, uniformly, that they "didn't want to advocate my lifestyle." At that point, as she writes in *The Creative Connection,* "I used my anger to motivate me to self-publish" (p. 161). It was as if she had inherited her father's desire to make of oneself an example. What she gave the world is a record even more intimate than his own, a record of the personal cost of an overreaching humanistic psychology.

[57] *Life,* July 12, 1968, pp. 48, 56.

[58] *Journal of Psychology,* Volume 28, p. 277, Maslow's emphasis.

[59] *Emerging Woman,* p. 65, her emphasis.

[60] In J. T. Hart and T. M. Tomlinson, eds., *New Directions in Client-Centered Therapy* (Boston: Houghton Mifflin, 1970), p. 524.

[61] "Eupsychia" was his term for the society which would be created by a thousand self-actualizing people left alone to follow their nature.

[62] *Journals,* p. 1186, Maslow's emphasis.

[63] Reprinted in *Emerging Woman,* p. 30.

[64] *Ibid.,* p. 31.

6

Inferiority Complex and Response: Alfred Adler—Discoveries and Errors[1]

Josef Seifert

Adler has made several significant psychological discoveries, among them the discovery of the powerful role played by the striving for power and prestige as well as by feelings and complexes of inferiority both in private and public life. On the other hand, the discoveries made by Adler become fruitful only if one does more justice than he did to the phenomena which he has seen. And this is only possible if one breaks through his one-sided and partially mistaken philosophy of the human person. That applies already to Adler's central notion, the *feeling of inferiority*. What is the meaning of this term? What Adler has seen and expresses with this term is, in my opinion, an original phenomenon, or better: a complex of very different fundamental phenomena, which are summed up under the somewhat misleading umbrella term "feelings of inferiority." These feelings or the experiences which underlie these feelings, include the human person's response to disease, to handicaps, the experiencing of our own contingency, the experience of one's own not being loved, feelings of guilt as well as the despair over the lack of a meaning of life or over one's own moral condition up to the hatred of oneself. Phenomenology tries to understand all things in their own being and nature, to comprehend the diversity of the phenomena and the wealth of different realities. Now I want to elucidate phenomenologically feelings and complexes of inferiority and to disentangle Adler's insights into them from the limiting point of view his general theory of motivation imposed on his own interpretation of them. Freud had introduced as the foundational motive boundless concupiscence, a search for pleasure epitomised in sexual pleasure which he calls *libido*; and Adler put in its place a form of pride, namely the boundless quest for prestige and recognition. Therefore he conceives the feeling of inferiority chiefly as a frustration of this fundamental motive, i.e., as the frustration of the aspiration to prestige and social recognition. For the same reason, Adler also postulates an almost inseparable mutual connection between feelings of inferiority, on the one hand, and striving for power and prestige, on the other hand.

An analysis of the completely different phenomena which Adler groups under the category of "feelings of inferiority" will show that their interpretation in terms of a clash between reality and the striving for power is too one-sided an explanation of these phenomena. Making such a statement, I would like to emphasize at the same time, however, that Adler has seen and described well most or all the phenomena of inferiority discussed below somewhere in his works; but he has failed to see them each in their right place and order and to integrate them in a more comprehensive view of reality.

We pass on then to the analysis of the different meanings and roots of feelings of inferiority, and to point out completely different possible responses to them.

I. Inferiority as the Experience of Contingency and of Not Being God

The first and most fundamental objective phenomenon, which Adler recognizes and calls inferiority, and the corresponding subjective feeling, does not spring from striving for prestige and the aspiration to recognition through other persons. Rather the objective datum of inferiority and the correlàted subjective feeling of inferiority are tied here to the consciousness of our own finitude and limitedness. It is that which Adler has in mind, when he writes in 1933: I have emphasized long ago, that to be human means 'to feel inferior' (1973, p. 67)."

He explains this in the following manner:

> To this ... is joined his knowledge of death. Who can doubt seriously that this human nature so stepmotherly endowed has received as a blessing a strong feeling of inferiority, which demands pressingly security, overcoming obstacles? And this immense and forcefully produced rebellion against a sticking feeling of inferiority as the basis of the development of mankind is roused and repeated in each baby and infant ... (1973, p. 69)

Even if the first starting point of Adler's discovery lies in that of the Organ-inferiority, which he has described in *The Nervous Character*, or even in much more peripheral phenomena like the inferiority the dirty child (*der Schmutzfink*) experiences (1992, p. 70), the deepest level of inferiority he treats is the metaphysical inferiority of the human person as such. He says:

> There is no movement without a goal. This goal can never be reached. The cause of this lies in the primitive understanding of man, that he can be never the lord over the universe, so that this thought, once it emerges, is banished into the sphere of the miraculous or of the omnipotence of God. The inner life is dominated by the feeling of inferiority and this is easily understood in terms of the feeling of imperfection, which lives in man and of the continuous aspiration of human persons and of mankind (1992, p. 70-71).

That inferiority, which lies simply in man's finiteness, manifests itself particularly in three facts: (1) that each person must die and thus his life and his goals possess in death a boundary; (2) that man is not almighty, that he is not the lord of the world; (3) that he is not infinitely good, that he is not God, and that we find in man both limits of perfection and evil. The experience of one's own temporal limits, the passing away of each Now, the constant transition into the inactual past of all happiness and of all experiences, the not-yet-being-of-the-future, the non-necessity of his own existence, and above all mortality, form one's consciousness of the finitude of human life. Each one of us additionally experiences many other limitations, especially moral limits and moral evils.

To discover and to take the appropriate attitude to one's own finitude is not only a fundamental moral issue but also a question of supreme interest for psychology. Time-limits do not permit us to analyze carefully here the truly appropriate response to our own finitude, namely humility. Humility is a fundamental moral attitude opposed to the striving for prestige and it involves the tranquillity and joyfullness of accepting one's own limitations out of love for others and for the absolute good. As such it does not produce psychic conflicts, but contributes to the healing of neuroses and conflicts. Examples of negative and psychically dangerous attitudes, which can end in suicide or crime, are: depression and despair over our own limitations and over our mortality and moral imperfection, the flight into diversion, of which Pascal writes so impressively in his *Thoughts* (*Pensées*), and a repression of one's own death. Let us think about Kierkegaard's analyses of despair in his work *Sickness unto Death.* Here we find a description of a whole spectrum of attitudes which the human person facing his limits can take. Many of these attitudes are wrong from a moral point of view, for example the repression of one's finiteness or the will to admit as little as possible the awareness of one's own finiteness. The worlds of luxury and technology serve largely the creation of an illusion of a perfect world controlled completely by the human person, the illusion of a world in which man is reminded as little as possible of his own limits. Other attitudes, such as the hatred of God, the luciferic pride and the wish to dethrone God and all values, are not only evil, but are also sources of the worst psychic disturbances, as Dostoevsky has masterfully analyzed in the character of Stavrogin and in his suicide in *The Possessed.* Let us consider separately different possible responses to the three aspects of the metaphysical limitation of the human person distinguished above.

1. Think first of the proper response of the human person to that dimension of his limitation which lies in the own death and in the transitoriness of his life. Can I consider peacefully my own mortality and finitude without hope for an immortal life? Would and should I not fall into despair over my metaphysical inferiority of mortality if I take the destruction of all values in death as the last word? Certainly there is also a stoic composure in the acceptance of the assumed fact of my annihilation in death. But although this attitude might be called healthy in an immanent

psychological sense, it is radically unhealthy in a deeper personalistic sense. It appears to me that a rational positive attitude towards my own death cannot be seen in a mere willing acceptance of, and resignation to, my own mortality, but only in the discovery of the truth that the person is by his essential nature and vocation immortal and above all, that the beloved Thou is immortal. Here psychology and metaphysics (but also religion) are connected in a most intimate way. We do not have sufficient time at our disposal to discuss the anthropological ordination of the human person to immortality. I might just quote a few sentences pronounced by Stefan Trofimowich in Dostoevsky's *The Possessed* which summarize the essential core of the personalistic arguments for immortality:

> I must be already immortal because God will do no injustice; and therefore he will not existinguish the fire of love once it has erupted in my heart. What is more precious than love? Love stands higher than existence, love is the crown of existence, and how is it then possible that existence is not subjected to love? ... If God exists, I am immortal!"[2]

2. Also the feeling of our own weakness is without question an aspect of our finitude: to learn that we are not Lord of the universe. If one postulates a will to power, the will to be Lord of the world, *as the fundamental motive of man*, the question emerges as to how the human person can respond in a positive way to the inferiority and finiteness tied up with his being human. Adler's answer to this fundamental problem, an answer which mainly rests on the concepts of compensation, ambition and striving for power, is unsatisfactory. This is not to deny that Adler's concept of a feeling of community indicates a deeper level of his response to our question.[3] In any case, one must put the question, whether Adler is right in his explanation, according to which—in the last analysis—awareness of the human inferiority in virtue of his limitation as such cannot elicit any response except a constant and eternally frustrated fight against this human inferiority as a human person. Is it a correct vision of man to see him involved in a constant effort for compensation and overcompensation of his own inferiority in the sense of his powerlessness? Adler's general theory of motivation appears to exclude an alternative attitude: namely a childlike acceptance of our limits, springing from humilty. If man is marked by a restless quest for power and for becoming the master of the universe, how can we admit a happy person who is powerless? Through all possible forms of striving for prestige, Adler thinks, man seeks to overcome his inevitable inferiority as a human person. And this uphill battle against his metaphysical inferiority becomes for man that "sting that spurs him on" to higher performances.

If the human person were really dominated only by his will to power and prestige, then the inferiority of his power as a human person would have to become to him altogether hateful and an object of his rejection. And if it were man's only aspiration to overcome this factual limit of power, linked to his nature as a human being, through all possible forms of compensation and overcompensation, then we would have to say that the psychology of Adler which asserts this would be a psychology of despair, because it would put in front of the human person—as his necessary goal in life—an ultimately and eternally inaccessible and unapproachable end. This end would be—according to Adler's own statements—at the same time inaccessible for man and his supreme goal.

If Adler were completely consistent, he would have to assume indeed that the human aspiration to attain supreme metaphysical power and to become the Lord of the universe, if it does not lead altogether to an open despair, must unconsciously include the will to repress the fact of one's own finiteness and the constant effort to create illusions for oneself, through which one overcomes the feeling of one's own inferiority as human person and somehow attains an illusory feeling of one's own omnipotence and power over the world. Indeed, such a conclusion might not be altogether foreign to the fictionalism and philosophy of will to power which Adler inherited from Nietzsche and which reminds us of some of Sartre's ideas. In this sense one could say that, in the last analysis, man would be characterized with Nietzsche as "will to power and nothing besides," a dreadful position which could lead at any time to the justification of a new Hitler. A strictly logical consequence of a theory of motivation which would only recognize the will to power would also also be anti-theistic and lead to the powerless attempt to abolish any reality superior to oneself, and therefore also to obliterate the real Lord of the universe and the divine Being. Dostoevski's parable of the human race which throws God out of heaven (in the novel *The Demons*) or even the description of Satan's will in the *Apocalypse* could give here an outstanding clue for understanding such an attitude.

Considered in this light, one could launch a devastating ethical and psychological objection against the last consequences of Adler's *Individualanalyse*, although these are consequences never drawn by Adler himself.

Considered from an ethical point of view, Adler's position leads to a despairing and demonic will to be like God. Psychologically, it leads either to the "total flight from reality," a flight which Freud regards as the source of, or an essential summary of the essence of, neurosis; or else to a despair which could end in suicide.

3. This leads us to the third aspect of human limitedness, the finiteness of all human values and the reality of evil in us, a theme to which we will come back in another context. The deepest dimension of our finiteness reveals itself only when we consider the limits of the values and goods and the reality of evils in us. This is our most sensitive inferiority with respect to God, who is of infinite goodness. And how indeed should we be able to accept God's infinite superiority over us if our last motive can be nothing other than the will to our own power and greatness? How can we react to God with anything except envy or hatred, if we recognize that God is infinitely good and we are imperfect and often evil? Are then not an incurable psychosis and despair, in fact even the hatred of God, pre-programmed?

Of course it would be also possible, although, only if one gives up the Adlerian theory of motivation, that the recognition of our own finiteness would lead to a glad affirmation of the truth of our own finitude and to its acceptance and experience not as a curse, but as a gift gratefully to be accepted: the immense gift that I, although I do not exist by any necessity, nevertheless do exist. That one can discover a positive meaning in his own finiteness is only possible, however, if a striving for prestige and power is not our last and only motive; for such a motive would necessarily lead to the hate and envy of the infinite good. Only if love, and what von Hildebrand calls "value responses" are the ultimate motives for our inner responses and external actions, is it possible to love God rather than to hate or to use Him. Love could then also be present in the relationship to the absolute good. And it would play the most central role for the overcoming of egocentric feelings of unhappiness due to one's own inferiority in contrast with God.

Only if love and a value-responding affirmation of God *propter se ipsum* exist, is it possible that one can joyfully affirm the superiority of God and love Him for His own sake. In this view which differs wholly from Adler's interpretation, the experience of metaphysical inferiority would not give rise to attempts of overcompensation and rebellion, but to a full acceptance of the metaphysical truth about the human person and it would be integrated in a positive meaning. A philosophy and psychology of "selfism," to quote Paul Vitz, which sets up an image of man as destined for self-realization and self-satisfaction only, can never provide a clue for understanding this.

In a certain sense, one would be led therewith also to a diagnosis of neuroses similar to the one offered by Igor Caruso in his early writings, where he claims that the origin of neuroses lies in some absolutization of finite goods. If we are right, we find here also a clue to overcoming those moral and psychological disorders which stem from a flight and rebellion against our contingency and mortality; and we could arrive at a happy acceptance of divine superiority and of our own limitedness. In this way, one returns also to the doctrines of great philosophers and spiritual masters like Francis de Sales.

At the same time, one could concede to Adler, that in this inferiority of the human person qua finite person the origin of the most elementary and most dreadful feeling of inferiority is found, and is thus potentially the fount of the most radical rebellion. For this inferiority is an entirely insuperable condition, a condition which nobody can alter. At this point, we can also refer to the great insights of Max Scheler regarding *ressentiment.* He holds that the envy of the very being of a superior person, which I can never possess, is the most terrible envy and the most profound root of *ressentiment.*[4] If envy or an unbridled striving for prestige and for being free from every inferiority, if "being like God" were really the only human fundamental motive, then lucifer would be the only logical consequence of the motivational structure of the finite person. One could then never accept one's own finiteness or the superiority of God. For Goethe is right: "In contact with a greater one than we are there is only one remedy against envy: to love him." Therefore I am convinced that value response, the response to the truth, the self-donation and abandonment of self-seeking in love, and the *affirmatio personae propter se ipsam* (the affirmation of the person for her own sake) are those phenomena which provide the sole clue to a positive response to what Adler regards as the primary inferiority of man qua man. Dietrich von Hildebrand, Polish personalism in ethics, and other schools offer the ideas which allow a critical deepening of Adler's insights and an overcoming of his errors. Nevertheless, we must recognize the great discoveries of Adler regarding the primary metaphysical inferiority and limitedness of the human person as a fundamental problem of psychology. It was a pioneering achievement of Adler to recognize that the experience of our own finiteness and the inferiority resulting from it is a fundamental problem of psychology. Adler, in deviation from his pure principles, has also rightly seen that there are both completely egocentric and positive forms of response to this inferiority. Yet he does not develop a theoretical understanding of human motivation that can explain these differences or account for the factors in which this contrast of attitudes consists. While as psychologist he praises certain positive and psychologically liberating, as well as ethically and religiously valuable, responses to our metaphysical finiteness, he can hardly explain how such positive responses to the ultimate and first form of inferiority mentioned by him, i.e., our own finitude and inferiority, are possible. It takes a philosophy and psychology which renders intelligible the human capacity of love, of the transcendence of an act which affirms the other person for her own sake, it takes a religion which is theocentric to explain how the experience of the metaphysical *Urminderwertigkeit* (primordial inferiority), which one experiences as a finite and mortal person, and how the experience of the *Urunterlegenheit* (primordial weakness) and *Urendlichkeit* (original ultimate finitude) can be accepted in the context of a positive meaning. Only such a philosophy gives to these inferiorities a response which is both psychologically and morally positive and liberating, in the sense of the words of Stefan Trofimowitsch from *The Possessed* of Dostoevsky:

> Already the one continual thought, that something immeasurably more Just and Happier than I exists, fills me with unmeasurable emotion and unmeasurable thanks—, oh, who ever I have been, whatever I have done! ... The whole law of human existence rests only therein, that the human person bows always before something infinitely exalted. If one takes away from man that infinitely sublime, he ceases to live and dies of despair ... Even the most stupid person needs the sublime (p. 487). [5]

Nonetheless, one must concede that Adler expresses at times that transcendence of man which can be achieved only in a purely value-responding attitude: He was himself a Lutheran, a religious person. Adler has unquestionably in his concrete judgment on characters a critical relationship to the logical extreme of an unlimited will to power and prestige and of the egoism lying therein. Here is an especially beautiful example, where Adler speaks in a critical way of the boundlessness of ambition:

In the advancement of ambition there is no extreme boundary. It is interesting to observe, how both in the fairy tale, as in reality, just as in the overheated inner life of the vain person the increase of the aspiration to power can lead persons to a kind ideal of self-divinity. Often one does not need to investigate long to find that such a person behaves—as in the most serious cases of this kind—either directly so, as if he were a God or at God's place, or that he has such wishes and goals that, upon their fulfillment, he would be straightaway a God. This phenomenon, this striving to be like God, is the extreme point of a tendency in such a person which is noticeable in so many other ways, to cross the boundaries of his personality. Precisely in our days this becomes apparent unusually often. All efforts and interests which cluster around spiritualism and telepathy, point to persons who can not wait to go beyond their own given limits, who ascribe to themselves powers which human beings do not possess, who want sometimes even to make time stop in seeking to communicate across the limits of time and space with spirits of the deceased. If we search more deeply, we find that a majority of human beings have the tendency to secure for themselves at least a little place in the vicinity of God (1966, p. 189).[6]

Then Adler goes on speaking of the Bible and says:

Apart from psychological reasons, here also the circumstance plays a large role that a large part of humankind draws almost its first knowledge regarding the nature of human persons from those words of the Bible which explain that man is created in the "likeness of God," which leave behind significant, often momentous impressions in the child's soul. The Bible is of course a wonderful work, which one will always read with admiration, as soon as one has matured in understanding. If one wants to begin, however, with reading the Bible also to children, one must give them at least some commentary, so that they learn to humble themselves ... (1966, p. 189/190)

Here Adler opposes, even if not quite satisfactorily, an idea of the likeness of God which is joined with humility, modesty and acceptance of one's own finiteness, to a radically different type of will to be like God, which he characterizes masterfully and even magnificently in the quoted text and which he sees as a negative phenomenon resulting from an unlimited will to power. These passages thus make intelligible the fact that Adler was a Lutheran, a religious man, and reveal some consistency between his theology and his personal faith.

II. " Inferiority" in the Sense of Disease and Suffering

Let us discuss a further interpretation and a completely different kind of feeling of inferiority mentioned by Adler.[7] Here we are no longer dealing with the metaphysical finitude and the contingency of the human person as such, but rather with an inferiority in the sense of a reduced existence and "quality of life" due to emotional suffering or physical pains, handicaps or organ-inferiority, as Adler calls them. One can think here of all the crosses and sufferings which a person carries, not the least of them being aesthetic deficiencies, malformations or physical ugliness, etc. These evils are of course ultimately connected with the first form of inferiority, i.e., finiteness and they depend on it; for only a finite nature can be susceptible to these evils. Yet they are not a necessary consequence of the inferiority of contingency as such. Not even old age which results from the mere progression of the organism in time and inevitably gives rise to some form of decay and ugliness (even if old persons can possess extraordinary beauty of spiritual expression painted so lovingly in Rembrandt's magnificent paintings of his mother) is a necessary consequence of contingency. For while the Romans said: "Old age itself is a disease," old age as such is not tied to decay and decay does not result necessarily from the finitude of the human person, but rather the two are linked in a merely factual connection in a condition outside of paradise. At least a paradisiacal situation of the human person is thinkable where the progression of age would not produce the sufferings of old age, as we conceive of this in paradise or in heaven.

Finiteness, on the contrary, would exist also in paradise and will not cease even in heaven. Also this second kind of inferiority and suffering cannot be explained completely along the terms of Adler, namely from the tension between the striving for power and prestige on the one hand and their frustration on the other hand. For it is not the comparison with other human beings which constitutes or produces these evils.

If somebody has tormenting physical pains, these are in no way results of some frustration in striving for prestige, nor do they begin to exist through a comparison with other persons and their fate: They are simply given, and they are clearly evils. The same applies to psychic suffering or to grief. Naturally a tension between sufferings or physical deformities and the will to power or prestige can exist, but this tension is not of primary significance and nor is it constitutive for these evils. Striving for prestige can certainly be frustrated also through them. However, a deaf person unable to hear music, a state that afflicted Beethoven already when he composed the third of his nine symphonies, does not suffer because his striving for prestige is frustrated, but because, e.g., hearing music meant so much to him—and such sufferings have driven persons to the edge of suicide, as Beethoven describes so movingly in his *Heiligenstädter will.* The suffering here results from the tension between the consciousness that there is something of great beauty, which one once was able to hear, and now the consciousness that one does not and never will hear them again. And to how uncountably many further sufferings and inferiorities may the blind or the deaf person be subjected by virtue of his primary "Organ-inferiority!"

At this point a completely new critical question arises: Is really the *Urgefühl* (fundamental feeling) here that one is inferior because of these sufferings? Is Adler's explanation correct that through these inferiorities the *Selbstwertgefühl* (the feeling of one's own intrinsic value) is put into question? This question leads us again to the further question of the right and wrong attitudes towards this second kind of inferiority.

Is it really the fundamental tendency of the human person to achieve power and prestige through compensations? A power, which is prevented through these evils? Is it true that there is an irresistible urge to achieve highest results in the same area affected by the affliction or to compensate and overcompensate in another area?

We do not wish to deny such an attitude of defiance (*Trotzhaltung*) as we find it in Demosthenes who became the greatest living orator having stuttered and been afflicted by a weakness of voice as a child. But we ask: is there not another sense of suffering and grief? And do we not often understand that the inferiority in question does not decrease the value of our person? And that both this idea and the other one, that the organic inferiority is a cause of suffering because it frustrates our will to power, are shallow or at least very partial explanations of the phenomena? For in the first place, sufferings are much more complex evils than merely being frustrations of power or prestige.

Secondly, organ inferiorities cannot be correctly understood as suffering, at least those sufferings which cannot be overcome, if one only compensates in other ways and does not confront and accept them in a more direct and meaningful manner. Thus an elementary question poses itself here for anthropology and also for psychology: what are the meanings of life and of suffering which transcend the level of action and achievement and which cannot be explained in terms of techniques of compensation and overcompensation?

Let us think about the explanation of the meaning of suffering given by Karol Wojtyla both as pope and as philosopher. In my opinion *Salvifici Doloris* is an exceedingly excellent work on the salutary effects and values linked to suffering. There the author considers the deepest meaning of suffering as rendering possible a higher measure of love, both the humble love of him who suffers and sacrifices for others, accepts the love of the service they render him, offers his suffering up for others, as well as the love of him who renders services of love to the sufferer. The love realized in the care for the sick, in comforting them or in taking care of them, may exceed in value the evil of suffering itself, a truth expressed in the most powerful way by Dostoyevski in the description of the suffering, sickness and love between the brother of Staretz Zosima, Markel, and those who took care of him. Here an explanation of the full meaning of suffering is given that far surpasses that offered by Adler. The described meanings of suffering could obviously never be explained in terms of compensation and overcompensation. Also from a psychological point of view, the unfolding of the inner meaning in accepting the love realizable in suffering is much more helpful. For there are many cases of retarded human beings and of persons who lack certain talents who could only experience frustration if they attempted some compensation or overcompensation through achievements which would not be successful. If this were the only meaning of suffering they would recognize they might become victims of what Scheler calls *Krüppelressentiments*, resentments of handicapped persons against those who are free of similar handicaps.

Of course, Adler may be right that one should help handicapped persons to find creative possibilities of working or of producing something important they can do in spite of their handicaps. He may also be right that often the neurosis is the result of unsuccessful efforts at compensation and that the person who cannot draw attention to himself by objective achievements now gains this attention by neurotic symptoms. But if a patient is unable to face and accept his sufferings and to recognize a meaning more intimately connected with them, then his overcompensation or compensation takes on a neurotic character itself. It becomes a *Ablehnungsmanöver*, an atttempt to repress reality in which one fails to face fully the defect which emerges through one's own suffering. One cannot carry it and seeks to forget it by fleeing to diversions and to the creation of other satisfactions.

A third and more significant critique of Adler's ideas regarding compensation of the patient must be developed in the light of a distinction between ontological and qualitative values, as Hildebrand develops it in his *Ethics.*[8] We have to contest energetically the view that the inferiorities of organs etc. lead to an inferiority in that they could destroy or even reduce the *Selbstwert*, the intrinsic value and dignity of the human person.

This value of the human person—and this metaphysical insight has profound and liberating psychological effects—is much deeper than being a fruit of aesthetic and vital values such as health or even intellectual values such as brilliance of mind. Their absence or contrary can have completely different consequences, depending on the type of value at stake, but they cannot alter the ontological dignity of the person. Any idea of such ontological inferiority or reduction of the inherent dignity of the person through a low quality of life is superficial. If Adler's feelings of inferiority are interpreted philosophically along these lines, his ideas are extremely narrow, limited, and in part completely wrong.

Precisely regarding this point, a very important and interesting book is Max Scheler's, *Ressentment in the Construction of Morals*, because Scheler describes there the possible attitude of resentiment (*Ressentimenthaltung*) which the sufferer, the cripple, etc. can have. Resentment is a kind of wrong attitude towards suffering or other inferiorities and it is often related to essentially evil atttitudes such as envy and hate. Scheler also demonstrates some internal connection between the compensations and overcompensations described by Adler and *ressentiments.*[9]

III. Intellectual Inferiority: Lack of Talents and Stupidity

If Adler, regarding the arising of feelings of inferiority and of neuroses, attributes great weight especially to the *Organ-inferiority*, to handicaps, and perhaps also to sexual unattractiveness or frigidity, he seems to belittle the significant role a lack of gifts plays in the origin of feelings of "inferiority." These deficiencies appear to be an immense source of feelings of inferiority. They play possibly an even larger role here than physical weaknesses and aesthetic demerits: The lack of intellectual talent of the weak pupil, his bad memory, his inability to understand or to do well at school—all these are unquestionably causes of uncounted feelings of inferiority. It also makes sense philosophically, that precisely the intellectual values, which tower over purely vital ones, are more important than vital values to make a person feel "superior."

Much depends here also on the kind of environment in which someone lives. In a family that runs a circus, children may be more prone to feel inferior if they fall awkwardly off the rope, than if they are intellectually untalented. Feelings of inferiority may arise in a musical family, if the children are musical untalented, in an intellectually oriented family, if they are not gifted for intellectual achievements.

What is important here, is not only to find the right response to our own finitude and limits but also to our own obtuseness and lack of talent. In order to be able to respond to such deficiencies, we must first gain the knowledge that the ultimate value of the person does not depend on his intellectual brilliance. Hardly any work of literature demonstrates this more movingly than the Russian Folk Tale about the three old men contained in Leo Tolstoi's work, *Folk Tales*. The right attitude also calls for an acceptance of our lack of talent and the recognition that stupidity is never a mere fruit of lack of talent;[10] for the humble man who accepts his lack of great intelligence possesses a certain greatness and wisdom which even the proud genius does not possess. But the right attitude requires a difficult task for our freedom and formation of our affections through cooperative and indirect freedom. For we have to break through to an ungrudging acceptance and even love of persons who have more talents than we. The general theory of motivation presented by Adler's doctrines on the will to power and prestige as supreme goal, however, as well as his implicit philosophical anthropology does not leave room to recognize these things, although in his psychological analyses he often points in the right direction.

IV. Inferiority Through Guilt

A fourth and again a very different phenomenon, which Adler wants to subsume under the idea of inferiority, is that of moral guilt. Here we find a radically different and true meaning of actual inferiority, because it is in fact the guilt which causes an ugliness of the person, which is possible only through the abuse of freedom which alone can give rise to actual guilt. This moral ugliness or even atrocity Plato has called the *aischron*, that is, the "shamefully ugly" in the soul. We encounter here an ugliness for which we are responsible, which has sprung from our own deeds, our own freedom. In virtue of the mentioned elements of guilt, the inferiority of immorality is completely unlike any other kind of "inferiority."

Although Adler (who himself was a rather overmoralizing man) had a rather reduced theoretical understanding of the reality of moral conscience and guilt, he reached important cognitions regarding the relation between moral guilt and the ultimate value of the human person: If there is real guilt, then it affects the human person as such and calls forth a real "inferiority," and even a disvalue and unworthiness, a destruction of the moral dignity of the human person. Indeed, without being able to destroy the ontological dignity of the person, guilt nevertheless involves a moral unworthiness, which is an objective reality. This unworthiness and ugliness is of a completely different nature than the one that results from suffering or organic lesions.

To understand this lack of dignity and antithesis to the moral dignity to which the person is called, one would have to introduce a metaphysics of the human person in whose light one could recognize that the human person does not own his value and his dignity exclusively as if it were a firm possession never to be lost. Rather, the deepest dimension of the dignity of the human person is impossible without freedom and without a moral conquest—as Gabriel Marcel says: «Être une personne n'est pas une possession mais une conquête» (to be a person is not a possession, but a conquest). If, however, the deepest source of man's dignity as person lies in the correct use of his freedom and is entrusted to his freedom, then moral goodness, as the most central value of the human person, attains supreme significance. Then moral goodness has to be called with Platon's *Politeia*—the "proper good of the soul." And if this is truly the case, then guilt and malice give rise to a real unworthiness.

Here the question poses itself again: How does the human person respond properly to this real unworthiness he incurs through guilt? And precisely with respect to this question the most significant defects in Adler's theory become apparent. According to the general principles of Adler's theory, the guilty person would have to aspire to some overcompensations of the experienced unworthiness in consequence of his guilt; he would have to create substitutes for the moral satisfaction and the prestige linked to moral goodness denied to him. But through such a response, man would only forget his own guilt and the suffering inflicted on him by the pangs of conscience. But is that the right response? Certainly not. By its very essence, moral evil demands the response of inner repentence, of a regret and inner disovowal, of a distancing oneself from the evil deed, and of a resolution not to commit immoral acts, etc. This response is worlds apart from a mere compensation.

Another response to guilt would be the despair in which man regards himself as defiled and irreparably evil by virtue of the guilt. Think about Othello's words at the conclusion of Shakespeare's tragedy *Othello*. After he has murdered Desdemona, he utters grand and dreadful words in which he says that he is damned for eternity, that he will be chased away from the sight of Desdemona whom he has unjustly murdered by furious angels; and that he will be whipped away from the vision of God and from Desdemona's beauty. The horror of this despair of feeling lost forever is inseparable from real intuitions into the gravity of moral evils and into the objective ugliness and unworthiness they cause as well into justice of punishments due to this evil. Similar sentences of despair are spoken by Electra and Orest—after their matricide at the end of the tragedy *Electra* of Euripides. But is this the adequate response to guilt?

Is not a completely different repentence, permeated by the hope of being forgiven, possible? Can guilt never be deleted, or can one find meaning and even the moral dimension of the person's dignity again? Can it even be restored again fully by divine pardon and redemption? Psychology and even philosophy cannot help sufficiently in the answer to these questions because it is evident that mercy and pardoning as free acts of God, as well as redemption and deliverance from sin and guilt, involve divine freedom. Thus the innermost reason for psychic disturbances through the consciousness of moral guilt, and even more their cure, transends psychology, and even philosophy. If philosophy and psychology do not themselves degenerate into religion, forgetting the limits of their respective discipline, they will halt in front of the mysteries of faith. The Christian mystery of the deliverance from sin, of redemption, of free divine pardon, of the forgiveness of sin, etc., gives answer to these questions. So it is by no means devious or irrational, to understand one's task as psychiatrist in the context of a religious dimension of psychic conflicts which surpasses the authority of the psychologist and psychiatrist. It is an eminent act of reason and of a good philosophy of religion to understand why there are answers to the problem of the inferiority due to guilt which are inaccessible to pure reason alone. And it is reasonable to set up a psychotherapy on religious or Christian foundations which points out to believing and non-believing patients that there are higher levels of the question of guilt for which they cannot expect answers and cures from psychotherapy.

This could be argued for even in the light of the psychology of Adler. For if there is no human means against the deepest inferiority, the one incurred by guilt, then how should the psychologist as psychologist provide help? Paul Vitz, in his important book *Psychology as Religion* and still more in his fascinating study, *Sigmund Freud's Christian Unconscious* (1988, esp. pp. 101 ff., 172 ff., 207 ff.), has shown how, due to the insolvability of such problems in terms of "pure psychology," the non- or anti-religious psychology almost necessarily betrays its character of being pure psychology and of staying within its limits and boundaries, and turns instead into a *Religionsersatz*, defending a "secular humanism ... on the foundation of a denial of God and of an idolatry of Self." (1994, p. xii) [11] In the light of a Christian view of forgiveness and repentance, however, answers to the inferiority incurred through guilt are possible, which Adler was altogether unable to see, at least as long as he viewed the world from the point of view of his mistaken general theory of motivation in terms of the will to power and prestige, and in view of the bare response of overcompensation or compensation to inferiorities.

Already repentance is completely different from overcompensation. If one reads Scheler's essay on "Repentance and Rebirth" or Hildebrand's analyses of repentance, one understands that repentance is an entirely different response to guilt and to the unworthiness and "inferiority" incurred through guilt than the responses Adler has conceived: repentance involves a taking back and a disavowal of moral evil, a reversal, a special type of grieving and a new beginning, as well as peace despite guilt (1989). Repentance is also radically different from a flight from guilt, from a bare repression or forgetting of guilt, as well as from a resistance to guilt because one cannot bear the thought to be guilty. Think about Max Scheler's conversations with Hildebrand, which the latter outlines in his essays on Scheler. In them, Scheler said that he could not bear the thought of always appearing ugly, guilty and sullied before himself.

To flee into diversions, sports, amusements, as Pascal describes them powerfully in his *Pensées*—or to rebel against the reality and significance of guilt, not to recognize that one is guilty—all these are again distinct and wrong responses to the inferiority caused by guilt. Among them the most seriously wrong response is the accusation leveled against God for what is the effect of one's own responsibility; Adam says: "The woman, whom you have given me, has seduced me," God's creation of the "seductress" makes God himself guilty for Adam's sin of giving in to temptation.

Again another response to guilt is given by Nietzsche in his *Zarathustra*, where he refuses to accept the root of guilt itself, namely an objective moral good. Ethical relativism is also an answer to guilt. If one considers, with Freud, the nature of neuroses and of insanity as the flight from reality or as an evasiveness in front of reality, then one could identify plenty of forms of evasiveness in front of the reality of inferiority incurred by guilt. [12]

V. The "Inferiority Complex" as a Wrong and Irrational Feeling of Inferiority

Here a fifth and completely new phenomenon emerges, which one can consider as a feeling of inferiority which is a real but an irrational or at least an unjustified feeling of inferiority. We must make here a distinction clearly that is also found in Adler, but insufficiently carried through by him; namely, the distinction between feelings of inferiority and a complex of inferiority. The latter term again can mean three completely different things, each of which we can contrast with feelings of inferiority which are not complexes:

1. If we speak of a complex of inferiority, then we mean often a wrong feeling of inferiority, the illusion of our own inferiority in one of the previously distinguished meanings of this term. The first metaphysical inferiority can hardly be the object of a complex in this sense, because it exists always completely actually and can never be the object of bare illusions. The second kind of inferiority, however, above all with regard to aesthetic or intellectual defects, can very well be merely imagined: for example, a beautiful girl believes herself to be very ugly, or

a brilliantly intellectual woman or man believes herself or himself to be stupid. This is a complex, in contrast to the case where someone feels ugly because he is ugly.

2. We can also mean with "inferiority complex" that, due to disvalues or real limits of values, the illusory and wrong feeling of a person emerges that he is altogether worthless as person, that he is inferior as a whole. Here the deep philosophical question is to be treated whether a destruction of the value of the human person or a decrease of the inherent value and dignity of the human person himself is possible on the basis of his or her insufficiencies. Is it legitimate that afflictions or sufferings, that Organ-inferiority or frigidity, that aesthetic defects of one's own appearance, or that the metaphysical finiteness of the human person as such gives rise to a feeling of inferiority? In other words: the feeling that one's own life is meaningless, the feeling that one is robbed of all value, could be called a complex in the measure in which it rests on an error about the real implications of these partial inferiorities. It is a complex in this second sense if the human person believes that he or she is worthless because of deficiencies which do not touch the ontological value of the person. A complex of inferiority should indeed be overcome. Unlike the legitimate feeling of inferiority which reflects a reality and only should become an incentive to give the right response to the respective objective evils, a *complex* of inferiority in both senses is to be overcome simply through the truth. How one comes to the knowledge that the inferiority which one imagines does not exist really, is partially a philosophical problem, partly an empirical one of *Individualanalyse*, which recognizes no general prescriptions. Unquestionably, in order to overcome complexes of inferiority in the second sense, love and being loved possess here a primary meaning—as well as the mentioned religious dimensions, to which the physician of Lady Macbeth refers in Shakespeare's *Macbeth*.

3. Another meaning of the inferiority complex refers to the consequences and effects of real or imagined inferiorities. Thus Adler says:

> The inferiority [symptom] complex describes the attitude of an individual who by this complex expresses that he is not in the position to solve an existing problem. It must not be confused with the inferiority feeling. The inferiority [symptom] complex is the presentation of the person to himself and others that he is not strong enough to solve a given problem in a socially useful way ...The total mode with all its thoughts, feelings, and actions is continued into failure.

Adler adds that inferiority complexes (mistaken views of one's deficiencies or paralysing effects of real or imagined inferiorities) are usually connected with superiority complexes.

> ... We should not be astonished if in the cases where we see an inferiority [feeling] complex we find a Superiority complex more or less hidden. On the other hand, if we inquire into a superiority complex and study its continuity, we can always find a more or less hidden inferiority [feeling] complex (1956, p. 259).

The complex of inferiority is conceived here as a pathological response to inferiority feelings, as a state of paralysis and a paralyzing state which existinguishes activity, but which also consists in an attitude which leads to depression. Whether this feeling of inferiority rests on the truth, for example on genuine guilt which leads to this condition of depression, or whether there are imaginary sins at its root, plays no decisive role here. For the inferiority complex is in both cases an evil.

We have to distinguish therefore three completely different meanings of complex of inferiority or of complex of guilt. The first is the feeling of an ugliness or guilt, without real ugliness or guilt existing. Therefore we are dealing here with a feeling of guilt or of another partial inferiority based on illusions. Another meaning of "inferiority complex" is a wrong feeling of being a zombie or of feeling totally inferior or worthless as a person. Such a feeling can cause suicide and is never justified because the metaphysical dignity of the person continues to endow each person with an inalienable fundamental value. Thirdly, there is a feeling which leads to the generally paralysing condition which Adler has primarily in mind when he speaks of an "inferiority complex."

VI. Guilt Complexes, Feelings of Guilt, and Related Feelings of Inferiority.

A closely related field of problems, likewise touched upon by Adler's individual psychology, is the relationship between guilt complex and genuine feelings of guilt. We could interpret guilt complexes, as inferiority complexes, in three ways: In the first place, each idea or feeling of being guilty is a guilt complex if one is either altogether innocent or much less guilty than one feels himself to be. Secondly, one can understand by a guilt complex a feeling that one is worthless—as a whole person—possibly in virtue of a very real guilt. Completely different is the meaning of guilt complex when it means that somebody is paralyzed to the point of being unable to act or to work because of the depressing feeling of his own guilt. Such guilt complexes can lead to the sphere of the pathological.

A typical case of guilt complex in the first sense is given in the situation in which a woman would always feel guilty whenever she would experience sexual pleasure in marriage, and if she felt only pure and free of guilt when she would be wholly frigid. This would be typically a guilt-complex in which sexuality and moral guilt would be identified. In such a mind-set each pleasure, each ecstasy, each delight would be identified with sin or guilt. Some persons even feel guilty whenever they are happy. Another case of a widespread guilt complex is represented by the woman who feels guilty because she was raped. She feels as if she would have incurred personally the guilt for an act which in reality was committed by a criminal against her.

Another category within the first kind of guilt-complex would apply if somebody were to entertain completely exaggerated moral ideals by which he would feel bound. Feelings of guilt resulting from such idealizations are treated by Adler.

He describes such cases where, because of an excessive idealisation and exaggerated view of the moral imperative, someone always feels guilty. This is another type of guilt complex.

With regard to the second and third kind of guilt complex, many philosophically interesting differences are to be considered. Remember, e.g., the concluding scenes of Euripides' *Electra*, in which Orestes and Electra, after they have committed matricide, having killed their mother to revenge their father, outline the hopelessness of their situation and see their whole future life destroyed by their horrible guilt, from which nobody can wash them clean. Adler would have to speak here of a guilt complex.

The question poses itself, however, whether a purely psychological or philosophical answer can be given to the profound moral dilemma of Agamemnon's children (who believe they have committed a crime upon the order of some gods). It seems that only in a religious dimension an ultimate answer to their guilt as it has emerged through matricide is possible. For even the most onerous feelings of guilt and despair, when one excludes redemption, are perfectly normal. The psychologist has no right to call such feelings guilt complexes or pathological simply because he cannot provide a solution to their inextricable tragic character. Rather, if psychology pretends to offer salvation, it ceases to play its serving role; only on a deeper moral and even religious level an ultimate solution to guilt can be found.

Completely different from all guilt complexes described above is the feeling of genuine guilt. Only if one denies the evident moral phenomenon of guilt, which presupposes the wrong use of freedom and a violation of a morally relevant good can the difference between authentic feelings of guilt and guilt complexes in all the described senses be denied or overlooked.

And the problem of real guilt and moral good and evil always transcends psychology. The human person as person stands in need of meanings, values, goals. Even prior to Frankl, Adler sees that the human person is to be grasped as a being related to meaning, whose fundamental problem is to discover, recognize, and realize value in his life and in his acts.

Adler connects this quest for meaning with the classical tradition of ethics, expressed, for example, in some passages of Plato's *Theaitetos*, where the model paradigm is the perfect justice of God, which to imitate is the most profound vocation of each human person: the *homoiousis too theoo*, the becoming similar to God, is here regarded by Adler as the absolute ideal of perfection, although he rejects any opinion which claims that man can become like God in the sense in which the serpent speaks of this likeness, blurring the abyss which distinguishes the infinitely good God from sinful man. Adler writes:

> Man as an everstriving being cannot be like God. God who is eternally complete, who directs the stars, who is the master of fates, who elevates man from his lowliness to Himself, who speaks from the cosmos to every single human soul, is the most brilliant manifestation of the goal of perfection to date. In God's nature,

religious mankind perceives the way to height. In His call it hears again the innate voice of life which must have its direction towards the goal of perfection, towards overcoming the feeling of lowliness and transitoriness of the existence here below. The human soul, as a part of the movement of life, is endowed with the ability to participate in the uplift, elevation, perfection, and completion (1956, p. 107).

VII. "Inferiority" and Not Being Loved—Love and Value of the Person

The feeling of meaninglessness, the feeling of living in a world in which all values and all meaning-contents are pulled out, as Nietzsche expresses himself, would be unquestionably the most serious threat to human life and happiness—not only in the spiritual and moral sense of the term but also in the psychological one. Many forms of psychological conflicts and acts of suicide unquestionably can go back to such a destruction of the consciousness of the value of things and of the value and meaning of our own life.

Here we touch still another completely different meaning of the feeling of inferiority, about which Conrad Baars, has published extensively, going in a similar direction as Viktor Frankl. Baars has explored an extremely profound level of the feeling of inferiority, namely feeling unloved or, worse still, the feeling of not being worthy to be loved in the sense of lacking any value that could justify being loved. Here we touch the deepest problem posed by Adler: that of the ultimate value of the person qua person. A feeling of inferiority inasmuch as it puts this value into question is a completely different phenomenon than feelings of inferiority due to a lack of recognition and prestige. Turgeniew describes in the moving story from *Notes of a Hunter*, entitled "The Living Relic," a girl, who once was a vivacious beauty, but now is paralyzed, crippled and hardly cared for by others. Yet under these incredibly gloomy circumstances she experiences intense gratitude, love of nature and love of others so as to touch profoundly the hunter who visits her.

This girl could combine her justified feeling of not being loved and cared for by anybody with an intense feeling of love and gratitude. Yet even she believes in a love which she does not directly see, and does not doubt that preciousness in herself which allows for being loved. The person who believes that in him no value exists which calls for recognition and love, lives in some despair even if he is a world famous movie-star; he is poor even if he is the richest man on earth.

Adler's position on this is again ambiguous. Even though his general conception of human motivation in terms of will to power does not allow for love and affirmation, and the affirmability of a person for his own sake, he develops certain thoughts regarding the *Gemeinschaftsgefühl* in which he, too, recognizes the longing of man for ultimate affirmation and affirmability of his person. He sees this also on a more practical level. Alfred Adler himself sees this where he explores female sexual frigidity and male impotence as sexual phenomena. He claims that he always found their root to lie in an attitude, which only was interested in properties, or in a *Habenwollen*, an egocentric aspiration without love.

Yet, Adler moves partly on the mere level of what Styczen at the university of Lublin calls a pure doxology. His psychology regards the value of the human person dependent on recognition, fame, social evaluations, etc.—especially due to his fictionalistic tendencies.

At any rate, the deepest feeling of inferiority, which Adler puts in the center of his thought, is not the feeling of not being recognized in one's achievements in society but of being deprived of value as person in one's ultimate being which only the being loved by other persons can reach.

One could use here Gabriel Marcel's judgment in his book *Être et Avoir*, that the person strives to be affirmed in what he is and not only in what he has or produces. In question is the *persona est affirmanda propter se ipsam* (the person ought to be affirmed for his or her own sake). We transcend in love all the values which lie in a certain way on the outside of the human person. These we affirm for example in admiration, but love responds to the person as whole, it affirms the ultimate core of the person, the *Personkern*, as Scheler expresses it.

Thus we see also how intimately philosophy and metaphysics of the person are interconnected. There are, in fact, certain passages in Adler's writings which express this beautifully.[13]

VIII. Adler's Individualanalyse between Personalism and Subjectivism

Finally, I should like to address an important problem and clear up a widespread confusion which might threaten the Institute for Personalist Psychology and for which Adler has a considerable share of responsibility. The distinction I have in mind is the one between personalism and subjectivism. The two Ansbachers write the following:

> The psychological system with which Adler was most in sympathy, according to his biographer ... was that of William Stern. Stern defined his personalistic psychology as "the science of the person having experience ... The immediate subject matter of psychology, experience, is therefore to be identified and interpreted in terms of its matrix, the unitary, goal-directed person" ... Adler felt indebted to Stern "primarily for his great contribution of a philosophical foundation for finalism," that is, the interpretation of life processes in terms of their goals (Ansbacher 1956, p. 10).

The same authors mention (1956, pp. 11 ff.) in their book the close links between Adler, Gordon Allport, William Stern and other personalist psychologists in Harvard, and write:

> Among present-day psychologists Gordon W. Allport is particularly closely related to Stern, and although Allport hesitates to be labeled a personalistic

> psychologist ... he called his work on personality "a contribution to the same line of thought." Accordingly we are not surprised to find considerable similarity between Allport and Adler.

They attribute to Adler the discovery of meaning and of the significance of the human person's relation to meaning. Thus, we see in Adler a personalistic concern for the human subject.[14]

However, they use the expression "subjective psychology" for Adler and his school in order to refer to a completely different kind of subjectivism which is hidden in Adler's theory.

At this point the authors refer to the close kinship between Nietzsche and Adler. From Nietzsche Adler not only received his idea of the will to power as the *Grundmotiv* of the acting human person. From Nietzsche and Vaihinger he took also fictionalism and an "as if" philosophy. They designate the subjective psychology of Adler as characterized in its most essential kernel as a *fictio*:

> *Fictio* means, in the first place, an *activity of fingere*, that is to say, of constructing, forming, giving shape, elaborating, presenting, artistically fashioning, conceiving, thinking, imagining, assuming, planning, devising, inventing. Secondly, it refers to the *product* of these activities, the fictional assumption, fabrication, creation, the imaged case. Its most conspicuous character is that of unhampered and free expression (Ansbacher 1956, p. 78).

The authors clarify the *role* of fiction in Adler's thought in the following manner.

> For us the essential element in a fiction is not the fact of its being a conscious deviation from reality, a mere feat of imagination—but we stress the useful nature of this deviation. If we simply say, "The whole world is our idea and all forms are subjective," we get an untenable subjectivism. But if we say: "Conceptual forms and fictions are expedient psychological constructs," then these are closely related to "cosmic agencies and constituents" ... for it is they that call these expedient forms into existence in the organic being (Ansbacher 1956, p. 78).

Here they confuse personalism with subjectivism. But the subject in the sense of the person and his acts is the highest case of objective reality.

The Ansbachers write that this subjectivism is really the central idea in Adler's psychology:What we generally call "truth," namely a conceptual world coinciding with the external world, *is merely the most expedient error* (Ansbacher 1956, p. 83).

Adler himself writes about Kant and Vaihinger:

> The overwhelming number of passages from Kant which we have quoted and discussed sufficiently prove that the as-if view plays an extradordinarily important part in Kant. This side of Kant has hitherto been almost entirely neglected.

> The only writer to recognize and expound Kant's true doctrine in this respect was Friedrich Carl Forberg [1770-1848]. He clearly grasped and presented, at least in its basic principles, Kant's as-if doctrine, particularly in relation to the philosophy of religion (Ansbacher 1956, pp. 85-86).

Adler sounds here like Bultmann:

> "It is not the (theoretical) belief that the kingdom of God is coming, which constitutes religion; but the endeavour to make it come, even if we believe that it never will come. This and this alone is religion."

It is not possible here to investigate the pragmatic and Kantian roots of these views of Adler. Suffice it to remind ourselves that a philosophical discovery of the person, of personal uniqueness, individuality and personal unrepeatability, etc. is a discovery of the subject but in no way a lapse into psychologism. For the person is being in the primary sense and is as objective as any event in the material universe.

On the other hand, Adler's adoption of elements of the fictionalism and constructivism of Nietzsche, according to whom all values and meanings are *given to things,* and not discovered, is a radical subjectivism and precisely this subjectivism destroys personalistic philosophy and psychology, which can only exist if there is an objective nature and dignity proper to the person qua person, which is discovered by us, not made by us.

NOTES

[1] This text was delivered at the IPP conference under the less apt title: "Feelings of Inferiority and Meaning in Life. A Critical Study of Adler's Individual Psychology."

[2] Compare also Dietrich von Hildebrand, *Über den Tod* (Engl. "*Jaws of Death: Gate of Heaven*") where Dietrich von Hildebrand cites this precise passage from *The Possessed* and develops an extremely profound personalistic philosophy and religious vision of death and immortality.

[3] [Editor's note: With the phrase "feeling of community" Seifert refers to Gemeinschaftsgefuehl, which Buchholz-Kaiser translates as "social interest." It is this concept that she and her organization so value in Adler, and place at the center of their own work. Cf. chapter 3 of this volume.]

[4] See Max Scheler, *Das Ressentiment im Aufbau der Moralen*, in M. Scheler (1955).

[5] My own translation from the German edition.

[6] My own translation from the German edition.

[7] Cf. Adler (1973)

[8] Cf. Hildebrand, Ethics (1973); esp. Ch. 11

[9] Cf. also Hamburger (1993-1994).

[10] This is beautifully expressed by Johann Nestroy.

[11] The main theme of Vitz (1994) is certainly different, for it treats: "narcissims, egoism, self-worship (the "selfism") characteristic of most modern psychology," as the author says (pp. xi ff.).

[12] In a sense is it the main theme of Vitz (1988) to show that one finds in Freud personally such a repression and wrong answers to certain religious experiences and dimensions like those of guilt.

[13] Cf. Adler (1973) p. 166-167. Cf. also Buchholz-Kaiser (1991), especially p. 29 ff., where the author says: "Für uns Individualpsychologen ist das Gemeinschaftsgefühl das Kernstück der Adler'schen Persönlichkeitslehre" (p. 29), and where she discusses Adler's views on conscience and morality, thus unfolding certain personalistic tendencies in Adler.

[14] The very name of Adler's school "Individualanalyse" indicates a personalistic element.

BIBLIOGRAPHY

Adler, A., (1966) *Menschenkenntnis*, Frankfurt a. M.

Adler, A., (1992) *On the Nervous Character*, Frankfurt a.M.

Adler, A., (1965) *Praxis und Theorie der Individualpsychologie*, Darmstadt

Adler, A., (1973) *Über den Sinn des Lebens*, Fischer Taschenbücher, Frankfurt

Ansbacher, H. und R., (1956) *The Individual Psychology of Alfred Adler*, New York: Basic Books, Inc.

Buchholz-Kaiser, Annemarie, (1991) "Das Gemeinschaftsgefühl bei Alfred Adler im Vergleich zur Therapie der Psychosen" in *Individualpsychologische Bildungsarbeit. Aspekte der analytischen Bearbeitung von Persönlichkeitsproblemen in Gruppen; Das Gemeinschaftsgefühl bei Alfred Adler im Vergleich zur Therapie der Psychosen*, Zürich: Verlag Menschenkenntnis

Dostojewskijf. M., *Die Besessenen*, Verlag Martin Maschler, Berlin

Hamburger, S. J., (1993-1994) "Kritische Reflexionen über Max Schelers Ressentiment im Aufbau der Moralen," Aletheia VI

Scheler, M., (1955) *Vom Umsturz der Werte*, Bern-München: Francke-Verlag

Vitz, P. C., (1994) *Psychology as Religion. The Cult of Self-Worship*, 2nd edition, Michigan/Grand Rapids/Carlysle, UK: William Eerdmans Publishing Company/The Paternoster Press.

Vitz P. C., (1988) *Sigmund Freud's Christian Unconscious*, New York/London: The Guilford Press

Von Hildebrand, D., (1973) *Ethics*, Franciscan Herald Press: Chicago

Von Hildebrand, D., (1989) *Transformation in Christ*. Our Path to Holiness, New Hampshire: Sophia Institute Press

Von Hildebrand, D., *Jaws of Death: Gate of Heaven*,

III. Introductions to Systems

7

Personalist Themes in the Applied Thomistic Psychology of Anna Terruwe and Conrad Baars[1]

Philip Sutton

I. Introduction

The truth that we owe to man is, first and foremost, a truth about man. Perhaps one of the most obvious weaknesses of present-day civilization lies in an inadequate view of man. Without doubt, our age is the one in which man has been most written and spoken of, the age of the forms of humanism, and the age of anthropocentrism. Nevertheless it is paradoxically also the age of man's deepest anxiety about his identity and his destiny, the age of man's abasement to previously unsuspected levels, the age of human values trampled as never before. How is this paradox explained? We can say that it is the inexorable paradox of atheistic humanism. It is the drama of man being deprived of an essential dimension of his being, namely his search for the infinite, and thus faced with having his being reduced in the worst way.

> Thanks to the Gospel ... the truth about man ... is found in an anthropology ... whose primordial affirmation is that man is God's image.

This quote comes from an address by Pope John Paul II during the first visit of his papacy to the Americas. Conrad Baars uses this quote in the Postscript to the last book which he authored,[2] and he and Anna Terruwe also use this quote in the Preface of their last coauthored book.[3]

The quote is a fitting introduction to a discussion of the personalist themes in the applied Thomistic psychology[4] of Terruwe and Baars. In their efforts to restate, develop and apply the teachings of Thomas Aquinas on the human psyche[5] to the contemporary understanding and practice of psychiatry, first, Anna Terruwe, and then, Conrad Baars as her translator and colleague, have taught and practiced a modern psychology that is truly personalist. The key to understanding the work of Terruwe and Baars is realizing their dedication to presenting the "whole truth" about human persons to their clients, to the professionals of applied psychology and to everyone who seeks a true, freeing and encouraging understanding of human nature.

In this paper, some of the main ideas of Terruwe and Baars are presented as a concrete illustration of "personalist psychology" as understood by the Institute for Personalist Psychology. The philosophical principles for personalist psychology have been articulated most succinctly by the Institute's founder, James DuBois[6]. Specifically, personalist psychology accepts as fact that human persons:

> ... are ordinarily, and most properly, ***conscious, rational, free, responsible, related to a[n objective] world of values***, and ***capable of recognizing themselves as the subject of action.*** While fully recognizing that intellectual abilities and personality ***develop*** and ***change throughout life***, ... all human beings [are recognized] as persons." (emphases added)[7]

In addition, human persons are assumed to be innately *spiritual, self-determining, religious, social/familial,* and *limited.*[8]

Discussions of ideas and examples from the writings and lectures of Terruwe and Baars are used to illustrate a number of these personalist concepts.

II. Humans Are Spiritual, Rational and Emotional *Beings*

1. Humans are Psycho-Somatic Beings

According to personalist psychology, human persons are *spiritual* beings who, while dependent upon their brains and:

> intimately and mysteriously united to their bodies ... are not identical to their bodies or bodily processes ... As spiritual beings, [humans] may rise above the chains of causality found in the material world ... [9]

In the psychology of Terruwe and Baars, a human person is understood to be a "psychosomatic unity," a body-soul composite.[10] Human beings are not just "embodied souls " or "ensouled bodies." In their writings and lectures, Terruwe and Baars assert the integrity of human nature while emphasizing one aspect of human nature or another, depending on their audience.

Among professional colleagues, Terruwe and Baars have emphasized the spiritual nature of human beings. For psychiatrists and other psychological professionals have tended to ignore the spiritual aspects of their clients or to assume that religious practices and moral beliefs reflect immaturity, unhealthy psychological needs or maladaptive behavior. In addition, modern psychology often has viewed and treated human beings as if we are merely "clever animals" whose emotions are effectively "instincts" to be invariably and irresistibly followed.

But, among priests, religious and devout laypersons, Terruwe and Baars have emphasized often the physical and emotional aspects of human nature. For humans are not simply "angels," who have no need of emotions and who can ignore or escape awareness of their emotions without unhealthy consequences. Terruwe and Baars knew personally and professionally the great "gift" that emotions are to themselves and their clients. Because emotions are often misunderstood, unappreciated and either "demonized" or "idolized" by laypersons and by psychiatric/ psychological professionals, Terruwe and Baars have devoted their professional careers to teaching and applying truths about man's emotional life.

2. Emotions Are "Psychic Motors"

According to personalist psychology, human beings are *rational*, able to "apprehend not only what is true, but also what is good and of value" enabling persons "to transcend themselves and respond to reality appropriately."[11] According to Terruwe and Baars, "emotions" are psychic reactions to the external and internal world in which we live, including our own thoughts, feelings and memories. Our emotions are responses to "whatever information our senses provide concerning the goodness, lack of goodness, usefulness or harmfulness things or beings have for us."[12] Our emotions result from rational judgments about someone's or something's goodness or usefulness to us.

Our emotions serve as "psychic motors" that "cause us to *be moved* or *move* us to act"[13]. There are two different kinds of emotions: the *humane* and the *utilitarian.* The humane emotions of the pleasure appetite cause us to be moved, cause inner movement within our psyches. The utilitarian emotions of the utilitarian appetite move us to take effective action to obtain a good or to avoid what is not good for us. Our free will is our "chief mover," and our emotions provide us with energy so that we may possess and do what we will more easily.

Terruwe and Baars assert Aquinas' understanding of the proper relationship between the will and the emotions. Although religious pedagogy at times has emphasized the misunderstanding "that the will is supreme and must be exercised no matter how one feels,"[14] Baars corrects this misunderstanding. He asserts that while humans must decide with their wills what to do, their wills are not to be tyrannical:

> Man's will [is] not the absolute and supreme principle of human conduct as was generally believed. The will (Thomas Aquinas) said, was not to be trained to overcome and master our suspect and 'dangerous passions,' but rather to rule over them democratically, i.e., to listen to them respectfully and together with them strive for the good. He called the will a 'moved mover,' moved also by the emotion of desire for that good .... All good, also and precisely the moral good, appeals not only to the will through reason, but also directly to the emotions of love and desire through the senses .... A person is able to strive for the good with two motors—those of desire and will. Such a person can be said to have real will power, because his will is supported by the desire for the good."[15]

3. The Humane and Utilitarian Emotions[16]

Following Aquinas, Terruwe and Baars distinguish two sets of emotions: *humane* and *utilitarian*. The humane emotions move us to *be* and are more associated with our intuitive mind (*intellectus*). Our humane emotions and intuition constitute our psychological "heart". The utilitarian emotions move us to *do* , to *act* , to *effort* and are associated more with our thinking mind or reason (*ratio*). Our utilitarian emotions and reason constitute our psychological "mind." Our "mind" functions properly to support the function of our "heart". Our thinking, reasoning, planning, and doing properly serve our knowing and being.[17]

The first and most fundamental humane emotion, *love*, is stimulated whenever we know, believe or sense something is good or pleasurable for us. The emotion of "love" may also be called "liking" or fondness". What we love, we may come to *desire* (wish, want); and if we come to obtain or possess what we desire, we experience *joy* (happiness, delight, pleasure, etc.). The emotion of *hate* (dislike, displeasure, disdain) is stimulated when we recognize that something is not a "sense-good" or object of joy (a "sense-evil".) What arouses our emotion of hate may then arouse our *aversion* (repugnance, repulsion, loathing); and if we cannot avoid what we feel aversion for, we experience *sadness*. Sadness is also aroused if we fail to possess the good that we love and desire, and joy is aroused if we are successful in avoiding that which we hate and which repulses us.[18]

List of the Emotions [19]

Humane Emotions		Utilitarian Emotions	
love	hate	hope	courage
desire	aversion	despair	fear
joy	sadness	anger	

The utilitarian emotions are stimulated by what we know, believe or sense is useful or harmful to us. Our emotion of *hope* (confidence, optimism, etc.) is aroused when we are faced with obtaining a good that is difficult to achieve, that requires work and sacrifice, or that may not seem enjoyable or desirable in itself. Emotional hope strengthens our efforts to persevere in realizing the good once we have decided or willed to obtain it. Faced with the inability to obtain such a good, our emotion of *despair* (hopelessness, pessimism) is aroused. Emotional desperation may lead us either to initiate strenuous efforts to realize the good or to stop efforts that are perceived as fruitless.

When faced with what we judge to be harmful or threatening to our own wellbeing or the wellbeing of others, the emotion of *courage* (fortitude, boldness, etc.) is stimulated. Emotional courage aids our decisions and efforts to overcome the harm ("sense-evil") that we face. If we judge that we cannot overcome perceived danger, our emotion of *fear* (dread, anxiety, timidity, hesitancy, etc.) may be aroused to aid our decision and efforts to avoid or escape the danger. Finally, when a sense-evil has harmed us or we judge that it is about to, the emotion of *anger* (annoyance, irritation, upset, wrath, etc.) is aroused. Emotional anger serves to stimulate us to protect ourselves from harm, to overcome or to obtain restitution for any harm that has already happened, to prevent the harm from reoccurring in the future, and to deal effectively with what is causing our anger.[20]

4. Emotional Health and Maturity

Human emotions are psychosomatic realities, comprised both of psychic feeling and of physiological arousal that naturally accompanies the feeling. For example, in addition to a psychic *feeling* of fear, a person aroused to fear will experience a more rapid heartbeat, rapid and shallow breathing, flushed face, increased perspiration, higher blood pressure and blood sugar, and other related bodily changes. Healthy and mature persons have grown to *feel* comfortable with all of their emotions. The word "feel" has been underlined for emphasis because psychological health, human maturity and human freedom depend on our being able to recognize and to *feel* comfortable with both the psychic feeling and the physiological arousal which accompany every emotion.[21]

Baars asserts that every emotion in its "pure state" is "good and necessary for healthy living. There are no negative or bad emotions [, for] emotions are natural tools with specific functions, precisely as our eyes, ears, hearts, lungs, hands, etc. are men's tools possessing specific functions."[22] Terruwe and Baars recognize that some emotions are less "preferred" or more "uncomfortable" to feel, yet assert the necessity of allowing every emotion to develop fully.

Contrary to a common misunderstanding of present Western culture, emotions need not be "expressed" or "gratified" in order to be satisfied and to develop well. Emotional health and maturity do require learning both a variety of appropriate, healthy and moral ways to satisfy our emotions and the wisdom to know whether, when and how to do so at a given moment. In some situations, the wisest decision may be simply to decline to express or otherwise gratify an emotion and to allow the psychic and physiological arousal of the emotion to quiet down.

Terruwe and Baars also distinguish *emotions* such as hate and anger which are morally neutral from *behaviors* or *intentions* (will-acts) such as hatred and rage which are not. A biblical injunction such as: "Be angry but do not sin,"[23] when properly understood, expresses the necessary distinction between the emotion of anger and the sinful (or righteous) acting out of this anger. Many psychological difficulties have been experienced by persons who wrongly identified the emotion and feeling of anger (or any other emotion) as a sin.

III. Humans Are Social/Familial Beings Who Develop and Change.

Personalist psychology recognizes "that intellectual abilities and personality *develop* and *change* over time" and assumes that human beings are innately *social* and *familial*. Human intellectual, spiritual, emotional and moral development occurs "within a variety of social settings," and personalist psychology asserts as "psychological fact" that "the most basic and essential social structure for personal development is the family, including ...both mother and father...[in a] committed relationship."[24] These personalist truths are expressed most clearly in the psychology of Terruwe and Baars in their understanding of the development and maturation of the emotions and in their concept of affirmation.

1. Emotional Development

Terruwe and Baars recognize that our development and maturation as emotional beings occurs in familial and other social environments over time. Emotional maturity, as well as psychological health and moral virtue, require first that children are able to experience and observe emotional maturity in their parents, other caretakers and other persons. Emotional maturity requires also that children have ample time and opportunities for their emotions "to grow to full capacity and become integrated with and subordinate to reason and will"[25]. Finally, children need time to practice whether and how to gratify their emotions in a variety of circumstances. If these requirements are met, children's emotions will respond readily to their will guided by their reason.

If this integration among intellect, will and emotions is to occur, emotions such as love, desire and joy need to be "cultivated," "nurtured" or "educated."[26] Emotional cultivation occurs when the sense-goods are provided in a timely manner appropriate for a child's development. Just as the "taste" for good food, choice wine or classical music must be developed gradually over time, so do all human desires develop gradually. Fostering a sense of awe, imagination, wonder and expectation and waiting to satisfy a desire until the proper time allow the desire to mature.

When the object of a mature desire is realized, the joy experienced is greatly increased. Untimely gratification of a desire "spoils" the maturing of the desire and leaves a child or adult unfulfilled when the desire is satisfied.[27] For example, in addition to the moral and spiritual dimensions of teenage sexual intercourse, premature information about and gratification of sexual desires by teens spoil or hinder their developing sexual desires. This may prevent or limit their experiencing the great joy that is the fruit of mature sexual desire in marriage.

Human emotional maturity requires learning how to rationally guide and restrain our emotions. This occurs initially and primarily in our families. Ideally, parents and caretakers guide and protect their children from the premature and untimely gratification of their desires and other emotions in an atmosphere of "rational norms" and "mature parental authority." Baars asserts:

> Telling a child, 'Your emotions *need* and *want* to be guided and directed by reason, and we will help you to bring this about by our example and sensible teachings,' enhances the growth of the emotions and their ultimate integration with the higher faculties.[28]

Parents and other relatives, initially, and school teachers, religious educators, and other adults eventually, have special responsibility for influencing the emotional development of the children in their care through their example and words. Terruwe and Baars use the example of a young person learning to ride a horse to illustrate the process of emotional development.[29]

2. Affirmation

Terruwe and Baars assert that, along with food, clothing and shelter, *affirmation* is a "fundamental human need."[30] By "affirmation," they mean our experience of *feeling* our own goodness and knowing with our "hearts," not just our "heads," that we are loved and important as ourselves, for who we *are*, not just for what we may do. This experience of "being affirmed" occurs when our parents and other significant persons are present to us "with the full attention of their whole being."[31] Baars asserts:

> When a child is deprived in infancy, childhood, or puberty of the most fundamental element of emotional nourishment, namely, the unselfish, mature love of an adult person, he remains incapable of experiencing joy and happiness. As long as this fundamental need for being loved for what he *is* (as distinguished from for what he *does* or *achieves*) is frustrated, he hungers for feeling loved and wanted, for having a sense of belonging, for being loveable, for feeling worthwhile and significant, for being who he is, for being unique, yes, simply for existing [32].

Baars considers affirmation so fundamental that he calls being affirmed our "second or psychic birth."[33] Being affirmed involves our being confirmed or strengthened emotionally and intellectually. Emotional strengthening comes when another person is fully *present* and *attentive* to us to *recognize* our goodness, is *moved* by our goodness, and then is in *communion* with us, revealing their being moved by us in the visible, sensible, physical changes in their face, posture and voice.

Explicit communication or action need not (but may) follow another's being moved with love and compassion for us in order for us to feel this emotional strengthening. Emotional affirmation, or affirming living, is fundamentally a state of *being*, not doing, and implicit communion is necessary, and perhaps sufficient, for our psychic birth to occur emotionally. True affirmation is rooted in *affectivity*, our capacity to be affected and moved by our humane emotions.[34]

This requires a calmer, less hurried way of life, more contemplative solitude, and greater sensitivity than our Western culture readily allows and supports. Many children are affirmed only partially or not at all because their parents and other involved adults are physically absent too much and/or are too emotionally unavailable when physically present. Many such children are aptly called: "orphans of living parents." [35]

The contemporary preoccupation with raising the "self-esteem" of children reflects the increasing number of children not being affirmed in their families.

Unfortunately, instead of promoting, restoring and maintaining healthy families in order to improve children's self-esteem, school, community and government leaders often charge professionals and caretakers outside of the family to provide what families have not provided. Where and when it happens, the authentically affirming presence of many dedicated teachers, counselors and other non-parent adults needs to be recognized and appreciated.

But, Baars also recognized and criticized many modern efforts that attempt to stimulate "self esteem" in ways that actually weaken others emotionally.[36] Modern self esteem enhancement programs, even programs claiming to provide "affirmation," though well-intended, are often misguided because they are rooted in *effectivity*, the capacity and readiness to think and act effectively as stimulated by the utilitarian emotions.[37] Persons who are overly driven by effectivity tend to regard and relate to others according to how useful the others are.[38] The worthwhile intention of stimulating self esteem in others can lead to a utilitarian exercise in "pushing the buttons of affirmation"[39] when the intended esteemers/affirmers are not motivated primarily by genuine compassion.

Baars uses the name *pseudo-affirmation* for the unauthentic, self-defeating attempts to affirm others.[40] He noted that professionals, educators, parents, etc., can be so busy "psuedo-affirming" others that they fail to recognize, respect or be genuinely moved by the others' goodness as they are. So treated, the others may come to believe that their personal worth lies in their achievements, productivity, activity, or usefulness, and not in their intrinsic goodness.[41]

Terruwe and Baars maintain that authentic affirmation includes intellectual and moral strengthening, as well as emotional. Baars writes of the need for:

> balance between emotional and intellectual affirmation, between the giving of emotional health food and intellectual truths ... If one gives the emotional health food together with insufficient intellectual and spiritual food, the emotions are denied the necessary guidance and tempering. If, on the other hand, one gives an abundance of intellectual and spiritual truths together with emotional junk food, one offers only half-truths.[42]

Baars clearly includes "moral" and "spiritual" dimensions of affirmation when he writes about "intellectual" affirmation, although he typically uses *intellectual* affirmation to mean moral and spiritual, as well as intellectual.

In order for intellectual affirmation to occur, it is necessary for parents and other familial and social "educators" to teach rational and spiritual truths in the right time and the right way. Children need to be taught according to their maturity and ability to understand. Their educators need to teach by example as well as their words, and to live the intellectual and moral truth that they teach. Parents and other educators and caretakers of the young need especially to refrain from any immoral behavior toward them or in their presence. This requires "self-restraining love".[43]

In addition, children need their parents and other adults not to give what the children are not ready to accept and not to demand what the children are unable to do or give.[44] Well intended but unreasonable restrictions, premature advice, excessive fault-finding or intrusiveness are forms of "pseudo-affirmation" that weaken, instead of strengthen, children intellectually and morally. Such pseudo-affirmation may lead children to distrust both parental and objective, moral norms.

IV. Humans are Self-Determining *and* Limited.

Personalist psychology asserts that human beings are *self-determining* and are *limited* in their perfection. As self-determining beings, humans and their behaviors:

> are not merely the product of genetic, social, or unconscious factors. ...[And while] some human behaviors arise from compulsions or unconscious causes,... it is evident that some human behaviors, indeed those of the greatest significance, are free.[45]

Personalist psychology also assumes: "Human beings are by nature imperfect, and all human perfections are *limited*."

While much benefit may be derived from various therapeutic approaches, it is assumed that applied psychology is not sufficient for freeing human beings from "all personal and moral short-comings". Modern counselors, therapists and "social engineers" ought and need to be *realistically* hopeful in their goals and efforts to improve personal and social welfare.[46]

1. Developing the Virtue of Self-Determination

As a paradigm for therapy, as well as for human development, the psychology of Terruwe and Baars offers a realistic, yet hopeful guide for helping humans seek and find psychological healing and wholeness. As discussed in Section II above, human beings possess an intellect by which they come to know what is true and good, and a free will which enables them to choose between different goods and between good and evil. In developing virtuous will-power (what personalist psychology calls "self-determination"):

> ...the cultivation of the emotions is as important as the thorough education of reason and the strengthening of the will in the development of the virtues ...Aquinas explicitly said: 'Virtue is not only in the will and reason, but also in the emotions.' Cultivation of the emotional life in its entirety, not its extinction or repression, is a prerequisite for integration and cooperation between emotions, reason and will ...This process of integration and cooperation is not an easy one and requires considerable time, at least the first eighteen years of life. Our fallen human nature with its imperfections needs all the help it can get from parents, teachers, and spiritual directors."[47]

The process of emotional maturation takes time and intentional effort. Because of our human imperfection, mature will-power or self-determination requires the development of the virtues of self-control and generosity. In order to develop these virtues, "ascetical practices," acts of voluntary self-denial of the gratification of both the humane and the utilitarian emotions, are necessary.[48]

On one hand, the need to learn to guide and to restrain the gratification of humane emotions such as desires for food and sex may seem obvious. Persons who do not, and perhaps cannot, control when and how they gratify their hunger or sexual desire clearly need to acquire, or reacquire, self control. On the other hand, while the guidance and restraint of utilitarian emotions such as *fear* (despair and fear) or "*energy*" (courage and hope) may seem less obvious, they are also crucial in present culture.

Baars asserts that modern Western culture is so rooted in ***e***ffectivity that many persons are driven by irrational fearfulness or restless striving. Much workaholism, both paid and voluntary, is motivated by this excessive fear or energy, causing many people to "live to work" instead of "work to live." Living in excessive effectivity leads also to using others primarily as objects of gratification or avoiding others as occasions of inconvenience.

Spouses, children, extended family members and close friends commonly feel neglected by persons who are motivated by overdeveloped utilitarian emotions and underdeveloped humane emotions. People cannot be an affirming presence to others or be affirmed by the presence of others if they are too busily "working" or striving because of excessive fearfulness or emotional restlessness. Restraining these utilitarian emotions, learning to relax, seeking solitude and enjoying true leisure are fundamental ways for developing authentic will-power, which is rooted in ***a***ffectivity.[49]

2. Limitations on Self-Determination Due to Emotional Repression[50]

Neurotic Repression. Terruwe and Baars' discussion of neurotic repression highlights the personalist recognition that some human behaviors are not free and "arise from compulsions or unconscious causes."[51] Terruwe and Baars repeatedly emphasize the difference between *rational guidance* and *restraint* of the emotions, which are healthy and lead to mature will-power and self-determination, and *repression*, which is unhealthy and hinders or prevents self-control. "Neurotic repression" involves one or more emotions "burying" or "covering" another emotion in such a way that the repressed emotion is not able to be recognized, felt or acted upon by the will. As Terruwe and Baars write:

> Repressed emotions cannot be controlled by reason and will ... In repression, ... the pleasure appetite is governed, not by reason, but by the repressing emotion so that in the act of repression the use of reason is momentarily suspended ... The repressing emotion has been *wedged* between the repressed emotion and reason. Thus, the action of the repressed emotion remains outside the sphere of control by reason and will.[52]

Terruwe and Baars agree with the classical Freudian observation that a repressed emotion does not disappear but continues to influence the person in an unconscious, unwilled manner. But, Terruwe and Baars' understanding of the process of neurotic repression differs from classical Freudian theory. Freud maintained that the *superego*, which constitutes a person's internalized societal and moral norms and conscience, is the cause of repression.[53] But, Terruwe and Baars, allowing that a misinformed conscience has an indirect role in the repressive process, assert that an *emotion* is the direct cause of repression. Baars writes:

> it is not what a person *knows* or *believes* to be true about emotions, human drives and human nature that leads him to repress, but rather his emotional reaction to these beliefs. His *fear* or *emotional energy* constitute the repressive force which moves him to try to get rid of feelings and ideas which he is led to believe are socially unacceptable, if not morally wrong.[54]

This distinction, first hypothesized by Duynstee[55] and later developed and applied by Terruwe,[56] is fundamental. For Terruwe found that persons suffering from certain kinds of neurotic repression would not be helped through classical psychoanalysis which forced repressed emotions into consciousness. She also observed that informing or changing the neurotics misinformed superego (conscience) was insufficient for curing their repression and relieving their suffering.

Aside from its therapeutic value, Terruwe's writing on neurotic repression was invaluable to the psychiatric career of Baars. Before discovering Terruwe's writings, Baars considered that undermining a person's conscience in an attempt to cure a repressive neurosis was ethically and morally wrong, and he considered leaving psychiatry. But, his discovery of Terruwe's and Duynstee's writings on repression, gave him an ethically, intellectually and professionally satisfying resolution of his problem.[57] Baars found himself professionally renewed and subsequently became the leading English translator and champion of Terruwe's writing, coauthored several books with Terruwe and authored additional books, articles and lectures independently under the inspiration of Terruwe's applied Thomistic psychology.

Hysterical vs. Obsessive-Compulsive Neuroses. Terruwe and Baars accept the standard clinical distinction between "hysterical" and "obsessive-compulsive" neuroses,[58] but they explain the differences between these two kinds of neuroses according to their own understanding of the repressive process. *Hysterical neurosis* results when "the repressing emotion allows the repressed emotion to do as it pleases ...As a result the *repressed* emotion will be most pronounced clinically."[59] For example, hysterical neurotics who experience the repression of their sexual desire commonly act in ways that appear overly "sensual" or "flirtatious," while hysterical neurotics who repress their anger may appear overly sensitive to criticism or unreasonably "assertive."

Typically, hysterical neurotics are not aware of these emotions and show a lack of concern ("bland indifference") about their behaviors.[60] In such cases, the methods of classical psychoanalysis are customarily used to bring the *repressed* emotion into consciousness. Once they have learned to be comfortably aware of these formerly repressed emotions, the sufferers may be helped to learn how to deal with their emotions under the mature guidance of their reason and control of their will.[61]

The other kind of repressive neurosis develops differently and requires different treatment. *Obsessive-compulsive neurosis* occurs: "when the repressing emotion continues to influence the repressed emotion and to obstruct its further activity. In that case the clinical picture is determined much more by the *repressing* emotion." [62] For example, obsessive-compulsive neurotics who experience the repression of sexual desire or anger commonly appear excessively fearful or restless, depending on the repressing emotion.

After obsessive-compulsive neuroses develop, the affected persons typically feel overwhelmed by fear or energy when a repressed emotion (e.g., anger or sexual desire) has been stimulated. But, unlike hysterical neurotics, they also are aware of and concerned about their compulsive behaviors. In spite of their best intentions and efforts, obsessive-compulsive neurotics find themselves driven to act in ways (e.g., angry or sexual) that they wish not to act, as well as suffering from excessive fearfulness or restlessness.[63]

Baars and Terruwe have given diagnostic labels to different kinds of "obsessive-compulsive neuroses." They name the "single" repression disorders (i.e., caused by only one repressing emotion): *fear neurosis* or *energy neurosis*[64], depending on whether a fear (fear or despair) or energy (courage or hope) emotion, respectively, is doing the repressing. Baars uses the "Candy Parable" to explain how persons may develop such obsessive-compulsive neuroses.[65]

Terruwe and Baars also identify disorders of *double neurotic repression*[66], in which one repressing emotion is itself repressed by a third emotion. For example, Terruwe and Baars diagnose a *camouflaged fear neurosis*[67] when one emotion (e.g., sexual desire) is being repressed by fear, which in turn is being repressed by energy.[68] And, Baars describes another kind of camouflaged fear neurosis in which persons, who already are repressing their anger with fear, are unintentionally trained to repress their fear with energy during the misapplication of anger assertiveness training.[69]

While repressive neurotics lack freedom of self-determination concerning behaviors related directly to their repressed emotion(s), such persons retain freedom in two particular areas. First, they retain freedom regarding nonrepressed emotions. For example, people suffering from sexual compulsions may still choose freely whether to steal, gamble, or act in hatred or rage. Second, repressive neurotics retain the freedom to seek healing of their psychological condition and the subsequent restoration of freedom concerning their compulsive behavior. As Adrian van Kaam writes:

> I can always find a free inner orientation in situations which I cannot immediately change ... I can freely decide that my sin or neurosis is a challenge, an occasion

for growth in humility and self-understanding, a repeated opportunity for reaffirmation of my basic commitment to God.[70]

Terruwe and Baars treat obsessive-compulsive neurotics different from hysterical neurotics. Their therapeutic approach[71] for obsessive-compulsive neuroses is called *mortification therapy*. This approach has been described in detail for dealing with repressed anger[72] and repressed sexual desire.[73] Instead of first trying to help clients become aware of their repressed emotions, mortification therapy initially helps the clients to "mortify" or diminish their repressing emotions. For example, fear neurotics are guided not to indulge their fear, and energy neurotics are advised to slow down their lives.

Gradually, as the force of the repressing emotion diminishes, the repressed emotion emerges. Only then are clients supported emotionally and intellectually to become aware of and comfortable *feeling* whatever emotions emerge. And, only being able to feel these emotions comfortably are clients encouraged to learn whether, when and how to express these emotions or to act in response to their stimulation. Ideally, clients learn to live according to the emotional "laws of gradualness,"[74] waiting patiently for their emotions to emerge and to grow naturally and experiencing enough successes and mistakes to grow in wisdom.

3. Limitations on Self-Determination Due to Emotional Deprivation

Just as emotional repression may limit human freedom and self-determination, emotional deprivation due to lack of affirmation also may do so. As described above, the human need for affirmation is so fundamental that being unaffirmed leaves persons emotionally "malnourished"and weak. If the deprivation is severe enough, the emotional life of the unaffirmed persons may be severely underdeveloped, even infantile.[75] And, unaffirmed or inadequately affirmed persons are likely to seek the experience of being loved and loveable in many self-defeating ways.

The self-defeating action or habit of trying to make ourselves feel affirmed is called "*self-affirmation.*"[76] Although wholesome self-affirmation is possible for persons who have been affirmed and are emotionally mature, Terruwe and Baars use the term self-affirmation almost exclusively to mean "*pseudo*-self-affirmation" (similar to their use of the term *pseudoaffirmation* to mean presumably sincere but unauthentic attempts at affirming others.)

Pseudo-self-affirmation means "looking for love in all the wrong places." Pseudo-self-affirmers may seek the experience of being affirmed in many ways: amassing financial wealth or material possessions, acquiring status symbols such as professional degrees or credentials, excessive striving to achieve occupational success or community involvement, seeking political power, becoming famous or associating with others who are famous, engaging in sexual promiscuity, or abusing mind-altering drugs or other substances. Under-affirmed persons who are very talented, attractive or assertive may be particularly prone to pseudo-self-affirming lifestyles centered on seeking wealth, fame or power.[77]

The lifestyles of pseudo-self-affirmers are truly self-defeating "vicious circles". For, such attempts to create the experience of being loved or worthwhile only leave deeper feelings of being unloved or worthless, which lead to additional and more intense self-defeating efforts.[78] Some pseudo-self-affirming habits may be accurately classified as "secondary or psychological addictions." In such cases, the unmet need for affirmation is the motivating force behind a person's inability to limit or stop the "addictive" behavior. Of course, with a drug or other substance addiction, a "primary" addiction may also exist. Sexual compulsions may be a secondary effect of a lack of affirmation, as well as a primary effect of neurotic repression.

Persons may be so unaffirmed that they develop a full *deprivation neurosis.* Such persons typically have experienced a significant lack of emotional affirmation by their parents and caregivers while growing up. Common symptoms of deprivation neurotics include: 1. being unassertive; 2. lacking emotional rapport; and, 3. feeling uncertain, insecure, inferior and inadequate.[79] Such persons may feel guilty because they do not feel loving toward those it is their duty to love, suffer often from deep depression, and may experience chronic resentment and act hateful or rageful in response to not having received the affirmation that was their "birthright."[80]

As with repressive neurotics, deprivation neurotics may lack freedom regarding pseudo-self-affirming behaviors that have become compulsive. Yet, such persons also retain at least minimal self-determination to seek healing for the psychological causes underlying their compulsions. Deprivation neurotics and other unaffirmed persons will need to seek the presence of mature, emotionally, morally and intellectually affirming adults who are able to recognize and be moved by the goodness in these suffering persons. Hopefully, any therapists or counselors that are sought are able to be authentically affirming, in the words of Adrian van Kaam, able to answer the counselee's need and appeal: "Please be *with* me and *for* me" (emphasis added).[81]

Often, the first step which unaffirmed persons need to take to ready themselves for the authentic affirming presence of others is to stop or avoid any pseudo-self-affirmation. This is easier to do if they already have begun to experience an emotionally affirming person who truly cares for them with self-restraining love. Another step is to lead a calmer, less hurried, more patient and open lifestyle so that they become more able to be present to others and to recognize better the goodness in others and in themselves.

A third step involves becoming more assertive, stopping trying to please everyone, and being more open to risking "hurting other's feelings" while doing what seems right. Other steps include practicing "positive imagination" and self-restraining love. Baars encourages the unaffirmed to be gentle with themselves and their feelings that seem so "child-like," as they wait for their emotions to grow up in their own way and at their own pace.[82]

V. Humans Are Moral and Religious

Personalist psychology asserts that we humans are disposed intrinsically to discover objective goods and values.

> These goods may offer human life meaning and direction, as well as make demands upon human behavior. The moral life consists largely in the conformity of human responses to these goods as they exist in a hierarchy.[83]

To the extent that we are able to perceive objective values and to act freely in response to them, we are *morally responsible* for our actions.

Personalist psychology maintains both that some "feelings of guilt or obligation ... do not correspond to any true guilt or obligation" and that:

> any counseling activity which seeks to free persons from feelings of guilt must be accompanied by a sensitivity to instances of real guilt and a willingness to pursue themes of forgiveness and reparation.[84]

Finally, personalist psychology recognizes that we humans are intrinsically *religious*. Through religious beliefs and practices, we seek "adequate answers to the most fundamental questions concerning the nature and meaning of human life." While the beliefs or actions of some persons may be the "product of unhealthy psychological needs" or "underdeveloped patterns of thinking," it is asserted that religious belief and practice "has a healthy and legitimate place in the life of the individual and society."[85]

1. Teaching Moral Responsibility

Terruwe and Baars assert that authentic moral teaching and living is essential for emotional maturity and psychological health. They accept the objective moral good as found in the natural law and in the revealed law as presented by the magisterium (teaching authority) of the Catholic Church. They also distinguish between the truth of the moral law itself and the helpfulness or harmfulness of various manners of teaching morality by word or example. The harmfulness of not teaching moral truth, of teaching moral error, and of failing to live by the truth that one teaches, was mentioned above in the section III discussion of "intellectual affirmation."

Continuing the earlier discussion, intellectual affirmation involves respecting and teaching moral norms and providing guidance to children (and adults) when they make mistakes. Parents and other moral educators need to:

> have a reasonable trust in the basic goodness of every human being ... This trust implies that the educator believes that the child will learn also from his faults and mistakes, because they interfere with his finding what he really wants: that which is truly good and fulfilling of his nature.[86]

Following Aquinas, Terruwe and Baars assert that moral good is "intelligible, capable of being understood as reasonable and connatural to our being." The goodness and rightness of the moral laws which direct us to that good are meant "to be understood and loved, as well as obeyed with joy ..."[87] Recognizing and being attracted to the moral law as good often does not occur until a child or adult has actually lived morally because they "ought to". As our mind and heart become integrated, and as we become more emotionally and intellectually mature, the "oughts" of the moral law, previously imposed from without, come to guide, restrain and dispose us from within our own minds and hearts.

On the one hand, giving accurate information about the moral law to children before they are mature enough to understand it and giving inaccurate information have both led to emotional repression. For example, emphasizing moral behavior to younger children in a manner which suggests that "sinful behavior is always a sin" may result in children developing much irrational fear or restless striving about the moral law. Some sincere, sensitive and intelligent persons have developed fear or energy neuroses as a result of being taught moral truths prematurely, inaccurately or in an overly fearful manner. Such persons came to experience an habitual overstimulation of their fear or energy emotions in order to push out of conscious awareness emotions and bodily feelings, which they believed were wrong and sinful for them to *feel*. [88]

On the other hand, a form of pseudo-affirmation or denial of the personhood of children and adults occurs when psychological and spiritual educators, including parents, lower moral standards by giving the message that a given "sin is not a sin."[89] This may be communicated directly, in words or writings, or indirectly, through indifference, too permissive or absent guidance, and bad example. Such "open-minded" neglect leads children and adults to believe that they are "too weak" to live the moral life, that the moral life is too difficult or that the joy of the moral life is not worth the effort that may be required. Such intellectual and moral denial also leaves children and adults at great risk of suffering psychological and spiritual harm as consequences of immoral actions and lifestyles. Increased feelings of being unloved, worthlessness and depression typically accompany any compulsive, objectively immoral behaviors.

2. *Moral Guilt*

When emotionally mature persons knowingly and freely perform morally wrong actions, they are guilty of their actions. Their awareness of their guilt normally stimulates a proper *feeling* of guilt, a "feeling of discomfort and uneasiness" which is "an experience of the psychological incompleteness" of their human action.[90] Van Kaam calls this "authentic guilt" (vs. "neurotic guilt").[91] Like our emotions, guilt feelings function also as "psychic motors". Valid guilt feelings support our will in making restitution for wrong actions and in avoiding the same actions.

But, emotionally immature or disordered persons may experience too much or too little guilt. Some people feel guilty when they shouldn't. Scrupulous neurotics "may suffer from guilt feelings without having committed a crime or sin."[92] Their fear of committing immoral behaviors stimulates their guilt feelings, and their guilt feelings may further stimulate their guilt.

Other persons may not feel guilt when they should. For example, true "psychopathic personalities" are devoid of guilt feelings because of a constitutional lack of subordination of their emotions to their reason.[93] They may feel "bad" because of the consequences of being caught but not because of acting "wrong". Finally, persons may lack guilt feelings if they have been uninformed or misinformed about moral living. Clearly, different remedial responses are needed by each of these groups if they are to be helped to act more in harmony with their moral nature.

3. Promoting Sexual Morality

The psychology of Baars and Terruwe has provided timely insights for understanding and dealing with the contemporary moral issues of contraception, nonmarital sexual activity and abortion. In 1965, three years before the papal encyclical *Humanae Vitae* by Pope Paul VI which reasserted the Catholic Church's opposition to contraception, Baars wrote a psychological defense of the Church's teaching. He explains that contraception is immoral because it violates the self-restraining and unconditionally self-giving aspects of marital love.[94]

Baars consistently observed and pointed out the lack of affirmation underlying promiscuous sexual lifestyles, including homosexual.[95] He described the self-defeating vicious circle of unhappiness caused by such pseudo-self-affirming behavior.[96] He also criticized as "Guidelines to Quicksand" the "pastoral" advice by certain moral theologians who authored a book on human sexuality which assumed that there were no objective norms or unhealthy consequences for "deviant" sexual behavior.[97] Finally, Baars identified the increasing lack of affirmation in Western countries as the primary psychological cause of the pro-abortion and anti-life movements.[98]

Much of the work by Terruwe and Baars on moral behavior took place while counseling or educating priests, religious and devout lay clients or audiences. Common themes of therapy and lectures included presenting a balanced and accurate understanding of moral norms and undoing the effects of misguided religious pedagogy which taught moral norms prematurely, or in an atmosphere which led to false and sometimes repressing notions about the emotional life, or in a pseudoaffirming manner which compromised or denied the moral norms. Committed to abide by the moral authority of the Catholic Church, Terruwe and Baars submitted their writings for appropriate review to insure that they were teaching moral truth.

Some reviewers in the Holy Office had initial reservations about the manner of Terruwe's treatment for obsessive-compulsive sexual neurotics, many of whom were priests and nuns. But, Terruwe's belief in the moral integrity of her therapeutic methods eventually was vindicated, and her methods were declared to be "founded on sound and correct principles and of great value to all."[99] Also, Terruwe reported that Pope Paul VI told her in a private audience that her work was "a gift to the Church."[100]

Later, when writing their last collaborative book,[101] Terruwe and Baars wrote a summary of their treatment approach for obsessive-compulsive sexual neurotics and submitted this summary for review by three American moral theologians. All three judged that there was "Nothing against faith and morals."[102] And, one reviewer, Jordan Aumann, O.P., wrote: "The authors' mortification therapy ... is in full accord with the teaching of the Magisterium of the Church on faith and morals, and particularly on sexual morality."[103]

4. Promoting Spiritual Wholeness

Terruwe and Baars have worked to understand and help the church deal with the crises of vocation among priests and professed religious. Many of their clients and lecture audiences included priests, sisters and brothers. Both Terruwe and Baars attended the 1971 Synod of Bishops on the priesthood as psychiatric consultants. Translating some of Terruwe's writings and his own studies led Baars to write in defense of priestly celibacy[104] and of philosophy studies as essential for the intellectual affirmation and formation of seminarians.[105] He also wrote and lectured about psychological causes of the crises of vocation among vowed celibate and married persons and about the need for priests, religious and bishops to be authentic intellectual and emotional affirmers of the laypersons, religious and priests in their care.

Throughout their writings and talks, Terruwe and Baars advise their clients and audiences about both the spiritual and psychological benefits of regular religious practice. They encourage the practice of contemplative, as well as meditative, prayer and scripture reading in order to come to know God better so that we can love Him more with our "heart," our humane emotions and intuition, as well as with our rational mind and will.[106] They regard contemplative prayer as a way to preserve and nurture our affectivity which enables us to love our neighbors and ourselves in more affirming ways. Also, Baars composed meditation tapes based on scripture to aid in learning contemplative prayer.[107]

Terruwe and Baars encourage Catholic clients who are seeking treatment for sexual compulsions to have a psychologically knowledgeable confessor whom they are able to trust emotionally and intellectually. In such cases, they also advise therapists to develop collaborative relationships with their clients' spiritual directors.[108] Baars emphasizes the spiritual and psychological worth of the practice of mature forgiveness and the harm of *premature forgiveness*.[109] And, Baars encourages therapists to pray with and for clients as a basic aid in the therapy process.[110]

Terruwe and Baars' ideas drew the attention of leaders and participants of Catholic and Christian renewal movements in the United States in the 1970's and early 1980's. Baars was consulted by leaders in the faith healing movement. Baars advised the leaders to focus less on techniques, to "deemphasize *e*ffectivity" in prayers such as the "healing of memories" and to practice affectivity, especially compassion for the sufferer. He cautioned against forcing emotions or memories into awareness or expressing them unduly and taught about the "law of gradualness" of emotional growth, maturation and integration.[111]

Baars often reminded people who expected immediate results but were disappointed after praying for emotional healing that "the healing of the emotionally ill person takes place gradually and in stages."[112] He gave an example about learning to play the piano to illustrate the wisdom in cooperating with emotional healing as a gradual process.[113] Baars also composed several "self-help" audiotapes that "emotionally and spiritually troubled people" might use to cooperate in their healing process.[114]

Baars' support of clients' Christian beliefs and practices was atypical in the profession of psychiatry, but his openness to the possibility of demonic influence was even more unusual. Although initially skeptical, witnessing a number of prayer services for deliverance from demonic influences led Baars to allow "that evil spirits can play some role in the cause or aggravation of psychological disorders and can exercise an obstructive force to effective therapy." Baars came to believe that a client's lack of responsiveness to all available forms of therapy along with historical involvement in occult activities would allow a diagnosis of a possible "spirit-caused illness."[115] In serving laypersons who were disposed to pray for deliverance, Baars found that he needed to remind people that *all* of our emotions are "good and necessary parts of our nature"[116] and that people are not evil or in need of deliverance merely because they *feel* anger, hate, despair or sexual desire.

VI. Final Remarks

In this paper, key concepts of Anna Terruwe and Conrad Baars' development and application of Thomistic psychology have been summarized and conceptualized according to the major themes of personalist psychology. Their applied Thomistic psychology is a specific kind of personalist psychology, a concrete application of the philosophical assumptions which are the basis for all personalist psychology. Not all personalist psychologists were or are Catholic Christians, but Terruwe and Baars are unabashedly so.

In responding to the quote used to open this paper, Conrad Baars wrote that the task of every Christian psychiatrist (and by implication, every Christian counselor and practitioner of applied psychology) is:

> to assist the Church and all Christians in knowing more about man as the image of God, to lessen his anxieties, to save him from his own abasement, and to bring order and strength to his psychic life for optimal receptivity to God's healing grace.[117]

Baars' understanding of the role of the Christian counselor is similar to that expressed by Adrian van Kaam: "to fulfill the humble role of John the Baptist,...

preparing the way for Christ by helping their fellow Christians to explore the neurotic tendencies" which may "poison" one's motives and "cripple" one's psychological and religious development.[118]

Practitioners of Terruwe and Baars' applied Thomistic psychology serve as John the Baptist by "filling in" the psychological "valleys" caused by repressed emotions and by being unaffirmed through authentic, affirming living; by "laying low" the "mountains and hills" of repressive emotions through mortification therapy; and by "straightening" the "winding roads" and "smoothing" the "rough ways" through intellectual, moral and emotional affirmation.[119]

The psychology of Terruwe and Baars presents and applies faithfully insights about human persons taught by Thomas Aquinas in the 13th century. As we approach the 21st century, more than 700 years after Aquinas, these psychological insights remain "the truth about man" and are worthy of our personal and professional attention. The timely and expedient teaching and applying of these personalist truths can help both professionals and laypersons to understand and to cope better with the psychological, moral and spiritual challenges of today.

NOTES

[1] This paper is an expanded version of a paper entitled *Personalist Themes in the Work of Conrad Baars and Anna Terruwe,* presented at the Institute for Personalist Psychology (IPP) conference on "The Nature and Tasks of a Personalist Psychology," October, 1994 at Franciscan University of Steubenville, Steubenville, Ohio, USA. The author wishes to thank Rev. William D. Virtue, STD for his helpful comments on an earlier draft of this paper.

[2] Baars, *Feeling and Healing*, 269-70.

[3] Anna Terruwe and Conrad Baars, *Psychic Wholeness and Healing* (New York: Alba House, 1981), vii-viii.

[4] In her dissertation (*De neurose in het licht der rationele psychologie*) and in Baars' English translation of her dissertation (*The Neurosis in the Light of Rational Psychology*), Terruwe refers to "rational psychology" (*rationele psychologie* in Dutch), a name for Thomistic psychology among the neoscholastic scholars of the mid-twentieth century. But, "Thomistic psychology" is used in this paper because "rational psychology" is rarely used by contemporary philosophers and because "rational" may have ambiguous meanings for contemporary psychologists and laypersons.

[5] Thomas Aquinas, "Treatise on the Passions," *Summa Theologica*, I-II, QQ. 22-48, (New York: Benziger Brothers, 1947, Vol. I, 691-790).

[6] James DuBois, *Philosophical Principles* (Steubenville, OH: Institute for Personalist Psychology, 1994).

[7] Ibid., *Principles* 2.

[8] Ibid., *Principles* 3, 6, 8, 10 and 9, respectively.

[9] Ibid., *Principles* 3.

[10] Baars, *Feeling and Healing*, 34.

[11] DuBois, *Principle* 5.

[12] Baars, *Feeling and Healing*, 12.

[13] Ibid.

[14] Ibid., 69.

[15] Ibid., 70.

[16] Different names have been given to these two sets of emotions. In his "Treatise on the Passions" of the *Summa Theologica,* Aquinas distinguishes the emotions ("passions") of the *concupiscible* appetite from the emotions of the *irascible* appetite. In *Loving and Curing the Neurotic* and *Psychic Wholeness and Healing*, to avoid confusion over the terms "concupiscible " and "irascible," Terruwe and Baars substitute the terms *pleasure* and *utility* respectively for the appetites and their related emotions. In *Feeling and Healing Your Emotions,* Baars substitutes the name *humane* for "pleasure" to avoid confusion caused by the latter term. In private communication, Rev. William Virtue, STD of St. Mary's, Loretto, Illinois, USA, has suggested using "happiness" and "assertive" respectively to distinguish these sets of emotions because "humane" may imply that the other emotions are "inhumane," and "utilitarian" itself often carries a negative connotation. Nevertheless, the author prefers to distinguish these sets of emotions as the "being" and "doing" emotions, respectively. The terms *humane* and *utilitarian* are used here because Baars seems to prefer them and because non-professional, English-speaking readers may be more likely to encounter these terms in Baars' writings and in his audio- and videotaped talks. For the future, because psychic wholeness involves the mature and complementary development of both sets of emotions, further efforts are warranted to decide more appropriate modern names for distinguishing these emotions.

[17] Baars, *Feeling and Healing*, 75.

[18] Ibid., 15-16.

[19] Terruwe and Baars, *Psychic Wholeness*, 15.

[20] Baars, *Feeling and Healing*, 19-20.

[21] Ibid., 35.

[22] Ibid., 75.

[23] Ephesians 4:26, (*The New American Bible,* Nashville, TN: Thomas Nelson, 1987).

[24] DuBois, *Principles* 2 and 10.

[25] Baars, *Feeling and Healing*, 75.

[26] Ibid.

[27] Ibid., 99.

[28] Ibid., 68.

[29] Ibid., 76-78; Terruwe and Baars, *Psychic Wholeness*, 240-241; and Terruwe and Baars, *Loving and Curing the Neurotic* (New Rochelle, NY: Arlington House, 1972), 480-481. An expanded version of this analogy was presented as part of the author's paper at the Institute for Personalist Psychology conference, October, 1994. A copy may be obtained by writing the author at the Institute for Personalist Psychology, St. Joseph Center, Franciscan University of Steubenville, Steubenville, OH, 43952-6711.

[30] Conrad Baars and Anna Terruwe, *Healing the Unaffirmed: Recognizing Deprivation Neurosis* (New York: Alba House, 1976), 204.

[31] Baars, *Feeling and Healing*, 153.

[32] Ibid., 109-110.

[33] Terruwe and Baars, *Psychic Wholeness*, 24.

[34] Terruwe and Baars, *Psychic Wholeness*, 123.

[35] Pope John Paul II, *Letter to Families* (Boston, MA: St. Paul Books, 1994), 47.

[36] Baars, *Feeling and Healing*, 166 and 224.

[37] Ibid., 32.

[38] Terruwe and Baars, *Psychic Wholeness*, 123.

[39] Baars, *Feeling and Healing*, 166.

[40] Ibid.

[41] Ibid., chapters 7 & 8; also, Conrad Baars, *Born Only Once* (Chicago: Franciscan Herald Press, 1975).

[42] Baars, *Feeling and Healing,* 234.

[43] Baars and Terruwe, *Healing the Unaffirmed,* 185-189.

[44] Baars, *Born Only Once*, 58.

[45] DuBois, *Principles* 6.

[46] Ibid., *Principles* 9.

[47] Baars, *Feeling and Healing*, 71-72.

[48] Ibid., 76.

[49] Ibid., 70-71, 153-159.

[50] This section on emotional repression and the next section on emotional deprivation mention some of Terruwe and Baars' diagnostic labels for psychological disorders which they have identified and treated as psychiatrists (e.g., *hysterical neurosis, fear* and *energy neuroses, camouflaged fear neurosis*, and *deprivation neurosis*). Other diagnostic terms which they use (e.g., *pseudoneurotic reactions* and constitutional (i.e., primary) *personality disorders*) are not discussed in the interest of brevity. It ought to be noted that

diagnostic terms like "neurosis," although once commonly used, are rarely used now by the psychiatric and allied mental health communities. Baars writes: "The difference between the official psychiatric diagnos(tic labeling system) and mine is that the former is determined by the most pronounced clinical symptoms of the patient ..., while my diagnosis ... describes the nature and the kind of person who develops it" (*Feeling and Healing*, 130-131.) Clinicians who diagnose the psychological disorders identified by Terruwe and Baars will be challenged by the need also to apply one or more labels from one of the more symptom-based, diagnostic systems in current use (i.e., American Psychiatric Association's *Diagnostic and Statistical Manual of Mental Disorders*, Fourth Edition (DSM-IV), or the *International Classification of Diseases*, 9th Revision, Clinical Modification (ICD-9-CM), as of this writing). Further discussion of which DSM-IV or ICD-9-CM diagnoses most closely match the diagnostic labels of Terruwe and Baars is beyond the scope of this paper, but interested readers are welcome to correspond with the author about this issue.

[51] DuBois, *Principles* 6.

[52] Terruwe and Baars, 39.

[53] Sigmund Freud. *A General Introduction to Psychoanalysis* (Garden City: Garden City Publishing Co., 1943).

[54] Baars, *Feeling and Healing*, 122-123.

[55] W.J.A.J. Duynstee, CssR, "De verdringingstheorie beoordeeld van thomistisch standpunt' ("The Theory of Repression, Judged from the Thomistic Viewpoint."), 1935 lecture appearing in W.J.A.J. Duynstee, CssR., *Verspreide Opstellen* (Roermond-Maaseik: J.J. Romen & Zonen, 1963).

[56] Anna Terruwe, *De Neurose in het Licht der Rationale Psychologie* (*The Neurosis in the Light of Rational Psychology*), Dissertation, Leiden, 1949.

[57] Terruwe and Baars, xii; Baars, *Feeling and Healing*, 122.

[58] Terruwe and Baars, *Psychic Wholeness*, 63.

[59] bid., 63.

[60] Ibid., 64-65.

[61] Ibid. 89-91.

[62] Ibid., 63-64.

[63] bid., 33-34.

[64] Terruwe and Baars, chapter III.

[65] Conrad Baars, "Man's Psychic and Emotional Life," audiotaped lecture (8th Annual Workshop for Priests: Erie, PA, 1980). Note: An edited and expanded version of the "Candy Parable" was presented by the author at the IPP Conference, October, 1994. A copy of this version maybe obtained by writing the author at the Institute for Personalist Psychology.

[66] Baars, *Feeling and Healing*, 225.

[67] Terruwe and Baars, 76-79.

[68] Terruwe and Baars, 76-79.

[69] Baars, *Feeling and Healing*, 225.

[70] Adrian van Kaam, *Religion and Personality* (Englewood Cliffs, N.J.: Prentice-Hall, 1964), 104.

[71] A comprehensive overview of the therapeutic methods of Terruwe and Baars is beyond the scope of this paper. Mental health professionals are encouraged to read *Psychic Wholeness and Healing* and *Healing the Unaffirmed* to learn more about their therapeutic methods and clinical case examples. Nonprofessionals are encouraged to read Baars' books *Born Only Once* , chapter 6 and *Feeling and Healing Your Emotions*, chapter 7 for "self-help" insights.

[72] Baars, *Feeling and Healing*, 180-185.

[73] Terruwe and Baars, 111-127.

[74] Baars, *Feeling and Healing*, 80.

[75] Terruwe and Baars, *Healing the Unaffirmed*, chapters 1-2.

[76] Ibid.; Terruwe and Baars, *Psychic Wholeness*, 25; Baars, *Born Only Once*, 73-80.

[77] Baars, *Born Only Once.*

[78] Ibid., 92.

[79] Baars and Terruwe, *Healing the Unaffirmed*, chapter II.

[80] Ibid., 191-192.

[81] Adrian van Kaam, *The Art of Existential Counseling* (Denville, NJ: Dimension Books, 1966), 33.

[82] Baars, *Born Only Once*, 81-99.

[83] DuBois, *Principles* 4.

[84] Ibid., *Principles* 7.

[85] Ibid., *Principles* 8.

[86] Terruwe & Baars, *Psychic Wholeness*, 121.

[87] Ibid., 122.

[88] Baars, *Feeling and Healing*, 120.

[89] Baars, *Born Only Once*, 41-42.

[90] Terruwe and Baars, *Psychic Wholeness*, 26.

[91] van Kaam, *Existential Counseling*, 166-167.

[92] Baars, *Feeling and Healing*, 255.

[93] Terruwe and Baars, *Psychic Wholeness*, 27.

[94] Conrad Baars, "Rhythm - An Expression of Marital Love." In *Proceedings of the National Federation of Catholic Physicians' Guilds*, Second Annual Symposium, Kansas City, MO: December, 1965.)

[95] Conrad Baars, *The Homosexual's Search for Happiness* (Chicago: Franciscan Herald Press, 1976).

[96] Baars, *Born Only Once.*

[97] Terruwe and Baars, 1981, 251-254.

[98] Conrad Baars, "The Psychiatrist: Friend or Foe of the Pregnant Woman?, in *Child and Family* (Vol. 9, N;o.1, 1970). Conrad Baars, *Abortion and a World Split Apart* (Paper delivered to the Seventh Annual Alternatives to Abortion International Academy, St. Louis, MO, 1978). Conrad Baars, "Psychic Causes and Consequences of the Abortion Mentality," in David Mall and Walter Watts (eds.) *The Psychological Aspects of Abortion* (Chicago: University Publications of America, 1979).

[99] Baars, *Feeling and Healing*, 268.

[100] Ibid., 268; Terruwe and Baars, *Psychic Wholeness*, ix-x.

[101] *Psychic Wholeness and Healing.*

[102] Ibid., x.

[103] Ibid., 136.

[104] Conrad Baars, *A Priest for All Seasons: Masculine and Celibate* (Chicago: Franciscan Herald Press, 1972.)

[105] Conrad Baars, "Your Seminary: Right or Wrong?" in *Homiletic and Pastoral Review*, Vol. LXXXII, No. 4, January, 1982, 57-61.

[106] Baars, *Feeling and Healing*, 243-244.

[107] Conrad Baars. Audiotapes: *Fear is Useless—What is Needed is Trust*; *Don't Look at the Waves—Look at Jesus*; *Speak Lord—An Aid to Meditation*; and *Be Still—An Aid to Contemplation.*

[108] Terruwe and Baars, *Psychic Wholeness*, 113-114.

[109] Baars, *Feeling and Healing*, 191-195.

[110] Ibid., 152 and 191; Terruwe and Baars, *Psychic Wholeness and Healing*, 112.

[111] Baars, *Feeling and Healing*, 196-199.

[112] Ibid.

[113] Conrad Baars, "Piano Parable," in *Fear Not: What is Needed is Trust* (Catholic Charismatic Conference: San Diego, CA, 1980). An edited and expanded version was included in the author's paper at the IPP Conference, October, 1994. A copy of this version may be obtained by writing the author at the Institute for Personalist Psychology.

[114] Conrad Baars, Audiotapes: *Premature Forgiving—When to Forgive and How*; *Healing*

Prayer for Psychic Wholeness; *Affirmation and Psychic Incarnation—For Emotionally and Spiritually Troubled People* (undated).

[115] Baars, *Feeling and Healing*, 202-203.

[116] Ibid., 203-204.

[117] Ibid., 270.

[118] van Kaam, *Religion and Personality*, 159.

[119] Luke 3:5-6.

BIBLIOGRAPHY

American Psychiatric Association. *Diagnostic and Statistical Manual of Mental Disorders*, Fourth Edition. Washington, DC: American Psychiatric Association, 1994.

Aquinas, Thomas. *Summa Theologica*, I-II, QQ. 22-48. New York: Benzinger Brothers, 1947, vol. I, 691-790.

Baars, Conrad W. "Rhythm—An Expression of Marital Love." *Proceedings of the National Federation of Catholic Physicians' Guilds*, Second Annual Symposium on Rhythm. Kansas City, MO, December, 1965.

_____, "The Psychiatrist - Friend or Foe of the Pregnant Woman?" *Child and Family*, Vol. 9, No.1, 1970.

_____, *A Priest for All Seasons—Masculine and Celibate*. Chicago: Franciscan Herald Press, 1972.

_____, *Born Only Once: The Miracle of Affirmation*. Chicago: Franciscan Herald Press, 1975.

_____, *The Homosexual's Search for Happiness*. Chicago: Franciscan Herald Press, 1976.

_____, *Abortion and a World Split Apart*. Seventh Annual Alternatives to Abortion International Academy, St. Louis, MO, August, 1978.

_____, *Feeling and Healing Your Emotions*. Plainfield, NJ: Logos International, 1979.

_____, "Psychic Causes and Consequences of the Abortion Mentality," *The Psychological Aspects of Abortion*, Ed. David Mall and Walter Watts, M.D., Chicago: University Publications of America, 1979.

_____, "Your Seminary: Right or Wrong?" *Homiletic and Pastoral Review*, Vol. LXXXII, No. 4, January, 1982, 57-61.

_____, *Fear Not: What is Needed is Trust*. Audiotaped talk: Catholic Charismatic Conference, San Diego, CA, 1980.

_____, *Man's Psychic and Emotional Life*. Audiotaped talk given at the 8th Annual Workshop for Priests, Gannon University, Erie, PA, 1980.

_____, Undated audiotapes:

Affirmation & Psychic Incarnation -For Emotionally & Spiritually Troubled People.
Be Still—An Aid to Contemplation.
Don't Look at the Waves—Look at Jesus.
Fear is Useless—What is Needed is Trust.
Healing Prayer for Psychic Wholeness.
Premature Forgiving—When to Forgive and How.
Speak Lord — An Aid to Meditation.

_____, and Terruwe, Anna A. *Healing the Unaffirmed: Recognizing Deprivation Neurosis.* Staten Island, NY: Alba House, 1976.
Freud, Sigmund. *A General Introduction to Psychoanalysis.* Garden City: Garden City Publishing Co., 1943.

The New American Bible. Nashville, TN: Thomas Nelson, 1987.

Pope John Paul II. *Letter to Families.* Boston: St. Paul Books & Media, 1994.

Terruwe, Anna A. *De neurose in het licht der rationele psychologie.* Dissertatie: Lieden, 1949.

_____, *The Neurosis in the Light of Rational Psychology.* Translated by Conrad Baars. New York: Kenedy & Sons, 1960.

_____, and Baars, Conrad W. *Loving and Curing the Neurotic.* New Rochelle, NY: Arlington House, 1972.

_____, and Baars, Conrad W. *Psychic Wholeness and Healing.* New York: Alba House, 1981.

van Breeman, Octavia. *Wie is Dr. Anna Terruwe?* Duerne, Nederland: Bibliotheek Dr. Anna Terruwe Stichting, 1993.

van Kaam, Adrian. *Religion and Personality.* Englewood Cliffs, NJ: Prentice-Hall, 1964.

_____, *The Art of Existential Counseling.* Denville, NJ: Dimension Books, 1966 Virtue, William N. Personal communication, 1995.

PLEASE NOTE: Information on audiotaped and written materials by Conrad Baars, M.D. may be obtained by writing:

Michael Baars
801 D South West Street
Sikeston, MO 63801 U.S.A.

Information on the writings and talks of Anna Terruwe, M.D. in Dutch, English, German, French and other languages may be obtained from:

Bibliotheek (Library)
Dr. A. Terruwe Stichting (Foundation)
Vlierdensweg 109
5753 AC Deurne Netherlands

8

The Theology and Pretheology of Empirical Christian Character and Personality Formation[1]

Adrian van Kaam, C.S.Sp.
with Susan Muto

I. Introduction

I feel honored to be invited at this convention of psychologists interested in personalistic psychology. The commitment of the initiators, organizers, and participants of this gathering is to be admired. How dedicated you are to a Christian psychology of person and personality!

My own specialization and that of Dr. Muto is not primarily in a Christian psychology of personality. Our preferential focus is the transpsychological formation theology and pretheology of empirical-experiential Christian character and personality formation. I am sure, however, that there are many points of convergence between our shared concerns with Christian personhood as illumined by the doctrines and traditions of the Church.

Professor Paul Vitz' paper made it clear to me that I should clarify the position of my paper in relation to other presentations. First of all, I must make distinctions between different kinds of personality formation and theory. I shall introduce these distinctions under five headings, namely, theories that are: (1) non-transcendent, (2) pretranscendent, (3) humanistic transcendent, (4) Christian transcendent, (5) Christian transpsychological or formational-theological transcendent.

1. *Non-transcendent Psychological (Implicitly Philosophical) Theories of Personality Development.*

These theories reject the very notion of transcendence.[2] They are strictly behavioristic stimulus-response theories. An example is the theory of B. F. Skinner.

2. *Pre-transcendent Psychological (Implicitly Philosophical) Theories of Character and Personality Development.*

These theories do not exclude the transcendent dimension of human life. Their preferential focus, however, is our pretranscendent existence. At times they may take into account certain psychological aspects of the transcendent dimension of human personality. While they may be open to some findings of either the non-transcendent or transcendent psychological theories, they do not make either of them the central focus of their interest and elaboration. The same applies to the implicit philosophies that underlie their theories. They may refer briefly to them. They will neither discuss them at length nor analyze their impact on their theories. These pre-transcendent theories prepare implicitly, sometimes explicitly, for transcendent character and personality formation. Carl Rogers' client-centered personality theory is an example of this approach.

3. *Humanistic Transcendent Psychological (Implicitly Philosophical) Theories of Character and Personality Formation*

These theories focus primarily on one or the other kind of humanistic transcendent psychological personality formation. They take into account, if directly relevant to their considerations, the findings of non-transcendent and pretranscendent psychological theories but do not focus on them preferentially. At times they may be more attentive than non-transcendent and pre-transcendent psychologies are, to related philosophies and mythologies. However, they are inclined to psychologize them in terms of their own theories. They do not make them as such the focus of their research or theorizing. In some way they may prepare some of their audiences indirectly for a renewed interest in their own Christian transcendent traditions. Examples of humanistic transcendent psychological theories are Carl Jung, Abraham Maslow in his later writings, the transpersonal, existentialistic, and new age psychologies, the Esalon psychologies as well as some of the Western psychological offshoots of Far- Eastern religions.

4. *The Christian Transcendent Psychological (Implicitly Philosophical, Formational-Theological) Theories of Character and Personality Development.*

These theories strive to develop a transcendent psychological view of character and personality formation that is compatible both with the foundationals of the Christian tradition and the demonstrated factual findings of psychology. Their focus is the psychological aspect of Christian transcendence. It takes into account the findings and dynamics of non-transcendent, pretranscendent, and humanistic transcendent psychologies. It pays more attention than other psychologies do to underlying philosophies, theologies, and ideologies of its own and other psychologies. While it does not necessarily focus on their elaboration, it is more inclined to meet them on their own merits than some humanistic transcendent theories do. It takes into account in a consultative manner Christian formation theology, if directly relevant to psychological research or practice. It leaves the search for and the elaboration of the findings of formation theology to experts in that field.

The psychology of Christian transcendent personality prepares people implicitly for the transpsychological theology of Christian character and personality formation. Examples of this psychological approach would be, among others, the organizers and speakers of the Steubenville convention on personalistic psychology.

5. *Christian Transpsychological Form-Traditional Character and Personality Transformation and Theory.*

This is a theory and practice which—within a formational-theological frame of reference—focuses on the conditions, dynamics, and consequences of the transformation of people's character and personality in Christ. It takes critically into account—via its pretheological servant formation science—the findings of clinical, human, social, psychological, educational, historical, literary and similar sciences, arts and disciplines if they are directly relevant to formation theology. Christian transpsychological personality theory takes into account certain insights of informational theology. The conditions are, first of all, that they are clearly and proximately relevant to cmpirical-experiential character and personality formation. A second set of conditions is that they are acceptable to the church or ecclesia as compatible with its doctrine as explained, for instance, in its authoritative catechetical theology. The presenters of this paper represent this approach, I myself being the initiator of this new discipline and of the comprehensive, systematic formation theology it serves. I call it a science insofar as it takes into account the formationally relevant contributions of the sciences and may use some aspects of their scientific methodology if compatible.

I think these distinctions are helpful in preventing confusion between different disciplines. This confusion has led to attempts to create such false "hybrids" as theo-psychology or psycho-theology. This compelled me in 1944 in Holland to establish a pretheological science of formation. From the start I viewed it as related to, yet as clearly distinguished from, my budding formation theology. Both disciplines are now coming to their full expression in the research, publication, education, and resource development work we are doing at our ecumenical Epiphany Association Center.

A hybrid like psycho-theology or theo-psychology threatens the scientific autonomy of psychology. Worse still, it endangers the integrity of Christian theology. In the Netherlands Ms. Maria Schouwenaars, the Flemish initiator of the Christian Life Schools for Young Adults, invited me to develop and teach in the town of Gemert one of the two core courses focusing on a simplified version of my formation theology. This would complement her own core course which I compared with an elementary presentation of formation science.

A serious conflict arose when some teachers with advanced degrees in psychology tried to psychologize the program too much. This threatened our formational-theological approach. Our approach complemented but was not dominated by pretheological formation science. This pretheological formation science in turn was not dominated by psychology only.

Already in the same town, Gemert, in the seminary where I taught philosophical anthropology, I had successfully pleaded with my colleagues on the faculty to allow me to teach, on the side, as it were, a course in the social sciences. I wanted to alert the seminarians not only to the dangers to the faithful of false philosophies; I strove also to make them aware of the onslaught of popularized psychologism. The pull of popular psychologism (not simply psychology) had become familiar to me both as a student and as a professor, especially while hiding with all kinds of people during the last year of the war, that is, during the infamous Dutch Hunger Winter. They represented many faith groupings.

Some among them were not related to any faith tradition that was explicitly religious. This does not mean that they did not have any tradition at all. They usually represented faith traditions that were not religious but merely ideological or psychologistic. Among all these people I met also university students, some of whom seem somewhat confused about the meaning of life and of the troubles we had to face.

As my work and its defense against psychologism grew, it came to the attention of Monsignor Giovanni Baptista Montini, at that time secretary of state in the Vatican and later Pope Paul VI. Montini called the Papal Nuncio in the Hague asking him to request confidentially that my provincial superior make me available on a full time basis for as long as it would take to develop further my formational-theological theory to serve the emerging Dutch Life Schools. At that time I called my formation theology with its corresponding formation science "godsdienstige vorming," religious faith formation; "geloofs vorming," faith formation; or "geestelijke vorming," spiritual formation. This paper will address, therefore, the formation theology and pretheology of Christian character and personality formation.

II. Theology of Formation

I purposely chose the title of this talk because it points to my initiation of formation theology in Holland. I distinguished this approach to theology from that of informational theology.

These two basic theologies complement one another. Informational theology informs us about God's Revelation; it explains this "Divine Information." It probes and elaborates its depth of meaning; it proposes to the Church possible new interpretations; it points to the basic moral, pastoral and spiritual applications and implications of this Revelation. It defines such applications and implications basically. Usually it does not go into the detailed dynamics of their empirical-experiential implementation in Christian character and personality formation. This task is left for the most part to formation theology.

My formation theology starts out from the implications of scripture, tradition, and church doctrine for empirical-experiential Christian character formation.

Church doctrine includes the insights of informational theology, which the church has approved and integrated in its sacred doctrine. Formation theology asks what in church doctrine or in doctrinally compatible statements is relevant to their implimentation in Christian character and personality formation.

III. Christian Character Formation

Christians are called by their churches to transform their lives into the life of Jesus. The core of the transformation is what Scripture calls their heart. Our Christian character corresponds with our Christian heart because of its intimate interrelation with this ground and center of our Christian existence. Our human character has to be transformed into a Christian or Christlike character. Our character as transformed by Jesus, transforms our personality as a whole into a Christian personality.

Owing to original and personal sinfulness, we are unable by ourselves alone to transform our heart or its matching character. We are called to flow humbly with the transforming power of the Holy Spirit. For it is the Holy Spirit, our Divine Formative, who gives form to Jesus' life in us.

This work of the Spirit can be clarified by introducing the concept of the pneumatic-ecclesial dimension of Christian character about which I shall say more later. This highest dimension of our Christian personhood is a divine gift. Through it the Holy Spirit in and with the Church orients our life formation.[3]

The Holy Spirit not only gives us divine guidance through this dimension. The Spirit also enables each of us to treasure within this dimension the disclosures of our life call we have received so far. Such disclosures turn this pneumatic-ecclesial dimension also into what we might call a kind of "spiritual memory bank." That is why so many spiritual masters can recall vividly some of their decisive experiences. They become interiorized formation events, memorable key life situations, able to be narrated. Consider, for example, John Wesley's conversion experience, and that of St. Augustine. Such turning points are gradually granted to us during our divinely guided formation history. Our call, as a consequence, is disclosed to us over a lifetime.

New providential situations always keep arising. We have to meet them wisely and effectively. There the contents of our pneumatic-ecclesial dimension come into play. The Spirit of Jesus helps us by bringing to our attention contents of our spiritual memory that are pertinent to the situation at hand. These facilitate our search for a grace-filled response to such situations.

In my formation theology the pneumatic-ecclesial dimension is the supreme leading dimension of our Christian life. It orients all other dimensions of our Christian personality. I defined and elaborated these subordinated dimensions as the sociohistorical, vital, functional, functional-transcendent, transcendent, and transcendent-functional dimensions. They all have to be transformed by the forming presence of Jesus in us.

In the words of the Apostle Paul:

Clearly you are a letter of Christ [not merely of secular-humanistic personality theories] which I have delivered, a letter written not with ink but by the Spirit of the living God [who works through our shared and personal pneumatic-ecclesial personality dimensions], not on tablets of stone but on tablets of flesh in the *heart* [expressed in the love-filled character or core of our ongoing Christian transformation]. This great trust in God is ours, through Christ [hence Christian character]. It is not that we are entitled of ourselves to take credit for anything [for it is *graced* character transformation]. Our sole credit is from God who has made us *ministers* [graced ministerial Christ characters] of a new covenant, a covenant not of a written law [only] but of *Spirit.* The [informational] written law kills [if we try, by sheer information only, to give wholesome form to our heart or its expression in character], but the Spirit gives life [he is the ultimate transformer of our all too human character and personality; we flow with this transformation by the Spirit in inspired interaction with the informational law]. (cf. 2 Cor. 3:3-6).

IV. Essence and Existence in Creatures

My theology of character and personality formation is based on the distinction I made between informational theology and formation theology as explained briefly earlier in this paper.

What I want to do now is to clarify this distinction somewhat more. I will do so by relating it to Thomas Aquinas' famous distinction between essence and existence.

Essence refers to *what* is, existence refers to *how* creatures give form to and receive form from their essence in and by their unfolding or existing. For example, the essence of an oak tree is present in the seed of the tree. The moment an oak tree comes into existence its formation process starts. It is a process of ongoing actualization of its essential oak form-potencies. These form potencies are hidden by its loving Creator in its essence. When the Creator, after preformation, grants to this essence existence, a long journey of disclosure and actualization of these "form potencies" is set in motion.

V. Essence and Existence in Human Creatures

Unlike other creatures human persons receive from their Father in heaven the power to decide freely how they will give form to their essence. Each one's essence was—before its existence in space and time—eternally hidden in the loving heart and mind of God, our Father. I define in my formation theology our essence as our founding life form or soul eternally preformed and bathed in divine love. Once our essence is granted existence by the same eternal love, we are made ready by the Spirit of love to hear the mysterious call of our now "existing" essence. It is a call by our Father Creator to discover and actualize over a lifetime in and with Jesus the potencies he has planted in our unique-communal essence. This continual invitation of our Father to realize our essence is our life call. Later I will distinguish this life call from the various vocations in which we may realize this call.

Both informational theology and formation theology deal with essence and existence. Both theologies are in their own way concerned with informational Revelation about what is essential and what is existential in God's plan. Existential are, among other things, the formational problems of our slowly unfolding existence in this world. These problems are about "how" to implement the call of our divinely preformed essence in our everyday Christian life or existence, especially in its core: our Christian character.

These two basic types of theology differ, however, in the preferential focus of their theological attention.

The preferred (not exclusive) focus of informational theology is: the creative unfolding of the essential truths of Christian revealed information including, when appropriate, their basic implications for Christian life formation as formulated in Church doctrine.

My formation theology's preferred (not exclusive) focus is: the creative unfolding of lived Christian existence. I focus, first of all, on those basic findings of informational theology that have been elevated to the sublime status of the doctrine of the Church or are obviously compatible with this doctrine. My formation theology attends to these doctrinal formulations points insofar as they shed light on experiential Christian character and personality formation. I have called our participation in the Spirit's transformation of our character: the formative spirituality of the Christian.

This preferential focus of my formation theology thus implies, when suitable, sufficient attention to Church-accepted outcomes of informational theology. We use that sacred information gratefully if and when it touches the empirical character and personality formation of our existence in Jesus. St. Teresa of Avila, for example, meditates in her book, *The Way of Perfection*, on the revealed prayer "Our Father" to explain its experiential implementation in Christian forms of vocal, mental, and contemplative prayer.

The grounding of my formation theology in the Christian "essence-existence structure" explains my disagreement with atheistic existentialism. According to the Christian essence-existence structure: God-given essences precede and guide their existences or, in my terminology, essential information precedes formation. According to an atheistic existentialist, like, as for instance, Jean Paul Sartre, or a contemporary like the French psychiatrist, Jacques Lacan, existence precedes essence. In their view I create my own essence or character arbitrarily in absolute freedom. To distinguish them from my Thomistic view of what is "existential," I call them "existentialistic."

In this regard at least, many secular-humanistic personality theories are not merely existential but existentialistic, often without realizing it. They see absolutized self-actualization or becoming a person, or value-free education, or a humanly conceived higher self, a client-centered existence, a non-directive personality development, or merely human archetypes as preceding our God-given essence. In their existentialistic view, through these educational and psychological processes we, by ourselves alone, are the proud inventors of our own essence. We shape our essence just as we want to. Our psychological and educational techniques precede and define what we become as persons.

To restate their error—my self-made essence replaces my divinely preformed essence in whose loving light I am called to give form to my character and personality.

Educational personality theories, which are often unwittingly existentialistic, should thus be distinguished from their counterpart, namely, personality theories that are existential in the Christian sense. Examples would be books like my own *The Vowed Life*, and *Religion and Personality*, and our co-authored *Commitment: Key to Christian Maturity.*

Experiential personality theories are in some way necessarily existential (not necessarily existentialistic). They are empirical-experiential disciplines. This means that the focus of their attention should not be, first of all, or even exclusively on the philosophical or theological study of essences. They concentrate on the empirical-experiential dynamics of the implementations of these essences in human and animal life. This is as it necessarily should be. Experiential psychological theories should not pretend, however, that their approach tells the whole story of human formation. They should not leave their audiences and readers with the impression that they do not have an essence given to them in advance of their educational and formational attempts to become a person. Any attempt to become a person without taking into account this given essence with its ethical implications will fail in the end. It is doomed to give way to rampant individualism, to say nothing of the violent subjectivism that ignores all sense of community and erodes faith.

VI. Formation Theology and Formation Science

As a young boy I met often with nephews and nieces who were not reared like I was in Christian schools and families. They were not Christians, yet I was impressed by their high moral standards and their passionate dedication to social justice. Soon I realized that they had neither received baptism nor a Christian education. Therefore, they could not grasp the fine points of Christian faith that I tried to communicate in our ardent youthful discussions. This led to my conviction that I should give shape not only to a formation theology. I should complement it with a *preChristian, pretheological* discipline or science (science mainly only insofar as it also incorporates critically appraised findings of the sciences). I wanted my formation science and discipline to make sense to those outside of our churches, who genuinely pursued a transcendent character and personality formation.

This conviction deepened later. I learned that Thomas Aquinas had thought along similar lines in the 13th Century. He created a pretheological philosophy that could make sense to the philosophical human reason, even of those who were not believers. He incorporated findings of pagan philosophers in his pretheological philosophy. They also provided him with new philosophical concepts. He could use them for the systematization of his own informational theology. Later my own Church obliged all its seminarians to study first two years of pretheological philosophy before they were allowed to begin their study of theology. By then I had already been trying to do something similar for my formation theology. I initiated my pretheological formation science that could make sense to experiential human reason. It added to my formation theology—which I had already initiated—some concepts and constructs that were helpful in its systematization.

Later experiences in the last year of World War II confirmed the necessity of such a pretheological formation science. At that time I was trying to sustain spiritually bereft people adhering to religious or ideological traditions different from my own. I could only do any good to them by appealing to their experiential reason and spirit in the light of my unfolding pretheological formation science.

This conviction was reinforced again when I functioned as a counselor in the Dutch Camp Overberg for juvenile delinquents. Later in the USA, a contract offered to our Epiphany Association by the national office of all the USA Navy chaplains took me and Dr. Muto as team leaders all over the world to conduct conferences on spiritual formation and pastoral care for over 1,100 Navy chaplains representing 86 different faith groupings. My pretheological formation science proved to be a gold mine of basic ideas on transcendent character and personality formation. They made sense to the chaplains of all of these faith and formation traditions. They all could share this God-created human base for the very possibility of transcendent life formation for all people. We showed them also how they could graft on it their own diverse theologies.

Already before this Navy experience I had found the same when I had been invited by Professor Abraham Maslow to take over for a year his courses at Brandeis University and later by Professor Grauman to teach for a year at his department in Heidelberg University in Germany. Both audiences, composed of a wide variety of faith and formation traditions, were most receptive—thanks to my use of pretheological formation science.

One could compare this with, for instance, the courses on pretheological Thomistic philosophy taught by Professor Mortimer Adler, the creator of the Great Books program. These lectures, too, were at the time well received by the ideologically mixed audiences at the University of Chicago.

VII. Theology of Christian Character and Personality Formation

For brevity's sake, I usually refer to my theology as "formation theology." At present the term formation is used with an increasing variety of specified meanings, such as pastoral, missionary, liturgical, spiritual, monastic, apostolic, religious, lay, family, world and social justice formation, to give only a few examples. Such limited applications of the term "formation" are devised for the restricted audience one has in mind. It enables experts to focus their attention on the fixed conditions of one or the other specific kind of Christian formation.

Formation theology as such focuses on the ongoing fundamental spiritual transformation of our human character and personality into a Christian character and personality. Any specific Christian formation presupposes, first of all the transformation of our human heart with its matching character in the image of God. We are called as "little words" in the Divine Word.

This basic transformation of human heart and character by the Holy Spirit should be grasped, worked out, and consistently consulted first. Only after that can one safely enter into the specific kinds of Christian formation mentioned above. There is less danger then of one's becoming totally absorbed in one or the other limited type of formation. One will be less inclined to absolutize this specific formation to such a degree that one forgets one's own and others' primordial ongoing participation in the basic transformation of human character and personality by the Holy Spirit. This inner transformation of one's heart, as nurturing one's Christ-character, is the holy ground, the fertile seedbed, the sacred source of the fruitfulness of any particular kind of formation.

Beyond this foundation, any specialized type of Christian heart and character formation should be highly appreciated. Therefore, formation theology often refers in examples to specialized types of formation just as it refers to special schools of spirituality like the Benedictine, Franciscan, Carmelite, Ignatian, or Spiritan. In dealing with such schools I like to point out, when suitable, how their specific Christian character formation is related to and should be rooted in the basic Christian character formation that is the preferred focus of formation theology. This has been expressed in our video series entitled *Becoming Spiritually Mature* and in our book *Divine Guidance: Seeking to Find and Follow the Will of God.*

VIII. Core Form, Heart and Character in Terms of Formation Theology

God knows and wills from all eternity our overall unique-communal life call. This is the *first* aspect of our call. Before the universe began, Eternal Love knew and willed the specific possibilities for goodness with which he would endow us. The Eternal Father preformed our lives as a whole in the unique-communal image of holiness he lovingly chose and willed for us from the beginning. God is like a good gardener, who selects the seeds (our life call, our providential ideal character) that will blossom in the pristine sunlight of spring (our vocations, ministries, and professions).

Anything that happens to us during our lives is an opportunity, given or allowed by God, to make us a little more aware of what he has in mind for the unique Christian transformation of our heart-nourished character and personality. Each happening contains some expression of the mysterious meaning God intends for our Christian character and personality formation as a whole. This divine character transformation gradually unfolds between our birth and baptism and our transition to eternity after the short pilgrimage God planned for us on earth. In and through the Church, the Holy Spirit, our Divine Formator, illumines this transformation of our character into a virtuous Christlike character in accordance with the beatitudes. A good reference here is Dr. Muto's book, *Blessings that Make us Be*, and the previously mentioned, *Divine Guidance.*

The second aspect of our call to give form to a holy Christian character and personality is our vocation or calling to a special state of life. Each state of life adds its own specific virtues to our ongoing Christian character formation. Does God give a special profile to our Christian character by calling us to marriage or to the single life in the world, to be a priest, a minister, or a religious?

This general call then becomes more specific also in different kinds of ministry. Each ministry may again add a specific virtue to our Christian character. For example, a professional aspect of one's vocation might be expressed in volunteer work or as a pastoral associate, while a career might involve being a mill worker, fire fighter, cab driver, teacher, business person, artist, nurse, physician, scholar, or writer.

In other words, this vocational, ministerial, and professional aspect of our call to whole-hearted character unfolding in Christ defines the providential fields of our unique-communal personality formation. In coformation with the Holy Spirit, we give form in and through these fields of life to the virtuous Christ character basically intended for us by the most Holy Trinity.

The third facet of character unfolding in Christ is the facet of particularity. It is disclosed to us by the guidance of God as hidden in the changing demands that accompany our specific vocational and professional fields. For example, a seamstress may be called to console one of her clients. A research librarian may have to handle the predicament of a homeless person seeking shelter. This third aspect of our ongoing character and personality formation by the Spirit adds particular divine inspirations to the first two. Like the former these too enrich our love-filled character and personality with characteristic virtues of specific expressiveness of our basic Christian character virtue of love for God and neighbor.

All three aspects of our Christian character formation—the general; the vocational, ministerial or professional; and the particular—come together in a harmonious way that makes a person's life personally and socially effective.

With these remarks on Christian character formation, we bring to a close this admittedly limited introduction to the complex art and discipline of formation theology. In the meantime I am working on the first draft of my *Dictionary on Formation Science and Formation Theology* to be published in due course by Epiphany Books.

NOTES

[1]

[2] By contrast, this notion is central in formation theology and its pretranscendent formation science. Empirical-experiential transcendence means in our two disciplines that the spiritual experiences of persons can go beyond or rise above their merely pretranscendent ways of life and experience. Pretranscendent experiences are referred to within our frame of reference as sociohistorical, vital, functional, and functional-transcendent measurable experiences. If they are posed as ultimate, they exclude explicitly or implicitly the very possibility of transcendent experiences being ultimate. It is the latter presupposition that we uphold in both the theory and practice of our two disciplines.

[3] Christian empirical personality theory, as initiated in 1944 in the Netherlands, prefers the term "dimensions" to that of "levels." Our life dimensions are always already present in us either potentially or actually. This notion counteracts the contention of certain secular personality theories that the higher, especially the transcendent dimensions, are either merely sublimations or symbolic expressions of the lower pretranscendent dimensions. The Christian believes that the potency for the reception of our highest possible divine dimension is present in all people as a "potentia obedientialis," our potency for reception of divine information (Revelation) and graced formation. The realization of this highest form potency and its outflow into Christian character formation is a gift of the Divine Formulator, the Holy Spirit. During our lifetime the Divine Formator gives form to the unique-communal Christ-form of our character and personality. The Holy Spirit (pneuma) forms this Christ dimension in and with the "ecclesia." Hence I use the term pneumatic-ecclesia dimension.

FOR FURTHER READING

Muto, Susan. *Blessings that Make us Be: A Formative Approach to Living the Beatitudes.* Petersham, MA: St. Bede's, 1980.

_____. *A Practical Guide for Spiritual Reading.* Revised Edition. Petersham, MA: St. Bede's, 1994.

_____. *Womanspirit.* New York: Crossroad, 1992.

_____. and Adrian van Kaam. *Commitment: Key to Christian Maturity.* Mahwah, NJ: Paulist Press, 1989.

_____. and Adrian van Kaam. *Commitment: Key to Christian Maturity.* Workbook and Guide. Mahwah, NJ: Paulist Press, 1990.

_____. and Adrian van Kaam. *Divine Guidance: Seeking to Find and Following the Will of God.* Ann Arbor, MI: Servant Publications, 1994.

_____. and Adrian van Kaam. *Harnessing Stress. A Spiritual Quest.* Mineola, NY: Resurrection Press, 1993.

_____. and Adrian van Kaam. *Healthy and Holy under Stress. A Royal Road to Wise Living*. Mineola, NY: Resurrection Press, 1993.

_____. and Adrian van Kaam. *Stress and the Search for Happiness. A New Challenge for Christian Spirituality*. Pittsburgh, PA: Epiphany Association, 1993.

_____. van Kaam, Adrian. *Art of Existential Counseling*. Wilkes-Barre, PA: Dimension Books, Inc.

_____. *Dynamics of Spiritual Self-Direction*. Pittsburgh, PA: Epiphany Books, 1992.

_____. *Existential Foundations in Psychology*. Pittsburgh, PA: Duquesne University Press, 1966.

_____. *Formative Spirituality. Volume I. Fundamental Formation*. New York, NY: Crossroad, 1983.

_____. *Formative Spirituality. Volume II. Human Formation*. New York, NY: Crossroad/Continuum, 1985.

_____. *Formative Spirituality. Volume III. Formation of the Human Heart*. New York, NY: Crossroad/Continuum, 1986.

_____. *Formative Spirituality. Volume IV. Scientific Formation*. New York, NY: Crossroad, 1987.

_____. *Formative Spirituality. Volume V. Traditional Formation*. New York, NY: Crossroad, 1992.

_____. *Formative Spirituality. Volume VI. Transcendent Formation*. New York, NY: Crossroad, 1995.

_____. *Formative Spirituality. Volume VII. Transcendent Therapy*. New York, NY: Crossroad, 1995.

_____. *Foundations for Personality Study*. Denville, NJ: Dimension Books, 1983.

_____. *Living Creatively*. Denville, NJ: Dimension Books, 1972.

_____. *Religion and Personality*. Pittsburgh, PA: Epiphany Books, 1991.

_____. *The Transcendent Self*. Pittsburgh, PA: Epiphany Books, 1991.

_____. and Susan Muto. *Formation Guide for Becoming Spiritually Mature*. Pittsburgh, PA: Epiphany Books, 1991.

_____.and Susan Muto. *The Power of Appreciation: A New Approach to Personal and Relational Healing*. New York: Crossroad, 1993.

9

Vision for a Personalist Psychology: Contributions of Paul Tournier and John Paul II[1]

Keith A. Houde

Modern personalist psychology is rooted in the personalist philosophy which emerged among a generation of French thinkers in the early 1930s. It was spearheaded by Emmanuel Mounier, founder of the revolutionary journal, *Esprit.* Mounier's personalism emerged as a philosophy of social protest directed against the "established disorder" of post-WWI France and a profound crisis threatening civilization as a whole.[2] His personalism has been described as "a pedagogy: a philosophy of service and not of domination," a philosophy of dialogue, in that his purpose was " not to provide definitive solutions, but rather to serve, to raise questions, to challenge comfortable assumptions, to act as a catalyst in the making of personal decisions."[3] His is "a philosophy of combat" characterized by "engagement" in temporal affairs and the burning issues of his time; as a committed Christian, Mounier held to a "tragic optimism" in his belief that man must bear witness to eternal spiritual truths by committing himself in contemporary temporal concerns.[4] Mounier's personalism is an "open adventure," because, like the human condition, it is flexible, "it does not lend itself to any final or definitive schematization."[5]

Mounier noted that historically, Christianity introduced the first "decisive notion of the person," a radical scandal to ancient Greek thought and sensibility.[6] Biblical anthropology and the biblical doctrine of redemption, "elucidated little by little throughout the trinitarian and Christological controversies from the second to the sixth centuries,"[7] are the foundation of any genuine and comprehensive truths about the human person.

Gordon Allport, pioneer of the modern study of personality, noted the significance of the Christian Church in the radical redefinition of the word *persona* away from earlier meanings as false, external self: "The choice of certain Church fathers who used the term to designate the Members of the Trinity markedly advanced the equivalence between *persona* and the inner (true) self."[8] Christianity also contributed to conceptions of every human person as possessing superior dignity, ideals of ethical perfection, social equality, and legal personhood.[9]

Personalism might thus represent the ancient psychology of the personal, living God whose Spirit hovered over the face of the primeval waters, who fashioned mankind out of the dust of the earth and breathed into his nostrils the breath of life, who created humanity in his own image, with the invitation to personal relationship and dialogue.

I. Tournier and Wojtyla

This paper focuses on the thinking of two Christian personalists: Paul Tournier and Karol Wojtyla/Pope John Paul II.

Both men were forged in adversity, familiar with loss and hardship. Both have shown remarkable resilience, exceptional genius, and a generous spirit.

Both have demonstrated a strong personal Christian faith, yet both acknowledge and encourage the necessary and fruitful dialogue with the secular world.

Although there are some differences in emphasis and perspective, there is a remarkable convergence and similarity of thought, affirming the Thomistic notion of the unity of truth.

Paul Tournier and John Paul II have made important contributions to a vision for a personalist theory of personality, psychopathology, and psychotherapy. Their recovery and development of the ancient biblical paradigm represents a revolution or radical paradigm shift for contemporary psychology. The personalist psychology which they describe might best be characterized as: wholistic, personal, dialogical, vital, and integrative.

1. Tournier

Paul Tournier was a Swiss physician who was born on May 12, 1898, as the son of a pious Calvinist pastor and poet in Geneva, Switzerland. His father died when he was three months of age. He survived a serious illness in infancy. He was orphaned at the age of six when his mother died of breast cancer. He was a lonely introvert as a youth, but through the friendship of significant persons in his life, he gradually recognized his intellectual ability and eventually his own worth as a person.

As a young man, Tournier worked in the repatriation of Russian and Austrian prisoners of WWI. He founded an international child welfare organization and organized a famine relief effort for Russian children. He invented calculating machines. He co-wrote and co-staged a play. He trained at the University of Geneva Medical School, graduating in 1923 to establish a general medical practice.

In 1924, Tournier married Nelly Bouvier; the couple had two sons. In 1932, he was introduced to the Oxford Group movement, a pietistic group with emphases on personal conversion and small group sharing, which made his nominally

Calvinistic Christian faith real and prompted him eventually to dedicate his life to a Christian view of medicine. (This same Oxford Group was the ultimate inspiration behind Alcoholics Anonymous.) As he listened to his patients, he became interested in the personal and spiritual meaning of their illnesses, embarking on what would become his career as a psychotherapist. When his neutral country was hemmed in by the Nazis and the Fascists during WWII, he served in the Medical Corps.

In 1940, Dr. Tournier published his first book, entitled *The Healing of Persons.* Over the course of the next 44 years he wrote a total of 21 books and numerous articles and lectured internationally.

Tournier's theological influences include Calvinism, neo-orthodoxy, evangelicalism, pietism, and ecumenism. Psychological influences include classical psychoanalysis, familiarity with classical behaviorism, and particularly the broadly phenomenological approaches of existentialism, personalism, Piagetian constructivism, and Rogerian client-centered psychology. Just as Augustine reinterpreted Plato and Aquinas reinterpreted Aristotle from a Christian perspective in order to address contemporary concerns, so has Tournier reinterpreted Freud, Jung, Adler, Rogers, and others from a Christian perspective in order to address twentieth-century concerns, pioneering what came to be known as "The Medicine of the Whole Person."

2. Wojtyla

Karol Wojtyla was born on May 18, 1920 in Wadowice, in a newly independent Poland, to a hard-working, Catholic family, who were well acquainted with suffering. His father was a commissioned quartermaster in the Polish army and his mother was a schoolteacher and seamstress. His younger sister died as an infant. His mother died of heart disease when he was nine. When he was thirteen, his older brother, a physician, died in a scarlet-fever epidemic. He and his retired father were left alone.

In spite of these tragedies, Wojtyla was an active extrovert and a brilliant student with special aptitudes for language and reasoning. On the eve of WWII, he entered the Jagiellonian University in Cracow to study Polish language and literature. As the Nazi occupation progressed, his studies went underground. He co-organized and acted in an underground theater to promote Polish nationalism. Without a work card, he was caught and deported as a slave laborer under harsh conditions in a stone quarry. He was later transferred to a chemical factory, where he gained firsthand experience of the alienation of the modern industrial worker.

In 1941, Wojtyla's father died. That winter, he was struck and run over in a vehicle accident, sustaining a near fatal skull fracture and shoulder injury. During his slow recuperation, and through the influence of a lay Catholic evangelist, he discerned a call to the celibate priesthood. He transferred to theological study, still underground. While in seminary, he risked his life by working on an underground railroad for Jewish families. He was ordained to the priesthood in 1946. He earned his doctorate in divinity through the Pontifical University of St. Thomas (or Angelicum) in Rome, and completed his habiliation at the Jagiellonian in Cracow. He served for three years as a parish priest in Poland. He successfully established a number of new parishes despite the opposition of the new Communist rulers in Poland. During these years, Father Wojtyla also wrote poetry related to his experiences as a laborer and factory worker, with philosophical and theological overtones. He returned to the Jagiellonian University to pursue philosophical studies. He wrote and lectured in social ethics at Cracow Theological Seminary and in 1956 was appointed Professor of Ethics at Lublin University. With his work, *The Acting Person,* he became one of Poland's leading philosophers and established an international reputation among phenomenologists. He created a department of patristic studies at Lublin University.

In 1958, he was appointed auxiliary bishop of Cracow. In 1960, he published *Love and Responsibility*, a pastoral and ethical treatment of human sexuality. In 1963, he was elected as Archbishop of Cracow. He played a significant role in the deliberations of the Second Vatican Council. In 1967, he became a Cardinal. In 1976, he published *Sign of Contradiction*, a series of Lenten meditations for the papal household. In 1978, he became Pope John Paul II, a consummate pastor, prolific writer, church reformer, and charismatic leader.

Theologically, Wojtyla delighted in the thought of Thomas Aquinas and the mysticism of St. John of the Cross. Philosophically, he studied Kant and Max Scheler, and attempted to reconcile existentialism and phenomenology with Christianity.[10] As Tournier reinterpreted contemporary psychologists, so did Wojtyla reinterpret and bridge Thomism with contemporary existential and phenomenological philosophy to produce a Christian personalist perspective. Wojtyla, and later John Paul II, thus pioneered what has been described as a "Christian humanism" or "Christian personalism."[11]

II. Wholistic

Personalist psychology is *wholistic* in the best sense of the term. It affirms a structure of human nature which is an incarnational whole.

Emmanuel Mounier noted that personalism respects the wholeness of each person in all of his dimensions—"material, inward, and transcendental."[12]

Paul Tournier understood human nature to be the union of *two aspects*: *natural* and *supernatural*. His entire theory of personality considers these two aspects.

The *natural* aspect of the person involved the *body* (anatomical, physiological, behavioral, economic), the *psyche* (feelings, imagination, artistic), and the *mind* (intellectual, abstract thinking, judgment, reasoning). (Tournier sometimes used either "psyche" or "mind" in isolation to refer to the entire mental/psychological domain.)

Tournier called the *supernatural* aspect of the person the *spirit* or "heart." He understood this to be the essence of center of polarization of the person, that which gives each person his or her specifically human character. It is invisible, nonspatial, and not directly accessible. It is the realm of "moral consciousness" or "conscience."

The natural and supernatural aspects of human nature are inextricably interrelated. The physical, the psychological, and the spiritual are part of one and the same *whole person*.

Karol Wojtyla (e.g., in *The Acting Person*) and later Pope John Paul II (e.g., in *Redemptor Hominis* and in the *Catechism of the Catholic Church*) presents a view of the human person as a unified being in which natural and personal (or spiritual) modes of causality are inseparably integrated: "As an incarnate spirit, that is a soul which expresses itself in a body and a body informed by an immortal spirit, man is called to love in his unified totality."[13] "The spiritual and immortal soul is the principle of unity of the human being, whereby it exists as a whole—*corpore et anima unus*—as a person."[14] He blends and transcends Thomistic faculty psychology and phenomenology toward a truly personalist vision of humanity.[15]

Natural causality or "nature" involves the "psychosomatic dynamism," immanent movements of somatic, bodily reactions (the senses) and psycho-emotive reactions (the passions). It is akin to the sensitive faculties of Thomas Aquinas.

Personal causality or the "person" is spiritual and immaterial (a spiritual soul[16]). It involves the "personal dynamism" of self-determination and self-transcendence, through intellect and will. The person is conscious, intelligent, free, and self-creative. Intellect and will have the potentiality of attaining actualized personalistic perfections of truth and self-determination, respectively.

Contrary to Thomistic anthropology, which suggests the primacy of reason over will, for John Paul, will is not merely a rational faculty. Will is the source of freedom. It allows the person to transcend nature in his actions: "he is the one who is determined by himself, and ... his decisions make him become somebody, who may be good or bad."[17] Through will, he or she may overcome both internal natural appetites and external determinants.

For Wojtyla, the essence of the person is revealed in action. Human action is informed by knowledge (and conscience) and directed by will. John Paul elsewhere speaks of the "heart" as "the depth of human consciousness" and "the inward mystery of man."[18]

Tournier integrates dichotomy and trichotomy, and John Paul expands the traditional Thomistic dichotomy of body and soul to elevate volition. (St. Francis de Sales spoke of spirit as the "fine point of the soul.") Tournier viewed cognition as part of the natural, while John Paul sees it as part of the spiritual aspect of the person. In sum, Tournier and John Paul both speak of the whole person, a physical, psychological, and spiritual reality, whose life involves sensation, cognition, emotion, volition, and action.

III. Personal

Personalist psychology is essentially *personal.* In contrast to some modern approaches, it represents a restoration of the person within personality theory. It recovers the uniqueness, value, and mystery of human personhood. It is voluntaristic, moral, and existential, in that it restores attention to the uniquely human attributes of freedom, responsibility (or conscience), and the search for meaning.

1. Mystery

Tournier's distinction between the natural *personage* and the supernatural *person* shows a profound respect for the value of the human person.

Tournier referred to the natural aspect of human nature as the *personage*, since it represented the external roles or means of expression of the person. The personage is apparent, external, observable, and measurable. It is bound up with society and learned through socialization. It associates as an isolated individual. It is comprised of automatic, mechanical physical and psychical phenomena.

Tournier identified the spirit with the *person*, as the authentic unadulterated self, the center of personal existence, who one is in reality. It is deep, hidden, elusive, and non-measurable. It is bound up with God and can be fully known only by God. It communicates inwardly as a person in relationship, through "true dialogue." It transcends both conscious and unconscious mechanisms. It is also the center of creative decision-making, and, therefore, of sin.

In the best personalist tradition, Tournier's usage of the term, "person," shows a profound respect for the dignity of human personhood not commonly found in modern psychological theories. His theory of individual differences recognized the absolute uniqueness of each human person. Although he recognized the value of typology and diagnostic nomenclature (and advanced his own broad typology of *strong* and *weak* persons[19]), he acknowledged its limitations. Tournier held that the human person is an "inexhaustible mystery," who "fits into none of our categories of thought."[20]

John Paul similarly conveys a respect and wonder for the unique value of each individual human person, who is the focus of the Church's pastoral care:

> What is in question here is man in all his truth, in his full magnitude. We are not dealing with the "abstract" man, but the real, "concrete", "historical" man. We are dealing with "each" man, for each one is included in the mystery of the Redemption ... Her solicitude is about the whole man and is focussed on him in an altogether special manner. The object of her care is man in his unique unrepeatable human reality, which keeps intact the image and likeness of God himself.[21]

This dignity and worth is related to the reality of personhood:

> The Church cannot abandon man ... Each man in all the unrepeatable reality of what he is and what he does, of his intellect and will, of his conscience and heart.

> Man who in his reality has, because he is a "person," a history of his life that is his own and, most important, a history of his soul that is his own.[22]

This respect is seen in his frequent use of personalist language and his insistence of "the priority of ethics over technology, ... the primacy of the person over things, and ... the superiority of spirit over matter."[23]

2. Freedom

According to Mounier, personalism's central affirmation is "the existence of free and creative persons"[24]

Tournier's high estimation of the importance of human *freedom* or liberty is best summarized in his oft-repeated refrain: "To live is to choose."[25] Human choice gives direction to life: "It is through the making of successive and resolute choices that man traces out his life."[26] The capacity for volition demonstrates the supernatural character of the person. Although human freedom is an incarnate freedom, in choosing the person transcends natural determinism. Like Kierkegaard, Tournier emphasizes the primacy of volition over reason.

John Paul significantly influenced the Second Vatican Council in its consideration of human freedom, particularly religious freedom. He cites this passage repeatedly: "Genuine freedom is an outstanding manifestation of the divine image in man."[27] It contributes to human dignity: "Christ and ... his Apostles ... preserved ... a deep esteem for man, for his intellect, his will, his conscience and his freedom. Thus the human person's dignity itself becomes part of the content of that proclamation."[28] John Paul acknowledged that human freedom is incarnate and not absolute. He recognized that the behavioral sciences "have rightly drawn attention to the many kinds of psychological and social conditioning which influence the exercise of human freedom."[29] Although he notes that volition is not bound by reason, it can never be authentically exercised apart from the demands of the moral conscience.

3. Responsibility

For Tournier, freedom is inevitably related to *responsibility*: "I have often remarked that to live is to choose, that man is truly man only insofar as he chooses his ends and courageously shoulders the responsibility for his choices."[30] Responsibility implies a *moral conscience*, which Tournier understands as the interior God-given sense of what conforms to love and justice: "We believe that men are free and responsible in their behavior. Moment by moment they have a choice between obedience and disobedience to God, to the good, to the truth."[31] Conscience is inescapable and indestructible:

> There is no man living who can escape the inner voice which accuses him of violating the order of nature in using his instinct contrary to its purpose—for solitary pleasure instead of for a shared pleasure which generates community. A man can be moved to repress the voice of his conscience, but he cannot be freed from it.[32]

Choice and responsibility suggest the reality of sin and guilt. According to Tournier, ultimate moral responsibility for behavior is based upon one's degree of personal liberty.

John Paul also recognizes the importance of considering "the role of conscience in man's moral development" and its relation to responsibility: "The truth about moral good, as that truth is declared in the law of reason, is practically and concretely recognized by the judgment of conscience, which leads one to take responsibility for the good or the evil one has done."[33] Moral conscience is located "in the 'heart' of the person"[34] It is "an act of a person's intelligence, the function of which is to apply the universal knowledge of the good in a specific situation and thus to express a judgment about the right conduct to be chosen here and now."[35] It is "the interior dialog of man with himself" and "also a dialog of man with God, the author of the law, the primordial image and final end of man."[36] John Paul cites Vatican II's definition of conscience as "the sanctuary of man, where he is alone with God whose voice echoes within him."[37]

John Paul notes the importance of the formation of conscience, distinguishing between "good conscience" and "erroneous conscience."[38] For the attainment and preservation of human dignity, conscience is essentially grounded in objective truth: "Man's freedom is not negated by his obedience to the divine law; indeed, only through this obedience does it abide in truth and conform to human dignity."[39] When ignored, humanity becomes dehumanized. This truth is knowable. It is found most completely in the person of Jesus Christ:

> Jesus Christ meets the man of every age, including our own with the same words: "You will know the truth, and the truth will make you free." These words contain both a fundamental requirement and a warning: the requirement of an honest relationship with regard to truth as a condition for authentic freedom, and the warning to avoid every kind of illusory freedom, every superficial unilateral freedom, every freedom that fails to enter into the whole truth about man and the world. Today also, even after two thousand years, we see Christ as the one who brings man freedom based on truth, frees man from what curtails, diminishes and as it were breaks off this freedom at its root, in man's soul, his heart and his conscience.[40]

Human action is informed by conscience and directed by will. The essence and worth of the person is revealed through his or her acts: "Although being is prior to action, and thus the person and his value is prior to and more fundamental than the value of the action, it is in actions that the person manifests himself—a fact we have been stressing from the first."[41] "The `personalistic' value of the human action—that is, the personal value, is a special and probably the most fundamental manifestation of the *worth* of the person himself."[42] Human action has personalistic value if it promotes transcendence and integration:

> The personalistic value ... inheres in the performance itself of the action by the person, in the very fact that man acts in a manner appropriate to him, that self-determination thus authentically inheres in the nature of his acting and the transcendence of the person is realized through his acting. This ... leads to integration in both the somatic and the psychical sphere of man.[43]

4. Meaning

Tournier recognized the human person's inevitable search for existential meaning. This is related to his or her longing for God. In addition to studying the material and psychological causes of an event, the person "will also try to find its meaning—what God is trying to say to him through it, where God wishes to lead him."[44]

John Paul also acknowledged the validity of existential questions, citing Vatican II:

> What is man? What is the meaning and purpose of our life? What is good and what is sin? What origin and purpose do sufferings have? What is the way to attain true happiness? What are death, judgment and retribution after death? Lastly, what is that final, unutterable mystery which embraces our lives and from which we take our origin and towards which we tend?[45]

For him, these questions are ultimately answered in Christ: "In Christ and through Christ man has acquired full awareness of his dignity, of the heights to which he is raised, of the surpassing worth of his own humanity, and of the meaning of his existence."[46]

IV. Dialogical

Personalist psychology is *dialogical*, in that it understands that the human person is essentially a whole person in relationship.

Tournier noted that "there are then two parallel dialogues, two personal contacts—one with another person, the other with God."[47] He expanded upon this to identify the person's important relationships with God, others, and the world:

> Man, then, is to be seen in relation and interaction with himself and others, with the world and with God. Society, the world, and God are his external place; his body, mind, and spirit are his internal place.[48]

John Paul similarly wrote of the human person's vocations to "life with God" and "communion with his neighbor."[49] He noted the person's "identity as a spiritual and bodily being in relationship with God, with his neighbor and with the material world."[50]

1. God

Tournier recognized the human person's need for a personal relationship with God: "All men are looking, in fact, for God's support. Some are quite aware of the fact; in others it is only a vague nostalgic longing."[51]

John Paul noted the teleological orientation of the moral life toward God, as the supreme good and ultimate end of man.[52] He noted the spiritual hunger of the person which satisfies existential longings,

> that never-ending restlessness referred to in the words of St. Augustine: "You made us for Yourself, Lord, and our heart is restless until it rests in You." In this creative restlessness beats and pulsates what is most deeply human—the search for truth, the insatiable need for the good, hunger for freedom, nostalgia for the beautiful, and the voice of conscience."[53]

2. Others

In the person's social relationship with others, Tournier distinguished between "causal relationships" (according to an objective, mechanistic attitude) and "mystical relationships between persons" (according to a subjective, spiritual attitude).[54] The latter represents authentic dialogue and interpersonal communion.

Tournier offers a challenging discussion that the unique gifts of men (e.g., rationality, objective relationships) and women (e.g., affectivity, personal relationships) are complementary and that any false opposition between them must be overcome in order to reestablish a balance in modern civilization.[55] He speaks of marriage as "a great school of the person, through the level of personal commitment it entails and the exacting quality of the dialogue it demands."[56] He noted the importance of the family in the development of the person.

John Paul spoke of the person's "social nature" as a potentiality which may be actualized or perfected in the personalistic value of "participation." Participation is the capacity of the person to achieve individual self-fulfillment while simultaneously contributing toward the common good, avoiding non-participative extremes of individualism and totalism.[57] In this way can one attain "true communion of persons."[58]

John Paul recognized the full range of human social relationships:

> Man in the full truth of his existence, of his personal being and also of his community and social being—in the sphere of his own family, in the sphere of society and very diverse contexts, in the sphere of his own nation or people (perhaps still only that of his clan or tribe), and in the sphere of the whole of mankind—this man is the primary route that the Church must travel in fulfilling her mission ... [59]

He wrote on the complementary gifts and roles of women and men.[60] He presented a profound Christian personalist vision of marriage and family life, citing Vatican II's description of the family as "a school of deeper humanity."[61] It is interesting to note that a respected secular journal of family therapy has recognized the important contribution of John Paul's thinking to the field.[62]

3. World

Tournier recognized the significance of a person's situation or environment: "The medicine of the person considers man *in situ*, in his relationship with his environment."[63] He noted the existential significance of one's personal context: "Men and women have a vital need of a place."[64]

John Paul, the outdoorsman and sportsman, noted that "We cannot say we love the land and then take steps to destroy it."[65]

V. Vital

Personalist psychology is *vital*. It is dynamic and existential (in accord with a Semitic approach vs. a more static and scholastic Hellenistic approach) in that it represents a recovery of the human person who is alive and in motion. Within the context of the personalist conception of the struggle between *personalization* ("the living activity of self-creation, of communication and of attachment, that grasps and knows itself, in the act") and *depersonalization*, the person emerges in the "human struggle to humanize humanity."[66] Personalist psychology offers its unique perspective to discussions of human motivation, development, healthy personality, and psychopathology.

1. Personalization

The personalist understanding of personalization involves everything that contributes toward the development of healthy persons. It might be understood to involve vitality, the rhythm of life, the seasons of life, and virtuous life.

a. Vitality. Tournier speaks in positive terms of the "adventure of living."[67] He recognized a vital instinct at the core of human personality, a composite of cooperating (or competing) power and love needs, given by God (Compare 2 Tim. 1:7 "For God did not give us a spirit of timidity but a spirit of power and love and self-control."). These motives represent a personalist reinterpretation of Freud's aggressive and sexual instincts, respectively.

In a similar vein, John Paul speaks repeatedly of the human aspirations of "life and love."[68]

b. Power. For Tournier, the power need involved dominion ("have dominion" Gn. 1:28b), aggression (the aggressive instinct), the need for meaningful work (adventure, discovery, creativity), and self-preservation ("whoever would save his life" Mk. 8:35a).

John Paul acknowledged the person's freedom and responsibility for "the exercise of dominion over the world."[69] He recognized that this same gift of power may be used for good or evil: "Why is it that the power given to man from the beginning by which he was to subdue the earth turns against himself, producing an understandable state of disquiet, of conscious or unconscious fear and of menace ... ?"[70]

c. Love. Tournier described the love need as related to generativity ("Be fruitful and multiply" Gn. 1:28a), sexuality (sexual instinct), the need for personal relationship (support/security, understanding, trust), and self-sacrifice ("whoever loses his life" Mk. 8:35b).

John Paul noted the necessity of love for the human person: "Man cannot live without love. He remains a being that is incomprehensible for himself, his life is senseless, if love is not revealed to him, if he does not encounter love, if he does not experience it and make it his own, if he does not participate intimately in it."[71] He notes that the way of perfection involves self-sacrificial love: "Perfection demands that maturity in self-giving to which human freedom is called."[72]

We might note here that Mounier spoke of the interpersonal communion of love as the human person's surest certainty: "I love, therefore I am; therefore being is, and life has value (is worth the pain of living). Love does not reassure me simply as a state of being in which I find myself, for it gives me to someone else."[73] The person is more than his life; his highest dignity is exercised in a profound choice of self-denial and self-sacrificial love: "This *surpassing of the self* ... is the passion for life at any price, even at the cost of the values that give life its meaning. To accept suffering and death in order not to betray human values—this or any other heroic sacrifice is, on the contrary, the supreme act of the person."[74]

d. Rhythm of Life. Mounier described personal life as a rhythmic "alternation of self-affirmation and self-denial."[75] The person needs to participate in the development of both personal identity and interpersonal relationships.

Parallel to the needs for power and love, Tournier's developmental theory involves two movements or stages in the formation of the person: *natural enrichment* and *supernatural relinquishment.* These movements correspond to "two gospels" of self-fulfillment and renunciation, respectively.

e. Natural enrichment. Natural enrichment is the first developmental movement of self-fulfillment and self-assertion. It is the time for receiving and for the ascent and expansion of the individual. Tournier recognized that persons become *individuals* when they are able to see themselves as separate and distinct from others, as when a child recognizes that he or she has the power to keep a secret.

f. Supernatural relinquishment. Supernatural relinquishment is the second developmental movement of renunciation and self-denial. It is the time of giving and self-sacrifice of the person. Tournier believed that an individuals did not become *persons* until they were able to share personal secrets with another person, and ultimately with God.[76]

g. Rhythm of life. Tournier spoke of an inherent rhythm of life, a constant successive and complementary alternation between natural enrichment and supernatural relinquishment. He highlighted four important factors in human development: love, suffering, identification (with role models), and adaptation.

John Paul noted the importance of both the natural and supernatural development of the child within the family: "The Christian family, in fact, is the first community called to announce the Gospel to the human person during growth and to bring him or her, through a progressive education and catechesis to full human and Christian maturity."[77] He notes the personalistic value of both individual interest/self-fulfillment and active participation for the common good.[78]

h. Seasons of Life. Tournier's and John Paul's conceptualizations of individual human development are both rooted in an essentially Augustinian view of "the ages of man" through salvation history. This path of redemption involves four general stages: creation in the image of God and original innocence, the Fall and original sin, the opportunity for salvation and sanctification through Jesus Christ, and eternal life or perdition.

Within this context, Tournier spoke of the seasons of life, conceptualizing the life span as comprised of four major phases: childhood, adulthood, old age, and death. John Paul also advocated developmental sensitivity, noting that "*the church accompanies the Christian family on its journey through life* ... The church's pastoral action ... must follow the family, accompanying it step by step in the different stages of its formation and development."[79]

Childhood (spring), the age of idealism, is governed by the law of passive submission. For Tournier, childhood began with conception, included childhood proper, as well as adolescence. John Paul also spoke of the human person's "personal history," which begins "from the first moment of his existence on earth, from the moment of his conception and birth."[80] The personal character of human relationships is evident in the primordial gaze between mother and child immediately after birth. John Paul also pays particular attention to the formation of children and youth or young adults.[81]

Adulthood (summer), the season of dynamism, is governed by the law of action. Its criterion is "doing" and "having."

Old age (autumn), the season of wisdom, is governed by the law of contemplation. Its criterion is "being."

Death (winter) is the season of (potential) resurrection and eternal life.

Like the dynamic developmental theorists before him, Tournier believed that successful resolution of the crisis proper to one age allows a person to move on to the next age. Acceptance of one's age leads to life, while rejection of one's age leads to premature aging.

Tournier and John Paul thus expand the extremes of the life span in both directions, from conception to eternal life, which is beyond what psychologists normally consider. John Paul could draw from the *Catechism of the Catholic Church*, which states: "Endowed with a spiritual soul, with intellect and with free will, the human person is from his very conception ordered to God and destined for eternal beatitude."[82]

i. Virtuous Life. "True strength" is Tournier's term for the healthy personality. True strength is supernatural strength which comes from a personal relationship with God. True strength is Tournier's best representation of the ideal person, perfectly exemplified in Jesus Christ. It is the result of religious salvation and reversal. True strength transcends natural strong and weak reactions and transforms human nature. True strength balances "faith" and "realism," where persons abandon their fears to God and are able to accept the truth about themselves as they are. True strength involves "true morality," a balance between authority and liberty. It involves a balance between "self-assertion" and "self-denial." True strength represents the harmony of power and love and the reversal of the fundamental inner conflict (discussed below).

Wojtyla speaks of *integration* as the fruit of self-transcendence. It involves the unified relationship and harmony between the personal dynamisms of knowledge and will and the psychosomatic dynamisms of bodily reaction and emotion.[83] The Catholic tradition of John Paul II has a long history of extolling character formation and the virtuous life. The *Catechism of the Catholic Church* is replete with teaching on the beatitudes, the human or cardinal virtues (prudence, justice, fortitude, and temperance), the theological virtues (faith, hope, and charity), the gifts of the Holy Spirit (wisdom, understanding, counsel, fortitude, knowledge, piety, and fear of the Lord), and the fruits of the Holy Spirit (charity, joy, peace, patience, kindness, goodness, generosity, gentleness, faithfulness, modesty, self-control, chastity).[84] The *Catechism* defines human virtues and the virtuous life as:

> firm attitudes, stable dispositions, habitual perfections of intellect and will that govern our actions, order our passions, and guide our conduct according to reason and faith. They make possible ease, self-mastery, and joy in leading a morally good life. The virtuous man is he who freely practices the good.[85]

2. Depersonalization

Modern psychiatry speaks of "depersonalization" as "an alteration in the perception or experience of the self" which frequently results from extreme psychological trauma.[86] Personalists use the term in a broader sense to refer to all of the forces within and outside of the person which prevent healthy personal development and which contribute to psychopathology. Wojtyla spoke of "disintegration" as personal inability to possess and govern oneself.[87]

For Tournier, psychopathology originates in the interaction between the natural (or scientific) and spiritual factors of an illness. This interaction is not linear or simplistic, but is rather a complex interaction, which differs in different situations for different people. Tournier's theory of psychopathology thus allows the personalist psychologist to grasp the *diagnostic synthesis* of a person's illness, to find the diagnosis which fits all of the symptoms, both natural and spiritual.

a. Natural. The natural sources of depersonalization are external to the person or on the surface of personality. They include the physical, psychological (recall Tournier's notion of personage), and sociocultural influences.

For Tournier, the natural basis of psychopathology begins with the *inborn psychosomatic temperament*. As a person develops through the life span, he or she encounters various *accidental psychological traumas.* Tournier identified two particular types of traumas which have a significant impact: parental discord and negative education. The child has an inherent need for parental unity which is disrupted in the face of significant "parental discord." "Negative education" crushes a child's self-confidence by blocking the spontaneous force of life within him. It may be engendered by even the best parents and teachers. It preaches a moralism based upon social convention rather than personal conviction. Religious moralism within Christian churches may be particularly disturbing and may lead to a form of "ecclesiogenic neurosis." All of this occurs within what Tournier calls "this impersonal world" and what John Paul refers to as "a society that is running the risk of becoming more and more depersonalized and standardized and therefore inhuman and dehumanizing."[88]

According to Tournier, accidental psychological traumas may result in *pathogenic psychological complexes,* an interaction of "false ideas" and "disturbed affectivity." False ideas may become entrenched in a pattern of obsessive thinking. Tournier identified three major forms of disturbed affectivity: false guilt, violence (or anger), and unhealthy fears. False guilt is a neurotic, infantile, legalistic, social guilt. Unhealthy fears include a wide range of phobias. Psychological complexes may become entrenched in a *mode of life* or lifestyle. Pathology may eventually be expressed in either a strong or a weak *reaction,* generally based upon a temperamental predisposition. *Weak reactions* tend toward false guilt and repressed aggressiveness. *Strong reactions* tend toward repressed guilt and violence.

b. Spiritual. The spiritual sources of depersonalization arise primarily from within the person, at the most deeply personal level (recall Tournier on the "person"). They involve the meaning and purpose of an illness. Mounier observed that the human person is "beset by internal disharmonies."[89]

According to Tournier, the spiritual root of human psychopathology incorporates the relationship between sin or true weakness, true guilt, the fundamental inner conflict, spiritual complexes, and universal existential fear. The dynamics of the spiritual diagnosis are perhaps best expressed in the following passage:

> The truth is that human beings are much more alike than they think. What is different is the external mask, sparkling or disagreeable, their outward reaction, strong or weak. These appearances, however, hide an identical inner personality. The external mask, the outward reaction, deceive everybody, the strong as well as the weak. All men, in fact, are weak. All are weak because all are afraid. They are all afraid of being trampled underfoot. They are all afraid of their inner weakness being discovered. They all have secret faults; they all have a bad conscience on account of certain acts which they would like to keep covered up. They are all afraid of other men and of God, of themselves, of life and of death.[90]

The ultimate spiritual diagnosis of personal problems is *true weakness* or *sin.* This universal weakness is transmitted from generation to generation. It is rooted in *true guilt*—genuine spiritual guilt before God, adult or moral guilt. Tournier did not automatically equate sin with psychopathology, but recognized it as a foundational influence.

Sin is the root of the *fundamental inner conflict* between the *vital instinct* on the one hand, and the *moral conscience*, on the other. Sin cripples human liberty and clouds its ability to make choices between the vital instinct and the moral conscience which are in accord with God's will. Tournier also described this conflict as the conflict between two aspects of the vital instinct, *power* and *love* (as described previously). It is much easier for weak human beings to lust for power than to choose to deny self and love another person. A similar conflict is described in Vatican II's *Gaudium et Spes* (*Pastoral Constitution on the Church in the Modern World*), which was influenced by the then Karol Cardinal Wojtyla: "Man is divided in himself. As a result, the whole life of men, both individual and social, shows itself to be a struggle, and a dramatic one, between good and evil, between light and darkness."[91]

According to Tournier, this fundamental inner conflict results in certain existential or *spiritual complexes,* such as the "complex of rootlessness" and the "Paradise Lost" complex. The *"Paradise Lost" complex* is described as a universal "nostalgia for perfection" and "homesickness for Paradise."[92] It highlights the gap between who we are and who we were meant to be, as well as the discrepancy between the personage and the person. Again, *Gaudium et Spes* notes

> the deeper dichotomy that is in man himself. He is the meeting point of many conflicting forces. In his condition as a created being he is subject to a thousand shortcomings, but feels untrammeled in his inclinations and destined for a higher form of life. Torn by a welter of anxieties he is compelled to choose between them and repudiate some among them. Worse still, feeble and sinful as he is, he often does the very thing he hates and does not do what he wants. And so he feels himself divided, and the result is a host of discords in social life.[93]

The fundamental inner conflict also results in an *existential fear* of God, damnation, social judgment, life, and death.

VI. Integrative

Personalist psychology is an *integrative* or synthesized psychology of the living, whole person in relationship. It proposes a psychotherapy of the person which acknowledges the contributions of both psychology and religion. It recognizes a unity of healing which requires a collaborative team in the healing process. It promotes the parallel dialogues of psychotherapy and soul-healing.

Tournier recognized *two movements* in the healing of persons: *psychology* and *religion*. These two movements parallel the developmental movements of enrichment and relinquishment. Tournier described these movements as follows:

> There are, then, in fact, two movements—movements which are successive and complementary. We shall see that they correspond to the gospels of which I have spoken, that of self-fulfilment and that of renunciation, that of psychology and that of religion. They correspond, in general terms, to the respective tasks of the doctor and the psychologist on the one hand, and those of the priest and the pastor on the other. The doctor seeks to give to the deprived the thing they lack—health, strength, a place, integration in a social environment. The minister of religion sounds God's call to detachment from all earthly possessions, a call which he addresses to those who have them in abundance.[94]

1. Psychology

Psychology is the therapeutic movement of restoring what was never received in development or what was subsequently lost. It is concerned with physical, psychological, social, and environmental health. *Psychological salvation* facilitates the move from a weak reaction to a strong reaction, from neurosis to relative psychological health. Psychological salvation removes false guilt. It encourages appropriate self-assertion.

2. Religion

Religion represents the second therapeutic movement, the Christian "cure of souls," the move toward a freely chosen personal abandonment and love of God and others. *Religious salvation* offers a qualitatively different existence than psychological salvation. It is dependent upon divine grace, in dialogue with human response. Tournier's writings suggest a basic progression in the process of religious salvation from convicting grace to faith and repentance to saving grace to reversal and true strength. God's forgiveness provides the solution to true guilt.

3. Unity of Healing

Tournier recognized the complementarity and order of the two movements of psychology and religion: The first movement of self-assertion necessarily precedes and prepares the way for the second movement of self-denial. He also noted a rhythmic alternation between these movements of receiving and giving.

Tournier regarded the transition from psychotherapy to the cure of souls as inevitable. The ultimate value of technical psychology lies in its preparation for the cure of souls. John Paul acknowledged the benefits of the psychological sciences in pastoral care: "Considerable help can be given to families by lay specialists (doctors, lawyers, psychologists, social workers, consultants, etc.) who either as individuals or as members of various associations and undertakings offer their contribution of enlightenment, advice, orientation and support."[95]

It is often difficult to discern the boundaries between psychotherapy and soul-healing. Personalist psychology thus requires a collaborative and multidisciplinary therapeutic team for the healing of persons.

Ultimately, all healing is limited. Just as sin does not equal disease, salvation does not equal healing in a simplistic manner.

4. Psychotherapy: Dialogue with Persons

Tournier recognized the validity and value of an eclectic or multimodal approach which utilizes scientific/technical treatments of medicine (surgery, medication, etc.), psychodynamic therapy (discovery of truth and expression of emotion), cognitive therapy (healthy suggestion and preventive education), behavioral therapy (constructive activity and balanced lifestyle), and a more personal social atmosphere or environment ("hospital of the person," "clinic of the person").

Personalist psychotherapy moves beyond merely technical approaches in its personalist attitude which seeks the comprehension of the person and the development of persons. For Tournier, the essence of psychotherapy is *dialogue* between persons:

> The essence of psychotherapy is the open-hearted talk, the expression of one's thoughts in the confidence of being really listened to and understood, entry into personal communication and receiving a response—in short, the living experience of dialogue. (*Place For You*, 106).

Dialogue is the basis of all therapeutic change and the distinguishing feature of Tournier's psychotherapy. Tournier used other terms to describe the reality of dialogue: "true fellowship," "personal contact," "genuine encounter," "genuine meeting," "communion," and "transparency." (*Strong and Weak*, 172; *Listening Ear*, 10-11, 35-37; *Meaning of Persons*, 136). Dialogue is not intellectual discussion or religious exhortation. True inner dialogue between persons transcends false external dialogue between personages. Personal Socratic dialogue surpasses the technical Freudian monologue. Dialogue is true personal relationship, the "I-thou" relationship described by Martin Buber. The experience of dialogue in therapy generalizes to other interpersonal relationships. Personal dialogue is rare, yet is a foretaste of what life should be. Personal dialogue inevitably leads to questions of existential meaning.

The dialogue with persons has three primary characteristics: reciprocity, listening for understanding, and nonjudgmental acceptance. These three qualities are remarkably similar to Carl Rogers' three characteristics of an effective helping relationship: congruence or genuineness, accurate empathic understanding, and unconditional positive regard. It is worth noting that Tournier began identifying these characteristics as early as 1948, at least contemporaneous with and perhaps preceding Rogers.

Reciprocity is the foundation of the therapeutic relationship. It is synonymous with the moral equality of persons. Reciprocity involves the recognition of personal relationship and mutual weakness on the part of doctor and patient, while necessarily maintaining a certain amount of their respective roles. It involves *self-revelation* or self-disclosure on the part of the doctor. Self-revelation includes the practice of "concrete witness," doctor "confession," and the "phenomenon of communication" of virtue (social modeling).

Listening for understanding is also essential to therapy. The understanding which arises from dialogue is a mutual understanding, wherein the patient simultaneously is understood and understands self. This mutual understanding is the occasion of truth and personal transformation. Listening for understanding also involves *interest* or concern, and the possible use of "Socratic questioning." Listening for understanding also requires *patience* and a respect for silence in therapy.

Nonjudgmental acceptance is also important to the therapeutic relationship. He identified non-judgment as the sign of grace within psychotherapy. He recognized, however, the human inevitability of judging, for example, as implied with any diagnosis. Tournier believed that judgment was destructive. Nonjudgmental acceptance involves *respect*, which requires confidentiality, respect of the patient's personal freedom, and implies a non-directive approach in therapy. Nonjudgmental acceptance also involves *support* or love, which involves encouragement, even in the face of chronic illness.

5. Soul-Healing: Dialogue with God

The psychotherapist's involvement in the patient's *dialogue with God* is the practice of "soul-healing" proper. Human persons inevitably seek to be in communion with God, sometimes without being aware of it. Existential questions and issues may initiate the dialogue with God. The dialogue with persons already anticipates the dialogue with God. The second inner dialogue with God often takes place in the presence of another person, frequently the person of the psychotherapist. The dialogue with God establishes a personal relationship in which each person is called by name.

John Paul II acknowledges the importance of pastoral dialogue:

> The church in fact uses the method of dialogue in order the better to lead people—both those who through baptism and the profession of faith acknowledge their membership of the Christian community and also those who are outside—to conversion and repentance, along the path of a profound renewal of their own consciences and lives in the light of the mystery of the redemption and salvation accomplished by Christ and entrusted to the ministry of his church. Authentic dialogue, therefore, is aimed above all at the rebirth of individuals through interior conversion and repentance, but always with profound respect for consciences and with patience at the step-by-step pace indispensable for modern conditions.[96]

Soul-healing incorporates the spiritual resources of prayerful meditation, bible reading, the confession of sin, and church fellowship.

Prayerful meditation is an important component in the dialogue with God and the practice of "soul-healing." Tournier distinguished between prayer as a monologue and prayer as a dialogue. He strongly advocated prayer as a dialogue between God and the human person. He identified "silent meditation" with dialogue prayer. He advocated the practice of "written meditation" to serve as a bridge between prayer and everyday life. Prayerful meditation is the place where a person receives God's guidance for their life. Tournier highlighted the need for the psychotherapist's daily personal prayer. He encouraged the personal prayer of the patient in preparation for therapy. He recognized the value of common prayer with the patient within the therapy session (describing this common silent meditation as "silentiotherapy"). He also described a place for the doctor's prayer for the patient within the therapy session. He recognized the power of prayer and identified physical, psychological, personal/spiritual, and social effects of prayer.

Bible reading and study is valuable in the dialogue with God. The bible is a record of dialogues between God and human persons, rather than a simplistic and legalistic prescription. It is the primary source for catechesis. It is a resource for comfort in affliction. Tournier incorporated bible reading into his practice of the cure of souls.

Confession of sin contributes toward the healing of persons. Patient confession to God in the presence of the psychotherapist greatly facilitates healing. Tournier distinguished between "true confession" and "half confessions." He distinguished between "religious (or sacramental) confession" and "psychological (or therapeutic) confession."

Confession involves *absolution* from God. Tournier strongly recommended "sacramental absolution" for persons from confessional traditions, however, he also advocated the practice of "lay absolution" with non-Christians or with Christians from non-confessional traditions. He believed that confession and absolution have remarkable psychological effects.

John Paul II exhorts clergy to the faithful and diligent ministry of the *sacrament of reconciliation:*

> This is undoubtedly the most difficult and sensitive, the most exhausting and demanding ministry of the priest, but also one of the most beautiful and consoling ... Before the consciences of the faithful, who open up to him with a mixture of fear and trust, the confessor is called to a lofty task which is one of service and penance and human reconciliation. It is a task of learning the weaknesses and falls of those faithful people, assessing their desire for renewal and their efforts to achieve it, discerning the action of the Holy Spirit in their hearts, imparting to them a forgiveness which God alone can grant, "celebrating" their reconciliation with the Father, portrayed in the parable of the prodigal son, reinstating these redeemed sinners in the ecclesial community with their brothers and sisters, and paternally admonishing these penitents with a firm, encouraging and friendly "Do not sin again."[97]

Forgiveness of others is a primary interpersonal effect of confession and absolution. Tournier distinguished between "true forgiveness" and "false forgiveness," the former resulting from grace, and the latter related to repressed aggressiveness.

Church fellowship was also regarded by Tournier as significant in the dialogue with God and the cure of souls. The dialogue with persons in church fellowship may transform a monologue with self into a dialogue with God. Tournier accorded great value to the Church as a center of worship, orthodox Christian teaching, and sacramental life. Tournier believed that dialogue counseling lends itself more to individual therapy than group therapy, yet he recognized the emergence of small evangelistic communities characterized by dialogical relationships. These charismatic communities help to build true fellowship and the civilization of the person. Tournier recognized the merit of various Christianity-based support group therapies, such as the Blue Cross, the Salvation Army, Alcoholics Anonymous, and other Twelve Step programs.

John Paul II speaks of the communal and personalist benefits of the *sacrament of Eucharist*::

> *The authentic sense of the Eucharist becomes of itself the school of active love for neighbor.* We know that this is the true and full order of love that the Lord has taught us: "By this love you have for one another, everyone will know that you are my disciples." The Eucharist educates us to this love in a deeper way; it shows us, in fact, what value each person, our brother or sister, has in God's eyes, if Christ offers Himself equally to each one, under the species of bread and wine. If our Eucharistic worship is authentic, it must make us grow in awareness of the dignity of each person. The awareness of that dignity becomes the *deepest motive of our relationship with our neighbor.*[98]

VII. A Personalist Agenda

Paul Tournier and John Paul II offer us a coherent vision for a personalist psychology which is wholistic, personal, dialogical, vital, and integrative. A psychotherapist and a pastor, a psychiatrist and a pope present a deeper, broader, richer, and truer vision of humanity. They provide valuable insight into "the nature and tasks of a personalist psychology," as well as inspiration for future directions.

Toward the development of a personalist psychology, much work remains to be done, theoretically and practically. To engage in this task in a cooperative, coordinated fashion, many hearts, minds, and hands are needed. Personalist-friendly psychology and philosophy programs (such as the Franciscan University of Steubenville, and Duquesne's Institute of Formative Spirituality) and organizations of personalist psychologists and philosophers (such as the Institute for Personalist Psychology, the Christian Association for Psychological Studies, and the American Catholic Philosophical Association), in dialogue with clients and other professionals, need to better coordinate individual efforts toward the development of a comprehensive personalist theory of personality, psychopathology, and psychotherapy. The work of Tournier, John Paul II, and other Christian personalists needs to be systematized, refined, integrated, and enhanced to meet the practical needs of the psychotherapist and pastor and to contribute toward the healing of persons and the development of a civilization of the person.

A tentative personalist research agenda is proposed. For research methodology, an expanded empiricism which utilizes experimental, clinical, experiential, and bibliographic data (vs. pure natural scientific empiricism or positivism) is suggested.

1. Philosophical Psychology

A systematic and historical study of philosophical psychology and theological anthropology might be undertaken, considering the contributions of the Bible, Midrash, Mishnah, patristics (especially Augustine, and including the Eastern fathers), scholastics (especially Aquinas), reformers (especially Luther, Calvin, and Wesley), modern theological anthropologies (e.g., Adrienne von Speyer, Pope John Paul II), as well as historical and contemporary Christian personality theories.[99]

2. Psychology of Personhood

Personalist psychology would do well to engage in a study of the concept of personhood and the unfathomable mystery of the human person. A personalist developmental psychology could recognize both existential personhood given at conception and the development of mature personhood through the life span (e.g., development of both personal identity and self-sacrifice). Prenatal and life-after-death phenomena would also be worthy of investigation.[100]

3. Psychology of Volition

In a revival of the determinism-freedom debate, personalist psychology should be at the forefront of volition studies.[101]

4. Psychology of Conscience

Personalist psychology is in a prime position to investigate the human conscience or moral sense. This might include studies of true and false guilt. A personalist theory of moral development, conscience formation, and moral education holds promise.[102]

5. Psychology of Dialogue

Personalist psychology could study the relationship between therapeutic dialogue and positive behavioral change. In this era of managed care (and limited number of sessions), perhaps it could provide evidence of the importance of the quality of a personalist attitude in the therapy relationship. It could contribute a specifically personalist theory of marriage and family therapy, perhaps looking at such areas as sexuality, fatherhood, and motherhood. Other topics for consideration could include forgiveness and fidelity. Studies of personal relationship with God, spirituality, faith, and prayer might also be pursued.

6. Psychology of Vocation

Personalist psychology might undertake the study of work as call or vocation. A personalist organizational psychology could offer much to modern industry.

7. Psychology of Suffering

Personalist psychology would be in a good position to investigate the meaning and value of human suffering, considering such topics as resilience in the face of trauma, perhaps even a psychology of humor. Other areas of study could be correlates of pathological religious faith, as well as a psychology of hatred.

8. Psychology of Virtue

Personalist psychology might make exciting contributions to a psychology of virtue, including such traditional character traits as humility and chastity.[103] Experimental and phenomenological studies of such specifically human and positive attributes as love, joy[104], and hope might be pursued. The formation of character and the mental health correlates of healthy faith might also be researched.

The advancement of a personalist psychology should be both scholarly and popularized, both carefully researched and "taken to the streets." In this way, personalist psychology might contribute to what Tournier called a "civilization of the person" and what John Paul II referred to as a more "personalized" society.[105]

The goal of personalism is succinctly stated by the spearhead of the modern personalist movement, Emmanuel Mounier:

> The best future one could wish for Personalism is that it should so awaken in every man the sense of the whole meaning of man, that it could disappear without trace, having become the general climate of our days.[106]

NOTES

[1] The author gratefully acknowledges the generous assistance of the dean and Wellehan Library staff at Saint Joseph's College in North Windham, Maine.

[2] Mounier, *Personalism*, vii.

[3] Mounier, *Personalism*, ix.

[4] Mounier, *Personalism*, ix-x.

[5] Mounier, *Personalism*, x.

[6] Mounier, *Personalism*, xx.

[7] Mounier, *Personalism*, xxiii.

[8] Allport, *Personality*, 29.

[9] Allport, *Personality*, 30, 32, 35.

[10] See Kalinowski, "Edith Stein;" Kochler, "Phenomenology of Karol Wojtyla;" Seifert, "Karol Cardinal Wojtyla;" Williams, "Intellectual Portrait."

[11] Paul Johnson, *Pope John Paul II and the Catholic Restoration.* See Dulles, "Prophetic Humanism;" Gendreau, "Integral Humanism;" Lescoe, "Pope John Paul II;" and Woznicki, "Christian Humanism."

[12] Mounier, *Personalism*, xiii.

[13] John Paul II, *Familiaris Consortio,* par. 11.

[14] John Paul II, *Veritatis Splendor*, par. 48. See Wojtyla, *The Acting Person*; John Paul II, *Redemptor Hominis*; *Catechism of the Catholic Church,* pars. 1700-1802; Dinan, "Phenomenological Anthropology of Karol Wojtyla."

[15] See Modras, "Thomistic Personalism;" Valadier, "Jean-Paul II."

[16] *Catechism*, par. 1703.

[17] Wojtyla, *The Acting Person*, 113.

[18] John Paul II, *Redemptor Hominis,* par. 8.

[19] According to Tournier, *strong temperaments* tend to be naturally optimistic, self-confident, active, and predisposed to aggressiveness. *Weak temperaments,* on the other hand, are naturally disposed to doubt, passivity, contemplation, and fear.

[20] Tournier, *Person Reborn*, 107.

[21] John Paul II, *Redeemer of Man*, par. 13.

[22] John Paul II, *Redemptor Hominis*, par. 14.

[23] John Paul II, *Redemptor Hominis*, par. 16. See Mueller, "Review of *Labor Before Capital.*"

[24] Mounier, *Personalism*, xvi.

[25] Tournier, *Seasons of Life*, 45; *Meaning of Persons*, 198-216.

[26] Tournier, *Meaning of Persons*, 200.

[27] Vatican II, *Gaudium et Spes*, par. 17; John Paul II, *Veritatis Splendor*, pars. 34, 38.

[28] John Paul II, *Redeemer of Man*, par. 12.

[29] John Paul II, *Veritatis Splendor*, par. 33.

[30] Tournier, *Adventure of Living*, 189.

[31] Tournier, *Person Reborn*, 114.

[32] Tournier *Strong and Weak*, 80.

[33] John Paul II, *Veritatis Splendor*, pars. 30, 61.

[34] John Paul II, *Veritatis Splendor*, par. 54.

[35] John Paul II, *Veritatis Splendor*, par. 32.

[36] John Paul II, *Veritatis Splendor*, par. 58.

[37] Vatican II, *Gaudium et Spes*, par. 16. Cited in John Paul II, *Veritatis Splendor*, par. 55; cf. par. 58. See also *Catechism of the Catholic Church*, pars. 1776-1802.

[38] John Paul II, *Veritatis Splencor*, pars. 62-64.

[39] John Paul II, *Veritatis Splendor*, par. 42; see pars. 50, 60.

[40] John Paul II, *Redeemer of Man*, par. 12.

[41] Wojtyla, *Acting Person*, 265. See Min, "John Paul;" Muscari, "On Human Nature."

[42] Wojtyla, *Acting Person,* 264.

[43] Wojtyla, *Acting Person*, 264.

[44] Tournier, *Person Reborn*, 28.

[45] Vatican II, *Nostra Aetate,* par. 1; cited in John Paul II, *Veritatis Splendor*, par. 30.

[46] John Paul II, *Redeemer of Man*, par. 11.

[47] Tournier, *Meaning of Persons*, 160.

[48] Tournier, *Place For You*, 68.

[49] John Paul II, *Veritatis Splendor*, par. 52.

[50] John Paul II, *Veritatis Splendor*, par. 13.

[51] Tournier, *Place For You*, 197.

[52] John Paul II, *Veritatis Splendor*, par. 73.

[53] John Paul II, *Redeemer of Man,* par. 18; cf. *Familiaris Consortio*, par. 51.

[54] Tournier, *Listening Ear*, 54-55.

[55] Tournier, *Gift of Feeling*, 13; see 104-113.

[56] Tournier, *Meaning of Persons,* 139.

[57] Dinan, "Phenomenological Anthropology of Karol Wojtyla," 324-325, 330. See Wolicka, "Participation in Community."

[58] John Paul II, *Veritatis Splendor,* par. 51.

[59] John Paul II, *Redemptor Hominis,* par. 14.

[60] John Paul II, *Mulieris Dignitatem.*

[61] *Gaudium et Spes*, par. 52; cited in *Familiaris Consortio*, par. 21.

[62] G. H. Zuk, "The Parable of the Prodigal Son—John-Paul-II."

[63] Tournier, *Place For You*, 68.

[64] Tournier, *Place For You*, 210.

[65] John Paul II, quoted at Disney's EPCOT Center exhibit on "The Land."

[66] Mounier, *Personalism*, xviii, xix, 7.

[67] Tournier, *Adventure of Living.*

[68] *Gaudium et Spes*, par. 48, cited in John Paul II, *Familiaris Consortio,* par. 17; John Paul II, *Veritatis Splendor,* par. 23.

[69] John Paul II, *Veritatis Splendor*, par. 38. See John Paul II, *Laborem Exercens.*

[70] John Paul II, *Redeemer of Man,* par. 15.

[71] John Paul II, *Redeemer of Man*, par. 10.

[72] John Paul II,*Veritatis Splendor*, par. 17.

[73] Mounier, *Personalism*, 23.

[74] Mounier, *Personalism*, 66.

[75] Mounier, *Personalism*, 38.

[76] Mounier identifies five progressive actions leading to personalization: going out of the self, understanding, sharing, giving (and forgiving), and faithfulness. Cf. Mounier, *Personalism*, 21-22,

[77] John Paul II, *On the Family*, par. 2; see also par. 39.

[78] Dinan, "Phenomenological Anthropology," 324.

[79] John Paul II, *On the Family*, par. 65.

[80] John Paul II, *Redemptor Hominis,* par. 14.

[81] John Paul II, *Familiaris Consortio*; John Paul II, *To the Youth of the World.*

[82] *Catechism of the Catholic Church*, par. 1711.

[83] Dinan, "Phenomenological Anthropology," 323-324.

[84] *Catechism of the Catholic Church*, pars. 1716-1729, 1803-1845.

[85] *Catechism of the Catholic Church,* par. 1804.

[86] American Psychiatric Press, *Diagnostic and Statistical Manual of Mental Disorders, Fourth Edition* (DSM-IV), 766.

[87] Dinan, "Phenomenological Anthropology," 323.

[88] Tournier, *Meaning of Persons*, 28-45; John Paul II, *Familiaris Consortio*, par. 43. Similarly, Mounier warns against opposite depersonalizing sociocultural dangers of individualism and collectivism; see *Personalism*, 18, 43-44.

[89] Mounier, *Personalism*, xiii.

[90] Tournier, *Strong and Weak*, 20-21.

[91] *Gaudium et Spes*, par. 13; see also par. 10.

[92] Tournier, *Place For You*, 38.

[93] *Gaudium et Spes*, par. 10.

[94] Tournier, *Place For You*, 101.

[95] John Paul II, *Familiaris Consortio*, par. 75.

[96] John Paul II, *Reconciliatio et Paenitentia*, 29.

[97] John Paul II, *Reconciliatio et Paenitentia*, par. 29.

[98] John Paul II, *Dominicae Cenae,* par. 6.

[99] See Vande Kemp, *Psychology and Theology.*

[100] See Verny and Kelly, *Secret Life of the Unborn Child*; Moody, *Life After Life.*

[101] See Howard and Conway, "Can there be an empirical science of volitional action?"; Lazarick et al., "Practical investigations of volition"; Rychlak, *Discovering Free Will and Personal Responsibility.*

[102] See Vitz, "Towards a Christian Model of Moral Development."

[103] See Kreeft, *Back to Virtue.*

[104] See Myers, *The Pursuit of Happiness.*

[105] Tournier, *Meaning of Persons*, 133; John Paul II, *Centesimus Annus*, par. 49.

[106] Mounier, *Personalism*, xiii.

REFERENCES

Allport, Gordon W. *Personality: A Psychological Interpretation.* New York: Henry Holt, 1937.

American Psychiatric Press. *Diagnostic and Statistical Manual of Mental Disorders, Fourth Edition* (DSM-IV). Washington, DC: Author.

Dinan, Stephen A. "The Phenomenological Anthropology of Karol Wojtyla." *New Scholas., 55* (Summer 1981), 317-330.

Dulles, Avery. "The Prophetic Humanism of John Paul II." *America, 169* (October 23, 1993), 6-11.

Gaudium et Spes (*Pastoral Constitution on the Church in the Modern World*). In Austin Flannery (Ed.), *Vatican Council II: The Conciliar and Post Conciliar Documents.* Northport, NY: Costello, 1980.

Gendreau, Bernard A. "The Integral Humanism of Maritain and the Personalism of John Paul II." In *J. Maritain: A Philosopher*, edited by Jean-Louis Allard, 43-52. Ottawa: University of Ottawa Press.

Houde, Keith A. "The Christian Personality Theory of Paul Tournier." Ph.D. dissertation, Fuller Theological Seminary Graduate School of Psychology, 1990.

Howard, G. S., and Conway, C. G. "Can there be an empirical science of volitional action?" *American Psychologist, 41* (11), 1241-1251.

John Paul II. *Centesimus Annus (Encyclical on the 100th Anniversary of "Rerum Novarum")*. Boston, MA: St. Paul, 1991.

John Paul II. *Dominicae Cenae (On the Mystery and Worship of the Eucharist)*. Boston, MA: St. Paul, 1980.

John Paul II. *Familiaris Consortio (The Role of the Christian Family in the Modern World)*. Boston, MA: St. Paul, 1981.

John Paul II. *Laborem Exercens (On Human Work)*. Boston, MA: St. Paul, 1981.

John Paul II. *Mulieris Dignitatem (On the Dignity and Vocation of Women)*. Boston, MA: St. Paul, 1988.

John Paul II. *Reconciliatio et Paenitentia (Reconciliation and Penance in the Mission of the Church Today)*. Boston, MA: St. Paul, 1984.

John Paul II. *Redemptor Hominis (The Redeemer of Man)*. Boston, MA: St. Paul, 1979.

John Paul II. *To the Youth of the World.* Boston, MA: St. Paul, 1993.

John Paul II. *Veritatis Splendor (The Splendor of Truth)*. Boston, MA: St. Paul, 1993.

Johnson, Paul. *Pope John Paul II and the Catholic Restoration*. Ann Arbor, MI: Servant, 1981.

Kalinowski, Georges. "Edith Stein et Karol Wojtyla sur la Personne." *Rev. Phil. Louvain, 82* (November 1984), 545-561.

Kochler, Hans. "The Phenomenology of Karol Wojtyla: On the Problem of the Phenomenological Foundation of Anthropology." *Phil. Phenomenol. Res., 42* (March 1982), 326-334.

Kreeft, Peter. *Back to Virtue: Traditional Moral Wisdom for Modern Moral Confusion*. Harrison, NY: Ignatius.

Lazarick, D. L., Fishbein, S. S., Loiello, M. A., and Howard, G. S. "Practical Investigations of Volition." *Journal of Counseling Psychology, 35* (1), 15-26.

Lescoe, Francis J. "Pope John Paul II and Existential Personalism." In *Pastor of the Poles: Polish American Essays Presented to Right Rev. Monsignor John P. Wodarski*, edited by Stanislaus A. Blejwas and Mieczyslaw B. Biskupski, 80-92. New Britain, CT: Polish Studies Program Monographs, 1982.

Min, Anselm K. "John Paul the Second Anthropology of Concrete Totality." In *Proceedings of the American Catholic Philosophical Association, 58*, 120-129. Washington, DC: Catholic University of America, 1984.

Modras, Ronald. "The Thomistic Personalism of Pope John Paul II." *Mod Sch., 59* (January 1982), 117-127.

Moody, Raymond A., Jr. *Life After Life*. New York: Bantam, 1976.

Mounier, Emmanuel. *Personalism.* Notre Dame, IN: University of Notre Dame Press, 1952.

Muscari, Paul G. "On Human Nature: A Look at the Subject from Karol Wojtyla's Work 'The Acting Person.'" *J. Mind Behav., 9* (Winter 1988), 13-28.

Myers, David G. *The Pursuit of Happiness: Discovering the Pathway to Fulfillment, Well-Being, and Enduring Personal Joy.* New York: Avon, 1992.

Nostre Aetate (Declaration on the Relationship of the Church to Non-Christian Religions). In Austin Flannery (Ed.), *Vatican Council II: The Conciliar and Post Conciliar Documents.* Northport, NY: Costello, 1980.

Rychlak, Joseph F. *Discovering Free Will and Personal Responsibility.* New York: Oxford University Press, 1979.

Seifert, Josef. "Karol Cardinal Wojtyla (Pope John Paul II) as Philosopher and the Cracow/ Lublin School of Philosophy." *Aletheia, 2* (1981), 130-199.

Tournier, Paul. *The Adventure of Living.* New York: Harper & Row, 1965.

Tournier, Paul. *The Gift of Feeling.* Atlanta, GA: John Knox, 1981.

Tournier, Paul. *Guilt and Grace.* New York: Harper & Row, 1962.

Tournier, Paul. *A Listening Ear.* Minneapolis: Augsburg, 1987.

Tournier, Paul. *The Meaning of Persons.* New York: Harper & Row, 1957.

Tournier, Paul. *The Person Reborn.* New York: Harper & Row, 1966.

Tournier, Paul. *A Place for You.* New York: Harper & Row, 1968.

Tournier, Paul. *The Seasons of Life.* Richmond, VA: John Knox, 1963.

Tournier, Paul. *The Strong and the Weak.* Philadelphia: Westminster, 1963.

United States Catholic Conference/Libreria Editrice Vaticana. *Catechism of the Catholic Church.* San Francisco: Ignatius, 1994.

Valadier, P. Paul. "Jean-Paul II: Une Vision de l'Homme." *Etudes, 353* (November 1980), 527-542.

Vande Kemp, Hendrika. *Psychology and Theology in Western Thought, 1672-1965: A Historical and Annotated Bibliography.* Millwood, NY: Kraus International, 1984.

Verny, Thomas, and John Kelly. *The Secret Life of the Unborn Child.* New York: Dell, 1986.

Vitz, Paul C. "Towards a Christian Model of Moral Development." *New Oxford Review,* (September, 1981): 20-23.

Williams, G. H. "Intellectual Portrait of John-Paul-II." *Worldview, 22* (1-2) (1979), 21-26.

Wolicka, Elzbieta. "Participation in Community: Wojtyla's Social Anthropology." *Communio* (US), *8* (Summer 1981), 108-118.

Wojtyla, Karol. *The Acting Person* (trans. by Andrzej Potocki). Boston, MA: Reidel, 1978.

Wojtyla, Karol. *Love and Responsibility* (trans. by H. T. Willetts). New York: Farrar, Straus, & Giroux, 1981.

Woznicki, Andrew N. "The Christian Humanism of Cardinal Karol Wojtyla." In *The Human Person* (*Proceedings of the American Catholic Philosophical Association, 53*), edited by George F. McLean, 28-35. Washington, DC: Catholic University of America, 1979.

Zuk, G. H. "The Parable of the Prodigal Son—John-Paul-II." *International Journal of Family Therapy, 3* (2) (1981), 153-159.

Appendix: Philosophical Principles of the Institute for Personalist Psychology

In an effort to define its own *personalist* goals, IPP has drawn up a list of ten philosophical principles. IPP intends its conferences and publication efforts to further substantiate the truth of these theses, and to integrate them into psychological research, teaching, and clinical practice.

1. The Nature of Evidence. Because human beings are complex beings, and because each scientific procedure has its limitations, we encourage the use of a wide variety of methods of studying the person. This requires the psychologist to espouse a broad notion of evidence, to view evidence as any way in which a truth reveals itself. Such a notion of evidence will serve to justify supplementing the traditional empirical methods of psychology with the use of philosophical methods of research in psychology, particularly as one approaches peculiarly personal phenomena such as love, freedom, ethical action, and religious practice.

2. Human Beings as Personal Beings. Human beings must not be viewed simply as "higher animals, but must be seen in their specifically personal dimension. In referring to persons, we refer to beings who are ordinarily, and most properly, conscious, rational, free, responsible, related to a world of values, and capable of recognizing themselves as the subject of action. While fully recognizing that intellectual abilities and personality develop and change throughout life, IPP recognizes all human beings as persons.

3. The Spiritual Dimension of Human Persons. Recognizing the personal dimension of human beings entails that we view them as more than physical beings, as spiritual beings wich may rise above the chains of causality found in the material world, and preserve a self-identity which goes beyond the identity of their bodies. This is not to deny that persons depend upon their brains and are intimately and mysteriously united to their bodies. We emphasize only that persons are not identical to their bodies or bodily processes.

4. The Objectivity of Value. Human beings are capable of being motivated by goods and values which are objective insofar as they are discovered, rather than subjectively produced. These goods may offer human life meaning and direction, as well as make demands upon human behavior. The moral life consists largely in the conformity of human responses to these goods as they exist in a hierarchy. The task of counseling is not merely to enter the subjective world of the patient, but to help the patient turn to and conform to reality.

5. Rationality. Rationality arises from the ability of persons to transcend themselves and respond to reality appropriately. In its fullest sense, rationality presupposes that one apprehend not only what is true, but also what is good and of value. This feature of persons also contributes to the ethical life, in which not only our judgments, but our actions must conform to what is true and good.

6. Human freedom. Without freedom, a variety of personal acts such as taking responsibility, making promises, loving another person for his or her own sake, and many others, would be impossible. It is not denied that some human behaviors arise from compulsions or unconscious causes, but it is evident that some human actions, indeed those of the greatest significance, are free.

7. Moral responsibility. Intimately connected with the abililty to perceive values and to act freely is the responsiblity of the human person. Thus, it is correct to attribute guilt and praise to human persons and their action. Certainly there exist feelings of guilt or obligation which do not correspond to any true guilt or obligation. These must be identified as such, and worked through. However, any counseling activity which seeks to free persons from feelings of guilt must be accompanied by a sensitivity to instances of real guilt and a willingness to pursue themes of forgiveness and reparation.

8. The Religious Dimension. Religious beliefs and practices need not be the product of unhealthy psychological needs, nor a sign of superstitious or underdeveloped patterns of thinking. In fact, it may well be that a nonreligious person cannot find adequate answers to the most fundamental questions concerning the nature and meaning of human life. It is not the business of IPP to promote one religion as true, but only to affirm that religious practice has a healthy and legitimate place in the life of the individual and society.

9. The Limitations of Human Persons. A realistic understanding of the aims of counseling and research entails recognition of the fact that no amount of counseling or social engineering can free human beings of all personal and moral short-comings. Human beings are by nature imperfect, and all human perfections are limited.

10. Society and the Family. Human beings are social by nature, and develop intellectually, spiritually, emotionally and morally within a variety of social settings. IPP holds that the most basic and essential social structure for personal development is the family, including here both mother and father. Cases of death, divorce, unexpected pregnancy, severe abuse and the like, often prevent this ideal from being realized, but the committed relationship of a man and a woman remains the ideal. This assertion is not intended as a political judgment, but rather as a psychological fact, and a consideration for individual and marriage and family counselors.

About the Authors

Annemarie Buchholz-Kaiser, Ph.D., serves as the director if the counseling division of Verien zur Förderung der psychologischen Menschenkenntnis (VPM, Zürich) and is a member of the VPM's interdisciplinary committee. Buchholz-Kaiser has written works on anthropological psychology and counseling based on a personalist theory of personality, and is the author of *Social Interest: Its Formation and Significance for Human Development* (English translation forthcoming).

William R. Coulson, Ph.D., is the director of the Research Council on Ethnopsychlogy. A former colleague of Carl Rogers, Coulson is now engaged in presenting the defects of humanistic psychology, particularly as an educational psychology. Coulson is the author of numerous articles and books, including *Groups, Gimmicks, and Instant Gurus* and *A Sense of Community*, and was the co-editor of a series of books with Carl Rogers.

John F. Crosby, Ph.D., chairs the department of philosophy and is director of graduate studies in philosophy at Franciscan University of Steubenville. Crosby has written numerous articles on the philosophy of the person, engaging critically the work of Karl Marx, and synthesizing insights from von Hildebrand, Wojtyla, Newman, and others. Crosby's forthcoming book is entitled *An Essay on Personal Selfhood.*

James William DuBois, Ph.D., teaches in the Viktor Frankl chair of philosophy and psychology at the International Academy of Philosophy in Liechtenstein, and is the director of the Institute of Personalist Psychology. DuBois has published a book on Adolf Reinach's phenomenology, as well as several articles on psychology and ethics, logotherapy, and the philosophy of the mind.

Keith A. Houde, Ph.D., has taught psychology at St. Joseph's College in Maine, and is a practicing clinical psychologist. Houde is director of the Eastern region of the Christian Association for Psychological Studies, and is the author of *The Christian Personality Theory of Paul Tournier* (UMI).

Josef Seifert. Ph.D., is the rector of The International Academy of Philosophy, Liechtenstein, where he also serves as a professor. Seifert has written numerous articles and books in German including *The Body Soul Problem in the Contemporary Debate; What is and What Motivates a Moral Action?*; *Objective Truth: The Transcendence of the Person in Knowledge*; and in English, *Back to Things Themselves: A Phenomenological Foundation for Classical Realism.*

Philip Sutton, Ph.D., is licensed as a clinical and school psychologist, and as a marriage and family therapist. Currently engaged as a practicing family psychologist in South Bend, Indiana, Sutton was the inaugural director of the MA Counseling program at Franciscan University of Steubenville. Sutton has assisted in the development of a series of videotapes on marriage preparation and on the work of Conrad Baars.

Fr. Adrian van Kaam, Ph.D., and **Susan Muto, Ph.D.**, teach at Duquesne University in Pittsburgh, and are the co-founders of the Epiphany Association. Fr. van Kaam has been a pioneer of existential psychology from a Chrisitian perspective, with numerous books, including *Existential Counseling* and *Religion and Personality.* More recently, Fr. van Kaam has worked to develop the Science of Formative Spirituality and has produced a series of textbooks on the theme. Muto has worked closely with Fr. van Kaam on many of these projects, and she is the author of numerous books and studies on spirituality and personality, including *Care for the Caregiver* and *Womanspirit: Reclaiming the Deep Feminine in Our Human Spirituality.*

Paul C. Vitz, Ph.D., is a professor of psychology at New York University and a practicing psychologist at St. Michael's Institute in New York. Vitz is the author of numerous articles in empirical and theoretical psychology, as well as several books including *Freud's Christian Unconscious* and *Psychology as Religion: The Cult of Self-Worship.*